THE COMPLETE GUIDE TO
BUYING, OWNING *and* SELLING A HOME
in Canada

THE COMPLETE GUIDE TO
BUYING, OWNING *and* SELLING A HOME
in Canada

Margaret Kerr
&
JoAnn Kurtz

JOHN WILEY & SONS CANADA, LTD

Toronto • New York • Chichester • Weinheim • Brisbane • Singapore

John Wiley & Sons Canada Ltd
22 Worcester Road
Etobicoke, Ontario
M9W 1L1

Canadian Cataloguing in Publication Data
Kerr, Margaret Helen, 1954 –
    The complete guide to buying, owning and selling a home in Canada

Includes index.
ISBN 0-471-64191-X

1. House buying — Canada.   2. Home ownership — Canada.
3. House selling — Canada.   4. Home ownership — Law and legislation —
Canada.   5. Vendors and purchasers — Canada.
I. Kurtz, JoAnn, 1951 –   . II. Title.

HD1379.K47 1997   643'.12'0971   C96-932059-0

Production Credits
Cover & text design: Christine Rae
Printer: Tri-Graphic Printing Ltd.

Printed in Canada
10 9 8 7 6 5 4 3 2 1

CONTENTS

ACKNOWLEDGEMENTS

We thank the following for their help:

Michael Kerr, Elaine Chelin, Joe Agostino, Michael Engelberg, Joan Emmans, Sophie Ouellette, J. Brian Cornish, Denis Noel, W. Richey Clarke, Darryl Drover, Terence Morrison, Herbert Suderman, Bryan Salte, Jack Webster, Jane Eagleson, Insurance Bureau of Canada, Canada Mortgage and Housing Corporation, Canadian Real Estate Association, Canadian Gas Association, Canadian Standards Association, Canada Post Corporation, Consumer's Gas, Monnex Insurance Brokers Limited, Sedgwick Limited, Armor Moving & Storage Ltd., AbbeyWood Moving and Storage Inc., Abell Pest Control, Addiction Research Foundation, Nova Scotia Real Estate Association, Ontario Real Estate Association, Prince Edward Island Real Estate Association, Ontario New Home Warranty Plan, Ontario Association of Architects, Office of the Land Registrar of Ontario, Halifax and Dartmouth Real Estate Board, Greater Toronto Homebuilders' Association, Toronto Humane Society—and a special thanks to anyone in Canada who didn't interrupt us while we were working.

buying a
home

1 A MANUAL FOR HOMEOWNERS

DECIDING TO BUY A HOME (OR AT LEAST THIS BOOK)

If you've picked up this book and you don't already own a home, you're probably thinking about buying one. But buying a home can take a long time and you've got the itch to buy something *right away*. So now you're thinking about buying this book. We want to encourage you to do that. You may think that we are acting only out of self-interest, but in fact we're doing you a tremendous service. After all, if you're going to buy something on impulse, it's better to buy a book about buying a home than it is to buy a home. Actually, even a lot of people who put a great deal of time and effort into finding a home might as well be buying on impulse, for all they really know about buying, owning, and eventually selling a home.

That's where this book comes in. You wouldn't buy a car without researching the available models, their features, and price, and you wouldn't drive the car without first having a look at the owner's manual. A car only costs a fraction of what a house costs, yet the kind of information that you can easily get about cars is difficult, or even impossible, to get about houses. We think that you should have access to at least as much information about your home as about your car.

ONCE YOU OWN A HOME

If you already own a home, you still need this book. Your relationship with

your home is a complex one and is just starting when you buy a house. Buying is the first stage, but it's followed by owning and then selling. Each stage has its joys, problems, and concerns. You don't need our help to experience your own kind of joy, and you don't need our help to find the problems either—they'll find you. But this book should help you cope with the problems as they arise, and help you identify and deal with the important concerns.

Some of the problems and concerns of home ownership are legal, some are practical, and some are both. Practical books on home ownership tend to focus on hands-on matters like financing or plumbing. Legal books on home ownership are written for lawyers, and even lawyers don't always understand them. This book, on the other hand, is both legal and practical. It's designed to help you avoid problems as much as to solve them. And it's designed to give you the information you need all in one place and in language that you can understand. And, unlike other books written by lawyers, it has pictures!

However, this book is not a substitute for legal or other professional advice. There are times when you need a real estate agent, home inspector, mover, insurance broker, contractor, exterminator—even a lawyer. We try to tell you when it's time to hire a professional. And we try to send you off with enough knowledge to make sure that the person you hire serves you well.

QUESTIONS THIS BOOK ANSWERS

Here's a sampling of some of the questions this book answers.

About Buying a Home

- When's a good time to buy a home?
- What does it cost to buy a home?
- How much can you afford to pay for your home?
- How much of a down payment will you need, and where on earth will you find the money?
- How much will you pay for your home each month?
- What should you look for in a neighbourhood and a house?
- What can a real estate agent do for you, and can you do it yourself instead?
- How do you make an offer to purchase a home?
- Do you need a lawyer to buy a home?
- What is a mortgage and how do you get one?
- How can you survive moving day?
- What do you do if there are problems with your new home?

About Owning a Home

- What kind of home insurance do you need and how do you get it?
- How do you make an insurance claim?
- What renovations will increase the value of your home?
- How do you find a reliable contractor?
- How do you live through a renovation?
- What are construction or builders' liens and how do you avoid them?
- What steps can you take to make your home secure?
- How can you prevent accidents in your home?
- What happens if someone gets hurt on your property?
- Who is a trespasser and what can you do about one?
- How do you get rid of stray and wild animals?
- What do you do about noisy neighbours?
- Can you get your neighbour to pay for part of your fence?
- Can your neighbour cut down your tree?
- Can you object to your neighbour's construction project?
- Can you do anything if your property taxes are too high?
- What happens if you can't pay your mortgage?

About Selling a Home

- When is the best time to sell?
- Should you buy first or sell first?
- Do you need a real estate agent, or can you sell your home yourself?
- How do you make your home attractive to purchasers?
- Do you need a lawyer to sell your home?
- What must you leave behind when you move?
- How much money will you get from your sale?

Having the answers to these and other questions dealt with in this book should help you prevent many potential problems and solve others, either on your own or with professional help.

IT'S GREAT TO LIVE IN CANADA ... BUT ...

Canada is a big country and the law may vary considerably from province to province. (And don't even get us started about the weather.) Because we've tried to write a book for all of Canada, we've often had to talk in very general terms. This means that we haven't been able to take provincial variations into account on every topic. If you need specific legal advice, don't just rely on this book. Speak to your lawyer.

2 WHAT CAN YOU AFFORD?

No matter how much money you have, the house of your dreams will always cost more than you can afford. That's one of the universal truths of looking for a new home.

We know it's hard to put up with someone telling you to be realistic when you are trying to make your dream come true, and a lot of people don't listen. But a lot of people also buy the house of their dreams, only to have it turn into a nightmare—once they wake up and realize how much they have to keep paying for it.

You can avoid this nightmare by knowing what you can afford. This will help you concentrate your house-hunting efforts on homes in your price range. The best way to keep yourself from buying a home you can't afford is *not to look at* homes you can't afford. You can take comfort from knowing that while the home you end up buying may not be *your* dream home, it is probably the dream home of someone who has even less money than you do.

To know what you can afford, you have to know

- what it costs to buy and maintain a home
- how much money you have for a down payment
- how large a mortgage you can afford

The most complicated of these three things is calculating how large a mortgage you can afford. This means preparing a budget (something you've probably put off longer than cleaning your oven—and you're probably moving to get away from that dirty oven). Well, you can run, but you can't hide. It's either cleaning your oven and staying put, or doing a budget.

WHEN IS THE BEST TIME TO BUY?

People often wonder whether they can get a better deal on a house if they buy at a certain time of year. The answer is maybe yes, maybe no. There are times (like Christmas vacation) when almost no one wants to go house-hunting. If you find a house that you like at that time of year, you may be able to buy it for a good price because there are very few purchasers competing with you for that house. There are other times of the year when almost *everyone* is out looking for a house. The house you find at that time of year may cost you more because other purchasers are interested in it too.

You may think, then, that it makes sense to shop when no one else is shopping. But sellers also know that they may get less for their home during slow periods, so there will probably be fewer houses on the market for you to choose from. Sellers are more likely to put their houses up for sale when they think there will be a lot of buyers. So you can choose between a smaller selection of houses at (maybe) a lower price, and a larger selection at (maybe) a higher price. If you want to try to buy during a slow sales period, ask a real estate agent for advice about when that might be in your area.

Finding a house takes time, so even if you think you know when to buy to get the best price, you have to start looking before then. The best time to start looking for a house is when you've decided you want to own a home. And if you find a house that you like at a price you can afford, that's the house to buy and that's the best time to buy it.

WHAT DOES IT COST
TO BUY AND OWN A HOME?

The cost of buying and running a home is probably higher than you think. The actual cost of buying the house includes more than the purchase price, and the ongoing monthly costs of owning the house include more than your mortgage payments. If you make the mistake of failing to take these additional costs into account, you will end up buying a more expensive house than you can afford.

What Are the One-Time Costs of Buying a Home?

The one-time costs of buying a home are all the things you pay for at the time the house is purchased. They include

- the purchase price
- sales taxes
- lawyer's fees and related expenses
- professional home inspection
- mortgage costs
- adjustments
- new home warranty costs
- relocation costs
- renovation costs

The Purchase Price

This is the price that you agree to pay for the house itself. Most people think of this amount as what their house will cost them. While it is the major part of the cost, it is not the only cost. Read on.

Sales Taxes

In every province there is a special kind of sales tax charged on the sale of real estate, called a **land transfer tax.** This tax is calculated as a percentage of the purchase price and can be thousands of dollars. You pay this tax to the provincial government at the time you buy your house.

The purchase price of your house may include things like appliances and curtains, which will be sold with the house (these are called **chattels**). If so, you will also have to pay **G.S.T.** and provincial **retail sales tax** on the value of the chattels.

If you are buying a newly constructed home, you will also have to pay G.S.T. on the purchase price. If your house costs less than $450,000, you can apply for a G.S.T. rebate of up to 2.5 per cent of the purchase price.

Lawyer's Fees and Related Expenses

Your lawyer will charge you for legal services provided in helping you buy your home. The amount of these fees varies greatly, but you can expect to pay anywhere between several hundred dollars and several thousand dollars. We'll discuss the role of the purchaser's lawyer in more detail in Chapter 6.

Inspection Fees

Some people have their home inspected by a qualified home inspector before they complete the purchase, to make sure that the house is in good structural condition and has no plumbing, wiring, or other problems. These inspections can cost several hundred dollars or more.

Mortgage Costs

If you are borrowing money by taking out a mortgage, the mortgage lender may insist on having the property appraised. Sometimes mortgage lenders charge an appraisal fee in the range of $100 to $200. If you get your mortgage through a mortgage broker instead of an institutional lender, the broker may charge a brokerage fee. The amount charged would depend on the circumstances, but it would probably not be higher than 1 to 2 per cent of the amount borrowed.

Monthly mortgage payments are usually due on the first of the month. If your house deal is closing on another day of the month, the mortgagee may deduct from the mortgage money that is being given to you, an amount to cover the interest for the time from the closing date to the first day of the next month. (This is called the **interest adjustment date.**) You may have to come up with some extra money on closing day to cover any shortfall in the amount of money that the mortgagee actually gives you.

If your mortgage is for more than 75 per cent of the purchase price, you may have to get mortgage insurance, which is arranged through the Canada Mortgage and Housing Corporation (CMHC). If you need mortgage insurance, you will have to pay an insurance application fee of $75 if your lender provides an appraisal, or $235 if your lender does not. You will also have to pay a one-time premium for the mortgage insurance. The amount of the premium varies with the value of the house and the size of the loan. The highest rate charged is 2.5 per cent of the amount of the loan.

There's much more about mortgages in Chapter 7. Flip there now if you can't stand the suspense.

Adjustments

If the person selling the house (the **vendor**) has paid such things as property taxes and utilities in advance, you may have to pay the vendor for your share of these expenses. You have no way of knowing how much this will be at the time you decide to buy your home. Your lawyer will tell you the exact amounts involved just before the sale closes.

New Home Warranty Costs

All provinces have warranty programs for newly constructed homes. Participation in these programs is optional in all provinces except Ontario. If your home comes with a warranty, there will be an enrolment fee that the builder will pass on to you, either by including it in the purchase price or as a separate charge. So, if you are buying a newly constructed home, be sure to find out whether there is an additional charge for a warranty and how much it will be. Depending on the province, the charge can be between $200 and $1000.

Relocation Expenses

You should budget for your moving costs. The amount will depend on whether you hire a mover or boldly go yourself. If you hire a mover, the cost will go up the more things you have to move and the further you have to move them. Moving can cost several thousand dollars. We tell you all about moving in Chapter 9.

Once you are in your new home, you will have to get telephone and cable television service, for which you will have to pay an installation fee. You may also have to pay a fee to transfer any gas, electric, or water service to your name.

Renovation Expenses

Not many people move into a house that is in perfect condition, so don't forget to budget for renovation, repairs, redecoration, painting, and cleaning. Also, be sure that you have left yourself enough money to pay for any new appliances or furniture that you may need.

What Does All This Mean?

As you can see, some of the money you thought you could use for a down payment has to be used to pay these one-time costs. So you either have less money for your down payment than you thought, or you will have to borrow more money than you planned.

What are the Monthly Expenses of Owning a Home?

Everybody knows there will be monthly mortgage payments after they buy a home, but many people forget about the other regular monthly expenses they will have to pay. These other expenses include

- property taxes
- utilities
- home insurance
- maintenance and repairs

Mortgage Payments

A mortgage is a loan that is repaid in instalments, usually on a monthly basis. The mortgage payments include an amount to repay the loan principal and an amount to pay the interest on the principal. The amount of the payment will therefore depend on how much you borrow and the interest rate.

Property Taxes

Every municipality charges property taxes that are used to pay for municipal services and for local schools. They are payable in instalments over the course of the year, sometimes monthly and sometimes at other intervals. Yearly property taxes can be many thousands of dollars, so it is important to find out what the property taxes will be and to budget for them. Some mortgage lenders pay the property taxes for you and require you to repay them on a monthly basis.

Utilities

You should find out the approximate monthly cost of heating, water, and electricity for any home you are interested in buying to make sure you can afford these utility payments. Since they can vary greatly from house to house (especially heating costs), it's a good idea to find out what the current owner has paid in the last year.

Home Insurance

Every homeowner needs home insurance. The cost will vary from house to house but will probably be $500 to $1000, or more, per year.

Maintenance and Repairs

If you don't want to spend time in the great Canadian outdoors shovelling your own driveway or mowing your own lawn, you should budget for snow removal and lawn care.

You should also keep in mind that things in your new home will break and have to be repaired or replaced—usually when you can least afford it. Make sure that your budget allows you to deal with these unexpected but necessary expenses.

What Does This Mean for You?

Once you have figured out how much you can afford for your house on a monthly basis, don't plan to spend it all on just your mortgage payments. If you spend too much on mortgage payments, you won't have enough money for all your other expenses.

HOW MUCH MONEY DO YOU HAVE FOR YOUR NEW HOME?

When you buy your new home, you should pay only what you can afford. (It's amazing how often books like this one give you the same advice as your mother.) What you can afford depends on a combination of how much of a down payment you have, plus how much of a mortgage you can afford to carry.

TABLE 1: WHAT YOU CAN AFFORD		
Your down +	A mortgage =	What you can afford
payment	you can afford	to pay for your new home

Once you find out how large a mortgage you can afford, add that amount to the money you have available for a down payment. The total is the maximum amount you can afford to pay for your new home.

DOWN PAYMENTS

A down payment is the part of the purchase price that you pay in cash at the time you buy your home. The rest of the purchase price is financed by a mortgage.

It's usually easy to calculate how much you have for a down payment. It's the money you have saved in the bank, or the money you can beg or borrow from your family (we don't recommend stealing), or the money you can raise by selling property that you already own. Remember, though, that this money has to cover not only your down payment but all of the other one-time costs of buying a house.

Minimum Down Payments

For most people, a large part of the purchase price will be financed by a mortgage, but you won't be able to get a mortgage from an institutional lender unless you have a certain percentage of the purchase price to pay as a down payment. Institutional mortgage lenders prefer you to have a down payment that covers at least 25 per cent of the purchase price of your home. A down payment of this size will qualify you for a **conventional mortgage**.

You may be able to buy a home with a down payment as small as 10 per cent of the purchase price, leaving up to 90 per cent to be financed by a mortgage. A mortgage for more than 75 per cent of the purchase price is called a **high ratio mortgage**. If you are a first-time home buyer, you may even be able to qualify for a high ratio mortgage with a down payment as small as 5 per cent.

Finding the Down Payment

If you already own a home, your down payment will come from the money you have left from the sale of that home after paying off your mortgage and paying the other expenses of the sale.

If you don't own a home, you must look to other sources for your down payment, such as:

- savings in your bank account, bonds, or GICs
- any other investments
- gifts or loans from your family
- RRSPs
- provincial home ownership savings plans

RRSPs

The Canadian government will allow you to withdraw, without tax penalty, up to $20,000 per person or $40,000 per couple from your RRSPs for the purchase of a home. You must repay the amount you withdraw within fifteen years, repaying a minimum of one-fifteenth each year, or there will be a tax penalty.

You can only borrow from your RRSP if neither you nor your spouse has owned and lived in a home as your principal residence within the last five years, and if you have never borrowed from your RRSP before to buy a house. There are other restrictions on borrowing as well. For more information, speak to the institution that holds your RRSP.

Provincial Home Ownership Savings Plans

Some provinces have home ownership savings plans. If you save for your down payment by depositing money into such a plan, you will receive a credit against your provincial income tax for the year. You must meet certain requirements to be eligible. Ask your bank or trust company whether your province has a plan and what the details are.

HOW LARGE A MORTGAGE CAN YOU AFFORD?

A mortgage (a **hypothec** in Quebec) is a special kind of loan available to home purchasers, usually from a bank or trust company. Banks and trust companies are called **institutional lenders**. The amount of money that you borrow by way of a mortgage is called the **mortgage principal**.

An Affordable Monthly Payment Equals an Affordable Mortgage

When you take out a mortgage, you should borrow only the amount of money you can afford to repay. The amount you can afford to repay is governed by the monthly mortgage payments you can afford to make. The monthly mortgage payments for any mortgage depend on

• the amount being borrowed (the mortgage principal)
• the mortgage interest rate

The higher the amount being borrowed and the higher the interest rate, the higher your monthly mortgage payments will be.

The first step in figuring out how much you can afford to borrow is to figure out how much of a monthly mortgage payment you can afford. In order to know what mortgage payment you can afford to make, you have to calculate your net monthly income and then deduct all your other monthly expenses to see what you have left for a mortgage.

TABLE 2: MONEY AVAILABLE FOR MORTGAGE PAYMENTS

Net monthly income	−	{Monthly living expenses { (other than housing) + {Monthly housing expenses { (other than mortgage)	=	Money available for mortgage payments

What is Your Net Monthly Income?

To know how large a monthly mortgage payment you can afford, you have to start by calculating your net monthly income.

What is Income?

Income is money that is earned at regular intervals. If you have a job, your salary or wages are your income. If you are self-employed, your income is the fees you collect for the goods or services you provide. Other forms of income include

• commissions
• tips
• interest
• dividends
• rent received

Gross Income and Net Income

If you are paid wages or a salary, your employer makes deductions from your pay cheque every pay period. Common deductions include income tax, unemployment insurance premiums, Canada Pension Plan contributions, union dues, insurance payments, and private pension plan contributions. These amounts are deducted automatically. The amount you are paid before the deductions are made is called your **gross income**. The small amount you actually receive (after the deductions are made) is called your **net income**.

Since you can only spend the income you receive after these deductions are made, you should use your net income rather than your gross income for the purposes of calculating what you can afford.

Calculating Your Monthly Income

Different people receive their income at different intervals. You may be paid weekly, every two weeks, bimonthly (which is different from every two weeks), or monthly. Self-employed people may receive their income at other less regular intervals.

Because mortgage payments are normally made monthly, it's necessary to figure out what your income is on a monthly basis, no matter when you are actually paid. To convert your net income to a monthly amount, use the following table:

TABLE 3: CALCULATING YOUR MONTHLY INCOME	
If you are paid:	Multiply the net amount of your pay cheque by:
weekly	4.33
every 2 weeks	2.165
bimonthly	2

If you are self-employed or can't accurately predict your regular income, you should estimate what your income will be for the current year and then divide that figure by 12 to give you an estimated monthly income. To be safe, make your estimate on the low side rather than on the high side.

What Are Your Monthly Living Expenses (Other than Housing)?

Once you have figured out your net monthly income, the next step in figuring out what you can afford to pay for your mortgage is to deduct your monthly living expenses (other than housing). Before you can deduct these expenses, you have to know what they are.

Identifying Your Living Expenses

These are the places your money goes when you're not looking. It's all the money you spend on things other than the roof over your head, such as groceries, transportation, clothing, and entertainment. If you have receipts for the past year, go through them rather than relying on your memory of what you've spent. There's a chart in this chapter to help you identify your monthly living expenses.

Calculating Your Living Expenses on a Monthly Basis

CONVERTING YOUR EXPENSES: Some expenses are incurred on a *weekly* basis, the most common example being groceries. To calculate your monthly expenses for these items, estimate what you spend in an average week, then convert this weekly amount to a monthly one by multiplying it by 4.33. People are always tempted to simply multiply the weekly amount by 4, but that doesn't work because the average month has more than twenty-eight days in it. If you calculated every month as having only four weeks, you would end up with a year of forty-eight weeks instead of fifty-two. (Now you know why bimonthly is not the same as every two weeks.)

Some expenses are incurred on a *monthly* basis, such as telephone and cable TV. Just use the monthly amount from your bill. Some expenses are incurred on a *yearly* basis, such as insurance premiums, car licence fees, and membership dues. To convert these annual amounts to monthly amounts, simply divide by 12. Finally, some expenses—car repairs, clothing, and vacations—are incurred on an *irregular* basis. The simplest way to deal with these expenses is to estimate the total amount for the entire year (or add up what these things cost last year) and then divide by 12.

TOTALLING YOUR EXPENSES: After you have converted all of your expenses to a monthly figure, total them. Deduct this total from your net monthly income. What you have left out of your monthly income (if anything) is what you have to spend on mortgage payments *and* other housing expenses. This will probably be very depressing.

It is at this point that many people realize they will have to make some sacrifices in order to own a home. (There we go, sounding like your mother again.) So the next step is to go through your living expenses again and see where you can make cuts. It's very important to be realistic here, because the money you decide you won't be spending on these other expenses will be committed to paying your mortgage.

It's not a good idea to reduce basic expenses like groceries and child care. Be careful in reducing other expenses as well. Are you sure that you can live through a Canadian winter without a vacation in the sun? Do you want to go through the year with fewer new clothes or dinners out? Once you are committed to paying for a mortgage, there's no going back!

You can use the following table to help you figure out both the expenses you have now and the adjustments you would be willing to make in order to own a home.

TABLE 4: MONTHLY NON-HOUSING LIVING EXPENSES

Expense	Actual monthly amount	Slash-and-burn monthly amount
Household expenses	$ _____	$ _____
Groceries	_____	_____
Household supplies	_____	_____
Household help	_____	_____
Telephone	_____	_____
Cable TV	_____	_____
Loan payments	$ _____	$ _____
Credit cards	_____	_____
Bank loans	_____	_____
Car loan	_____	_____
Other	_____	_____
Transportation	$ _____	$ _____
Car insurance	_____	_____
Licence fees	_____	_____
Maintenance	_____	_____
Gasoline	_____	_____
Parking	_____	_____
Public transit	_____	_____
Other	_____	_____
Clothing	$ _____	$ _____
Self	_____	_____
Spouse	_____	_____
Children	_____	_____
Personal grooming	$ _____	$ _____
Haircuts	_____	_____
Dry cleaning	_____	_____
Other	_____	_____

Health	$ _____	$ _____
Insurance (health, disability, life)	_____	_____
Uninsured medical services	_____	_____
Drugs	_____	_____
Dentist/orthodontist	_____	_____
Other	_____	_____
Entertainment	$ _____	$ _____
Eating out	_____	_____
Movies, plays, and sports events	_____	_____
Newspapers, books, and magazines	_____	_____
Club fees	_____	_____
Vacation	_____	_____
Sports equipment	_____	_____
Gifts	_____	_____
Other	_____	_____
Children's expenses	$ _____	$ _____
Day care	_____	_____
Babysitting	_____	_____
School fees	_____	_____
Lessons and activities	_____	_____
Summer camp	_____	_____
Other	_____	_____
Savings	$ _____	$ _____
Charitable Donations	$ _____	$ _____
Total	$ _____	$ _____

Money Available for Monthly Housing Expenses

After you deduct your adjusted living expenses from your net monthly income, what you have left is what you can spend on all your monthly housing expenses, *including* mortgage payments.

TABLE 5: MONEY AVAILABLE FOR MONTHLY HOUSING EXPENSES

Net monthly — Adjusted living = Money available for
income expenses monthly housing expenses

The non-mortgage expenses of owning a home include

• property taxes
• utilities
• home insurance
• maintenance and repairs

Your monthly housing expenses will depend on the particular house you buy. Some houses have low property taxes, cost little to heat, and will require relatively little maintenance; others will be very expensive to run on a monthly basis. Some of the expenses of running the house may be set out on the house feature sheet prepared when a house is listed for sale. You can get a general idea about property taxes and utilities for houses that have caught your eye in the real estate ads by calling the agent mentioned in the ad. Other things you may have to estimate, based on your own experience or on friends' experience.

As with your non-housing expenses, you must figure out how much you will spend on each of these items on a monthly basis. Use the following table:

TABLE 6: ESTIMATED MONTHLY HOUSING EXPENSES

Expense	Monthly amount
Property taxes	$ _____
Water	_____
Electricity	_____
Natural gas	_____
Fuel oil	_____
Home insurance	_____
Repairs and maintenance	_____
Gardening	_____
Snow removal	_____
Condominium common expenses	_____
Total	$ _____

The less you have to spend on these monthly housing expenses, the more money you will have available each month to pay your mortgage. The more money you can pay each month for your mortgage, the larger the mortgage you can afford.

Money Available for Mortgage Payments

You are now ready to calculate how much money you have available to make your monthly mortgage payments. Just take the amounts from your previous calculations and insert them into the following table:

TABLE 7: MONEY AVAILABLE FOR MORTGAGE PAYMENTS	
Net monthly income	$ _____
less:	
Monthly non-housing living expenses	$ _____
Monthly housing expenses	$ _____
Total available for mortgage payments	$ _____

Calculating the Principal Amount of Your Affordable Mortgage

You now know how large a monthly mortgage payment you can afford. Next, find out what your mortgage interest rate will be by checking your local newspaper's business or real estate sections, or telephone some banks or trust companies for the current interest rates.

Using these two figures (the monthly payment you can afford and the probable interest rate), calculate how much mortgage principal you can afford to borrow. Use Table 8 on the next page. It shows mortgage principal, based on different monthly payments and interest rates.

THE MAXIMUM PRICE TO PAY FOR YOUR HOME

Once you have found a home you want to buy, ask the real estate agent or current owner the amount of the monthly housing expenses (other than mortgage payments) of that house. Insert this amount at "Monthly housing expenses" in Table 7 to calculate the total amount that you have available for mortgage payments for that particular house. Take this amount and, using the current interest rates, go to Table 8, which will tell you the maximum mortgage amount that you can afford to borrow for this particular house. Add this amount of mortgage money to the money you have for a down payment. The total of these two amounts is the maximum price you can afford to pay for that particular house.

TABLE 8: HOW MUCH MORTGAGE PRINCIPAL YOU CAN BORROW AT VARIOUS INTEREST RATES AND MONTHLY PAYMENT AMOUNTS

Interest Rate / Monthly Payment	4%	5%	6%	7%	8%	9%	10%	11%	12%	13%	14%	15%
$ 500	$ 95,050	$ 86,000	$ 78,125	$ 71,425	$65,525	$60,375	$55,875	$51,925	$48,450	$45,375	$42,125	$40,125
600	114,060	103,200	93,750	85,725	78,625	72,475	67,050	62,300	58,150	54,450	51,100	48,150
700	113,070	120,400	109,375	100,000	91,750	84,550	78,200	72,700	67,825	63,525	59,625	56,175
800	152,080	137,600	125,000	114,275	104,850	96,625	89,375	83,075	77,525	72,600	68,150	64,200
900	171,090	154,800	140,625	128,575	117,950	108,700	100,550	93,450	87,200	81,675	76,650	72,225
1000	190,100	172,000	156,250	142,850	131,050	120,775	111,725	103,850	96,900	90,750	85,175	80,250
1250	237,625	215,000	195,300	178,575	163,825	140,975	139,675	129,800	121,125	113,425	106,475	100,325
1500	285,150	258,000	234,375	214,275	196,600	181,150	167,600	156,775	145,350	136,125	127,775	120,375

Amortized over 25 years
Figures rounded off to the nearest $25

A Word of Warning

Think carefully before you spend the maximum amount you can afford. All the mortgage calculations you do in this chapter are based on current interest rates. However, as you will see in the chapter about mortgages, any mortgage you get will probably have to be renegotiated before you have paid it in full—perhaps several times. If interest rates have gone up at the time your mortgage is due, your renegotiated mortgage will have a higher interest rate and your monthly payments will go up. You might want to leave yourself some leeway for such a possibility.

The Price Range of Houses You Should Be Looking At

The amount you can afford each month for your mortgage will depend on the particular house you buy. So, you might be asking yourself: How can I know what price range of house I should be looking at? To figure out this price range, fill out the following table:

TABLE 9: TOTAL MONEY AVAILABLE FOR MORTGAGE AND ALL HOUSING EXPENSES

Net monthly income (from Table 3) less:	$ _____
Monthly non-housing living expenses (from Table 4)	$ _____
Total available for mortgage and all housing expenses	$ _____

Go to Table 8 to find out how much mortgage money you could afford to borrow if you could use all this money to pay your mortgage. The amount you get from Table 8 will be quite a bit more than you can in fact afford, because you will also have to pay all non-mortgage housing expenses out of it. Take the amount of mortgage principal you calculated using Table 8 and add it to the money you have for a down payment. Start looking at houses *below* this price range.

Pre-Approved Mortgages

Many banks and trust companies will allow you to apply for a mortgage before you have found the home that you wish to buy. Getting pre-approval for a mortgage lets you know in advance the maximum amount of money that will be available to you.

While the bank or trust company will not actually give you the money until you buy the house, they will commit themselves to lending you a maximum amount at a specified interest rate, so long as you buy a suitable home within a fixed period of time (usually no more than 60 days).

Now that you know what you can afford, you can start to think (rather than dream) about where you want to live and what kind of house you want.

3 WHERE DO YOU WANT TO LIVE?

Now you know what you can afford, you can start to think about where you want to live: what features you want in a home and what location. For some of you the size and appearance of a house are the most important things. For others, location is everything. What you want may not be what you can afford. In the end, your choice of a house will involve a trade-off among price, features, and location.

THINK ABOUT WHAT YOU WANT

Before you start to look at houses, you should have an idea of what you want. Make a wish list for your ideal home. Then have a preliminary look around to see whether or not what you want is available in your price range. You may have to make changes to your wish list to reflect what you can actually afford.

A home is both the house itself and where it is located. You may start with an idea of the house you want or an idea of its location, but wherever you start, before you buy, you have to think about both.

Location

When we talk about location, we don't mean where in Canada you want to live. We assume that you already know both the province and the general area. Within that general area, you still have a wide choice: Would you prefer to live right in the city, in a suburb, in a smaller town, or in the country? You should also think about the kind of community you want to live in, how close to your family and friends and place of work you want to be, and the services you want nearby.

Features

When we talk about features, we mean the size and appearance of the house. How large is the lot? How many bedrooms are there? Are there new bathrooms and kitchen? Is the house in move-in condition or is it a handyman's special? When you list the features you want in a home, don't just think about whether a house meets your present needs. Think about your future needs as well.

The Wish List

To help you identify your wishes and needs for your new home, use the following checklists. Distinguish between the things that you absolutely must have in a home and the things that you would merely like to have if you could.

HOUSE FEATURES

	Must have	Would like
Single-family detached	_____	_____
Single-family semi-detached	_____	_____
Multiple family	_____	_____
Townhouse	_____	_____
Condominium	_____	_____
Number of storeys	_____	_____
Exterior (brick, wood, siding)	_____	_____
Large property	_____	_____
Backyard with fence	_____	_____
Swimming pool	_____	_____
Trees and landscaping	_____	_____
Deck or patio	_____	_____
Attached garage	_____	_____
One- or two-car garage	_____	_____
Private drive	_____	_____
Number of bedrooms	_____	_____
Number of bathrooms	_____	_____
New bathrooms	_____	_____
Master ensuite bathroom	_____	_____
Large kitchen	_____	_____
New kitchen	_____	_____
Family room	_____	_____
Separate dining-room	_____	_____
Sunroom	_____	_____
Fireplace(s)	_____	_____
Finished basement	_____	_____
Basement apartment	_____	_____
Nanny's quarters	_____	_____
Lots of closet space	_____	_____
Type of heating	_____	_____
Central air-conditioning	_____	_____
New plumbing	_____	_____
New electrical system	_____	_____
Municipal water and sewers	_____	_____
Move-in condition	_____	_____
Other (list)	_____	_____

HOUSE LOCATION

	Must have	Would like
Type of location		
city		
suburb		
small town		
country		
Easy commuting		
distance to work		
close to public transit		
snow plowing		
adequate parking		
Character of the neighbourhood		
size and appearance of houses		
restrictions on activities		
quiet street		
compatible neighbours		
safety		
mature trees		
sidewalks		
wildlife		
Services		
close to good schools		
close to shopping and other services		
nearby emergency services		
recreational facilities and programs		
close to parks		
snow removal		
garbage pick-up		
mail delivery to door		
water and sewage systems		
Low property taxes		
Stable property values		

Have a Preliminary Look Around

Once you have some idea of the kind of home and location you would like, you should have a look around to see whether what you want is available in your price range. Do this by looking at real estate ads, by driving around to see what houses are listed for sale, and by going to open houses. You can call the agent named in the ad or on the sign (or you can call any real estate agent) for more information about any house that catches your interest.

Fine-Tune Your Wish List

After some preliminary looking around, you should have a realistic idea of what is out there. It's unlikely that you will have found an affordable house that fully satisfies your wish list.

You will have discovered that similar houses have different price tags depending on their location. Since what you can afford is fixed, you will probably find that you have to compromise either on the features of the house or its location. Have another look at your wish list and change it if necessary.

At this stage you should have a good idea of what kind of house and what location you can get for the price you can afford. You have narrowed your choice of location and choice of features. You are now ready to start serious house-hunting—with buying in mind.

GO HOUSE-HUNTING WITH A REAL ESTATE AGENT

Once you've got some idea of what you'd like to buy, then you are ready to start your serious house-hunting. Unless you are only interested in a house to be built in a new development, the best way to find houses is to look with the help of an experienced real estate agent. Now you probably want to know

- what a real estate agent can do for you
- the cost of a real estate agent
- how to find a real estate agent
- how to work with a real estate agent
- the legal relationship between you and your real estate agent

What a Real Estate Agent Can Do for You

A real estate agent can:

- help you fine-tune your wish list
- get special access to information about the many houses listed for sale
- screen those houses to choose the ones most likely to be of interest
- arrange appointments for you to view the selected houses
- get information about neighbourhoods
- help you evaluate the condition of houses you view
- help you decide how much you should pay for a particular house
- help you make up an offer to purchase and negotiate with the vendor
- put you in contact with building inspectors, mortgage lenders, contractors, movers, and other useful people

You may think that you don't need a real estate agent to find and look at houses that are for sale. But you're wrong. For one thing, real estate agents are hard to avoid. Most vendors use a real estate agent, and if you want to view a house that is listed with an agent, you'll either have to deal with that agent or some other agent. For another thing, using a real estate agent will get you access to a lot more information than you could find on your own and will also save you a lot of time.

If you were to look for houses on your own, you would only know about the ones you happen to see with "For Sale" signs, or which are advertised for sale in the newspaper or through the Internet. Most houses that are up for sale are put on a **multiple listing service** or **MLS**. Only real estate agents have full access to the information on the multiple listing service, which includes details about the price, location, and features of each house. So a real estate agent will know more about the houses that are on the market than you could ever find out on your own.

A real estate agent will review all the MLS information, zero in on the houses most likely to be of interest to you, and take you to see only those houses. That way, you won't waste your time looking at the wrong houses.

Cost of a Real Estate Agent

The general rule is that there will be no cost to you as the purchaser for using a real estate agent's services. The real estate agent involved in a purchase of a home is usually paid a commission by the vendor.

How to Find a Real Estate Agent

You will be spending a lot of time with your real estate agent and you need the agent to know and understand what is important to you in a new home. So you want to find someone you like, trust, and feel comfortable with, maybe someone who is of a similar age, background, and stage in life.

You also want an agent who is professional, has time for you, and will work hard. So it's best to find someone who has experience and works full-time. Try to avoid an agent who has so many houses listed for sale that he or she won't have enough time to spend with you. Look for an agent who is knowledgeable about the neighbourhoods that interest you the most. Finally, choose someone with a pleasant personality. It will not only be easier for you to work together, but the agent will be a more successful negotiator on your behalf.

The best way to find a real estate agent is to ask for a recommendation from people you know and trust. If family and friends don't have anyone to recommend, you might want to use a real estate agent you met at an open house or spoke to on the phone during your preliminary search. Feel free to interview several agents before making your choice. If the real estate agent you choose does not have enough time for you or does not seem to understand what it is that you are looking for, or if you simply feel uncomfortable with him or her, end the relationship and choose a new agent.

How to Work with a Real Estate Agent

Once you've found a real estate agent, you want the agent to do all the things that we told you a real estate agent *can* do, and to do those things really well. Tell your agent what you want and let him or her do the work of finding houses. As you look at different houses, explain what you like or don't like about each house so that the agent will be able to focus the search on houses that should appeal to you. Focusing the search works best if you work with just one agent at a time.

When you view a house, you have to examine its condition very carefully. Your real estate agent has seen many houses and may be able to spot problems that you miss. If you have specific questions about repairs that have been made or the cost of maintaining the house, ask your agent to get the answers from the vendor.

When you find a house that interests you, make use of your agent's expertise in getting information about the neighbourhood and the neighbours. A good real estate agent should be able to give you information about such things as the local schools, property taxes, and even the names of people living on the street.

If you want to try to buy one of the houses you've looked at, your agent should check sale prices of similar houses in the area to help you decide how much you should be willing to offer. The agent will help you draft the actual offer to purchase the house and may suggest that you include special clauses for your protection. The agent will write up the offer for you to sign.

Once the offer has been signed, your real estate agent will act as a go-between, taking the offer to the vendor and bringing you back the vendor's answer. During the negotiations, you won't meet with the vendor face-to-face.

Even after you reach an agreement to buy a house, your agent can still be useful to you by helping you find mortgage money, building inspectors, renovators, and so on. Your agent will also be the one who arranges any inspections of the house before the sale closes.

The Legal Relationship between You and Your Real Estate Agent

The real estate agent who hosts an open house, or who is named in an advertisement or on a "For Sale" sign, is the vendor's real estate agent, and is also the vendor's **agent** in a special legal sense. The real estate agent has a legal relationship with the vendor called an **agency relationship**. In an agency relationship, the agent has a duty to look after the best interests of the person he or she is working for (in this case, the vendor.) If the vendor's agent makes any statements to you about the property for sale, it is the same as if the vendor personally made the statement.

You may think that the real estate agent who has been finding houses for you to look at is *your* agent in the legal sense of the word, but most of the time that is not the case. Unless you have signed a special agreement with your real estate agent to make that person your legal agent (as a **buyer's agent** or a **dual agent**), the law says that he or she is the agent of the vendor. (This is probably a surprise to you, but take a deep breath and you'll soon get over it.)

For the most part, the fact that "your" real estate agent is really the vendor's agent will not have any effect on the services, advice, or expertise that your agent provides. However, as the vendor's *legal* agent, your real estate agent has a duty to pass on to the vendor any information that would affect the vendor's decision to accept your offer to buy the house. So be a little careful when you are negotiating the price of a particular house. *Don't* tell your real estate agent the maximum price you are willing to pay, if it is higher than what you have offered.

Houses for Sale by the Vendor

What if you find a house that is being sold by a vendor who doesn't have a real estate agent? There could be an advantage to you in buying privately, which is that the price *may* be lower. The vendor will not have to pay a real estate agent's commission and may be willing to share the saving with you. It is just as likely, however, that the vendor wants to keep that saving, in which case the price will not be any lower than if a real estate agent were involved. In fact, you may find that a vendor who wants to sell privately has an unrealistic idea about the value of the house and may want more than its market value.

There can also be disadvantages to buying privately. For example, the vendor may hover over you as you view the house (when you view houses being sold through an agent, the vendor has usually been persuaded not to be home). If you make an offer on the house, you may have to negotiate with the vendor face-to-face.

If you decide to buy privately, be sure to research the house and neighbourhood thoroughly. If you're not sure that the price of the house is fair, you can pay a fee to have a real estate agent give you an estimate of the house's market value.

Houses That Aren't for Sale

What if you've found a street that you really want to live on—but there aren't any houses for sale on it? Choose several houses that you like. Write a letter telling the owners that you are interested in buying, and hand-deliver it to the door of each home. Even though a house is not for sale, the owner may still be thinking about selling.

We've told you how to find houses to look at. In the next chapter, we tell you how to evaluate the houses you see so that you can decide which one you actually want to buy.

4

EVALUATING THE HOUSES YOU SEE

In the course of house-hunting, you will probably see many different houses. Some you will be able to eliminate from consideration immediately. Others you will want to think about. You may end up evaluating several houses to see how they compare with your wish list and with each other. In order to keep track of the houses you have looked at and are thinking about, use one or more of the following methods:

- Make a copy of your wish list for each house you view and check off the features and location of that house.
- Take notes by hand or by using a tape recorder.
- Photograph or videotape the house, if the vendor will let you.
- Keep a copy of any "feature sheet" giving details about the house.
- Use the pre-printed evaluation form that your real estate agent may have for you.

When you are evaluating the houses you see, think about the location of the house, its features, and its condition. Below we set out some specific things to consider.

LOCATION OF YOUR HOME

Some people fall in love with a house and buy it for its new kitchen and bathrooms, and they don't bother to look beyond the house itself. Once you're in love, it's hard to be objective. The fact that your garbage will only be picked up occasionally, or that the "nearest" school is not exactly near, will pale in importance as you look adoringly at the brand new cabinets and stove or the gleaming bathroom fixtures. But some day after you move in, when your love has started to fade, garbage pick-up and a school within walking distance will suddenly seem a lot more important. That's why we asked you to identify some things about the location of the house when you were creating the wish list.

Some of the "must haves" you identified on your location wish list will depend on the municipality that the house is located in. Each municipality has its own government, services—and taxes. The quality of the services, and their cost, can vary widely from municipality to municipality. Other "must haves" will depend on the neighbourhood. What a neighbourhood is varies from place to place: it can be a small town or a district within a city. Sometimes the choice of neighbourhood and the choice of municipality amount to the same thing. In large urban areas, however, there are so many different kinds of neighbourhoods that the choice of neighbourhood may be as important as, if not more important than, the choice of municipality.

Type of Location

The type of location means

• a city
• a suburb
• a small town
• the country

The decision about type of location is often a life-style choice, although the choice will also have an effect on the price of the home you buy.

Easy Commuting

Probably the question about location that concerns people most is: How long is it going to take to get to work? The only sure way of finding out is by making the trip at the usual time you travel, using whatever method of transportation you intend to use. Your neighbourhood may have traffic restrictions in place designed to limit rush hour traffic. These restrictions may limit your ability to get in and out of your neighbourhood during those times, so don't forget to take them into account too.

If you or members of your family rely on public transit, you should check with the municipal transit authority for information on the nearest transit line, including

• the nearest stop

• when service is available (evenings, weekends, and holidays)

• the frequency of service

• transit routes

• transit fares

Whether you walk, drive, or take public transit, you will want to know how quickly the neighbourhood is plowed out following a snow storm. Call the municipality and ask what plowing priority your street and neighbouring streets have been given.

If the house you are looking at does not have a garage or private drive, check to see whether street parking is allowed and whether you need a municipal permit to park on the street.

Character of the Neighbourhood

The character and appearance of the neighbourhood are major factors in deciding where to buy. First impressions are very important, but remember that one look at a neighbourhood is not enough. You may have done your neighbourhood shopping on weekends or in the evening. What you saw then may not be the same as what you would see on a different day or at a different time. Go back to the neighbourhood or street you are looking at several times. You will see different things at different hours and on different days of the week. Get out of your car and walk around because there are things to hear and smell as well as to see.

Size and Appearance of Houses

Every neighbourhood has a character. Some neighbourhoods are very urban, with houses close together and close to the street, while others are suburban, with houses more widely separated and set back on large lawns. Some neighbourhoods are strictly residential, while others have some shops or light industry. Some neighbourhoods have only single-family homes, while others have multi-family homes or high-rises.

The character of neighbourhoods was once simply allowed to evolve by itself. Now, however, municipalities use **zoning by-laws** to control the look of a neighbourhood. Zoning by-laws can preserve the character of a neighbourhood by restricting the rights of owners to change how their property looks, or they can allow the character to change by permitting owners to alter their property.

Municipal zoning by-laws may control

- the minimum size of the lots
- the size of the house on any lot
- the location of the house on any lot

If you like the present character of a neighbourhood and would like it to stay that way, you want to make sure that the zoning does not allow for any changes, such as

- your neighbour tearing down the house next door, which is just like yours, and replacing it with a "monster home"
- someone buying a neighbouring property and building two or three new homes on it

On the other hand, *you* may wish to

- build an addition to the existing home
- tear down the existing house and build a new one

If you want to be able to make changes, find out whether the existing zoning will allow you to do so. If it does not, you can apply for special permission from the municipality, but an application can be long and expensive, and there is no guarantee that you will get the permission you are asking for.

Restrictions on Activities

Municipalities also use zoning by-laws to control the activities in the neighbourhood. Zoning by-laws may prevent the carrying on of a business and may also control such things as

- the number of unrelated people who can live in a house
- whether or not apartments are permitted in a house
- the number and kind of pets a household can have

If you like what's going on in the neighbourhood right now, you may want to contact the municipality to make sure that the zoning by-laws do not allow for changes such as

- a neighbouring property being used for a business
- a neighbouring home being converted into an apartment building or boarding house

But if you think you may want to change the way the property is used after you move in, for example, to carry on your business from your home or to add a basement apartment, you should check that the existing zoning will allow you to do so. Again, if it does not, you can apply for permission, but getting permission is not a sure thing.

Quiet Street

If you're concerned about traffic noise, be sure to visit the area during morning and evening rush hour. Listen as well as look. While there may not be a lot of traffic on the street itself, there may still be a lot of noise if the neighbourhood is near a major street or highway. Check at other times of the day and night as well to see if noise will be a problem for you. If the street is near a place of worship, there may be a traffic or parking problem at times.

Traffic may not be the only source of noise. Listen for noise from neighbours, airplanes, trains, and any surrounding bars, restaurants, or factories. You should also check for unpleasant smells that might come from restaurants, factories, or farms in the area, or from neighbourhood cooking.

Compatible Neighbours

You may want to know what kind of people live on the street: Do they look after their homes? Are they young or old? Are they families or single people? You will have to go back to the area at several different times on different days to get a sense of who lives on the street. If you are house-hunting in the winter, you may get a sense that no one lives on the street at all!

If you want to know whether or not there are children in the area, make a visit just before school starts and just as school ends.

You can find out the names of people living on a street by checking a municipal directory that lists residents street by street or by checking the municipal assessment rolls. Ask your real estate agent about directories and assessment rolls. Also, ask your agent whether the houses in the immediate area are owner-occupied or rented. Owners often take better care of their property than renters.

Once you zero in on a particular house, pay attention to the next-door neighbours to see whether they're neat and quiet. These are the people whose garbage and noisy parties will affect you, and whom you'll have to deal with about fences and mutual drives.

Safety

Television and newspapers give a lot of coverage to violent crime and street prostitution, so you probably know what neighbourhoods have these problems. However, a lot of seemingly secure neighbourhoods have a high rate of burglaries and break-ins that you're not going to hear about in the media. You can find out the crime statistics of a neighbourhood by contacting the local police, a community newspaper, or a member of the local Neighbourhood Watch, if there is one.

Mature Trees and Sidewalks

While the presence or absence of trees and sidewalks is largely a matter of personal taste, there are some practical concerns. Sidewalks are handy for keeping small children from playing on the road and are safer if you enjoy taking walks. Mature trees can be expensive to maintain and clean up after, and their root systems can cause problems.

Wildlife

Most people realize that if you buy a house in the country, you will have to share the neighbourhood with animals. Even in the city you may have to share your neighbourhood with raccoons, skunks, rabbits, and foxes—in some western areas even with cougars. Call the municipal animal control department to find out whether or not local wildlife is a problem in this neighbourhood.

While we're on the subject of our animal friends, there are urban areas in Canada where termites or carpenter ants are a concern. In such areas, whole neighbourhoods tend to be infested. Call the municipal building department to see whether the neighbourhood where you are house-hunting has been targeted for take-over by insects.

Services

Think about the kinds of services and facilities that you need to make your life safer and easier. Explore the surrounding area to make sure that the services that you'll rely on are readily available.

Schools

If you are a parent with school-aged children, one of the most important considerations when you choose a home is the schools in the area.

Call the municipal school board to find out the name of the elementary, middle, and high schools that serve the neighbourhood. If the local school is not within easy walking distance, ask the school board whether or not bussing is available. Get as much information as you can about the particular school from the school board, from people with children there, or from your real estate agent. You can also call the school and make an appointment for a tour and a meeting with the principal.

Consider asking about

- the academic reputation of the school
- the availability of any special academic programs
- the availability of child care before and after school
- the availability of teams, clubs, and other extracurricular activities

While the local school is the most important consideration, there are good reasons to investigate the municipal school system as a whole. Call the school board associated with each municipality and ask them about the things that are important to you.

- If your child has special needs, is gifted, or simply does not thrive in the school nearest to your home, what programs are available and where are they?
- What is the board's policy about the integration of children with disabilities into the general school population?
- Are there specialized programs available at the elementary and secondary levels, such as French immersion or arts and drama, and where are they located?
- How many high schools are there within the school district, and will you have a choice among them?

If your children attend a private school, you may want to know whether or not there are other children in the neighbourhood who attend the school. You can usually get that information from the private school.

Shopping and Other Services

You should check the distance to the nearest stores, gas station, family doctor, place of worship, and other services you will need on a regular basis.

Nearby Emergency Services

Find out how close emergency services are.

- Is there a hospital within a short distance, and does it have a 24-hour emergency department?
- If there's no nearby hospital, is there an ambulance station with paramedics?
- How close is the nearest fire station, and how long would it take a fire crew to respond to a fire at your home?

• How close is the nearest police station, and what would their response time be to an emergency call from your home?

Recreational Facilities

You may want to drive or walk around the neighbourhood to see whether there are any nearby public

• parks
• playgrounds
• skating rinks
• tennis courts
• gyms
• swimming pools
• golf courses
• libraries

Some municipalities run instructional programs and sports leagues for both children and adults, and some do not. If the municipality has only a few facilities, you may find them crowded and the programs overbooked. Telephone the municipality and ask for information on community facilities and activities—and be sure to ask how difficult it is to register in programs. Will you have to line up at 6 a.m. to get your child into a swimming program, or can you just drop off an application and be assured of getting a spot?

Snow Removal

There are two kinds of municipalities when it comes to removing snow from the sidewalks: those that do and those that don't. But just because the municipality doesn't shovel your sidewalk doesn't mean that *you* don't have to. In fact, most municipalities have by-laws that require homeowners to remove the snow from the sidewalk in front of their house within a certain period of time after a snowfall. Some municipalities will remove your snow, if you don't, but will charge you for the service, usually by adding it to your tax bill. In addition, you may also be fined for not shovelling. Some municipalities, if requested to do so, will automatically shovel the sidewalks of homeowners who are elderly or disabled, usually at no charge or for a minimal charge.

Telephone the municipality and say that you would like information on snow removal.

Garbage Pick-up and Recycling

You put your garbage in the garbage can and leave it on the curb, and that's all there is to it, right? Wrong!

Every municipality has rules governing what garbage they will take, when they will take it, and how it must be packaged. While there are some municipalities that will pick up anything left at the curb that doesn't move (Beware, napping children and animals!), others will not pick up garbage if it is put out too long before pick-up, or in the wrong kind or size of container, or if it is not properly sorted into real garbage and recyclables. A homeowner we know, frustrated at having had her garbage rejected on several occasions, finally placed a big red bow on the garbage bag, with a note which read, "Will you accept this if it is gift-wrapped?"

There are some municipalities that do not pick up garbage at all, particularly in rural areas. Then it's up to you to take the garbage to the local dump, and you usually have to pay a fee for this privilege.

Telephone the municipality and ask for information on garbage removal and recycling. Some municipalities will provide you with written information and instructions.

Mail Delivery to Your Door

Most, but not all, Canadians have their mail delivered to their door. In many rural areas, Canada Post does not offer home mail delivery. Instead, mail is delivered to a local post office where it must be picked up. Even in some urban areas, usually in newer subdivisions or developments, home mail delivery is not available. In these areas, mail is delivered to community mailboxes. If you have any doubts about whether or not home delivery of mail is offered in the neighbourhood, call Canada Post's customer relations department.

Water and Sewage Systems

In most urban areas water supply and sewage disposal are provided by the municipality. While the municipal water supplies are almost always safe, there are some places where there have been problems with water purity. Call the municipality to see whether or not there has been a problem.

In most rural areas, each homeowner must rely on well water and must have a septic tank for waste disposal. If homes in the municipality rely on well water, the question is whether there is any groundwater contamination. Again, call the municipality for information.

Low Property Taxes

Property taxes vary widely from municipality to municipality. Strikingly similar houses in neighbouring municipalities can have very different tax bills. The factors that affect whether a municipality's taxes are high or low are many and complicated. Higher taxes do not necessarily mean that you will get more or better services. To get information about the general level of property taxes in a particular municipality, speak to a real estate agent familiar with that municipality.

Stable Property Values

When you buy a house, in addition to getting a place to live, you are making a very large investment. The days of making huge profits on the sale of your home are probably over, but you hope that when it comes time to sell your home, you will make some money, or at least not lose any.

There are certain areas where the houses tend to hold their value better, even if house prices are generally falling. In these areas, house prices also seem to rise higher when house prices are going up. No one can predict the future, but an experienced real estate agent can tell you about the history of house prices in the area.

FEATURES OF THE HOUSE

House-hunting can be a bit of a chore, but it is also an adventure. It gives you a chance to see how other people live (and whether their furniture matches). Even if you decide that a particular house is not for you, you can get decorating or renovation ideas you will be able to use in the house you do buy.

Now is the time that your wish list will be useful. Check how many of your "must haves" and "would likes" each house has. But don't just focus on features. When you go through a house, try to picture how you would feel living there. Is there enough room for all of your family and possessions? Will you feel comfortable there? Will the house suit your needs five years from now?

CONDITION OF THE HOUSE

Once you've found a house that has the features you're looking for, go over it carefully to make sure that it doesn't also have problems you'd like to avoid. It's not enough just to look at the house; you also have to ask questions of both the owner and the owner's real estate agent. And don't just ask questions about specific things you may notice: look the owner straight in the eye and ask if he or she is aware of *any* problems with the house.

The vendor and the vendor's real estate agent have a legal obligation to tell you about any problems they know about, whether or not you ask. There are some vendors who might not tell you if you don't ask—in spite of this obligation. But there are fewer vendors who can look you straight in the eye and lie in answer to a direct question. In fact, if the vendor does no tell you about a defect that he or she *knows* about (whether or not you ask about it) you may be able to sue the vendor later. For more information about this see Chapter 10.

You may be thinking that you will have any home you buy professionally inspected, so why should *you* ask questions about it and go over it like a detective? While a professional home inspection should uncover any defects that the vendor is trying to hide, it is too expensive to do on every house you look at. You will only have one done on a house you are serious about buying. We recommend that you ask questions and do an inspection yourself to eliminate houses that are in poor condition, so that you don't waste your time on them.

You can get a sense of the general condition of a house just by casually looking around. You'll notice right away if the house smells or if every room needs painting. But try to get a better idea of the potential repair and maintenance costs by focusing on the things in the following table:

EXTERIOR

Roof

Are shingles missing, cracked, or curled?

How old is the roof? Even heavy-duty grade shingles only last 20 years.

Chimney

Is it straight?

Is the brick crumbling?

Eavestroughs and downspouts

Are they rusted or corroded?

Do they overflow?

Foundations

Are there visible cracks or crumbling mortar?

Is there soil erosion around downspouts?

Do decks, patios, or the yard slope toward the house? If they do, you can expect water to run into the basement.

Brickwork

Are there cracked or loose bricks? This may be caused by settlement in the foundation.

Is the mortar crumbling?

Are the bricks flaking (spalling)? The underlying cause may be poor-quality bricks and poor construction.

Is there white powder (efflorescence) on the bricks? This is an indication that moisture has penetrated the brick either from outside or inside the house.

Siding

Is vinyl siding buckling?

Is wood siding splitting, rotting, or buckling?

Is metal siding dented, pitted, corroded, or buckling?

Is stucco cracked, chipped, or loose?

Paint

Is paint peeling or flaking?

Concrete stairs and walkways

Are they uneven or cracked?

Wooden stairs, decks, and patios
   Are they uneven, sagging, or rotting?
   Are boards loose or missing?

Pool and equipment
   Is the water cloudy or still? The pump may not work.
   Is the pump noisy?
   Are tiles loose?

Trees and landscaping
   Are trees and shrubs overgrown or dying?
   If house is exposed to the weather, are there trees to form a windbreak?

Fences and retaining walls
   Are they leaning or rotting?

Next-door neighbours
   Do they maintain their properties?

INTERIOR

Kitchen
   Is there space for your refrigerator, dishwasher, and stove? Measure.
   What is the interior condition of cabinets?
   Are there signs of leakage under the sink?

Bathrooms
   Is there mildew or mould in bathtubs and showers?
   Is there adequate ventilation?
   Are there cracked or missing tiles?
   Are fixtures stained, cracked, or chipped?
   Is paint blistering or peeling or is plaster soft?
   Are there signs of leakage anywhere?
   Check the water pressure by turning on the taps and flushing toilets.

Walls
   Are walls straight?
   Are there cracks or holes?

Is plaster bulging?

Is paint chipping, flaking, or peeling? Most homes built before the 1960s have lead paint on the walls—if not as the surface coat of paint then somewhere below. Lead paint is not a health hazard as long as the paint is not flaking or chipping off the walls or woodwork. If it is, there is a danger of small children or pets eating paint flakes and suffering lead poisoning. (Removing lead paint should be done by professionals since the stripping process releases lead dust into the air.)

Is paint faded?

Is wallpaper peeling?

Ceilings

Are they stained, cracked, or warped? Is paint peeling? Any of these things may mean water leakage.

Floors and stairways

Are floors or stairs uneven?

Do floorboards squeak?

Are there hardwood floors under the carpeting (ask, or check for yourself by lifting loose carpet)?

Are floor tiles chipped, missing, uneven, or discoloured?

Is carpeting worn or stained?

Doors and windows

Are doors and windows unevenly hung?

Do doors and windows stick or scrape?

Are window panes broken or missing?

Are window frames rotting or stained?

Is caulking missing from window frames?

Basement

Are walls stained or damp? Are they crumbling or do they have white spots? These are signs of a damp basement.

Does the basement smell damp or musty?

Are there signs of drain backup?

Heating

How high are heating costs? Ask.

What kind of heating system is used and how old is it? Find out. Then check with the manufacturer or its service representative how long such a furnace is designed to last. If the furnace is not natural gas but you would like to convert to natural gas, call the gas company to find out whether this kind of furnace can be converted.

Has the furnace been professionally serviced on a regular basis? Ask.

Do all the chimneys have liners? Ask.

Are furnace and pipes corroded?

Is there oil spillage around an oil furnace?

Is there a gas smell around a gas furnace?

Are there leaks around hot water radiators?

If the weather is cold while you're house-hunting, are there portable heaters around? Do you feel drafts in the house? Have doors and windows been left open to hide the fact that the house is cold even when the heat is on?

Air-conditioning

Is there central air-conditioning?

If not, is the heating system hot water? Not every hot-water heating system can accommodate a soft-duct cooling system.

Electrical system

What kind of wiring is in the house? Copper wiring is safer than the aluminum wiring that is found in many older houses.

Check inside the control panel to see whether there are circuit breakers or older style fuse boxes.

Insulation

Has the attic been insulated and vented? Attic insulation is more important than exterior wall insulation. An attic vent will draw off moisture and will keep the house cooler in the summer.

What kind of insulation has been used? If urea formaldehyde foam insulation (UFFI) has been used, the resale value of the house will be affected, even though recent studies suggest that UFFI is not a health hazard.

Insects and other pests

Check for evidence of termites or carpenter ants: Is there sawdust around exposed wood? If so, tap the wood to see if it sounds hollow.

Check for evidence of insects or rodents by looking inside cupboards and closets for dead insects or mice, droppings, or traps and poison bait.

Septic systems and wells

How old is the well?

When was the septic tank last inspected and cleaned?

When was the well water last tested for purity, and what was the result?

What is the capacity of the well, and is there a cistern?

How many gallons per hour can the well pump handle?

SPECIAL CONSIDERATIONS FOR CONDOMINIUMS

You may be thinking about buying a condominium. There are advantages and disadvantages to this kind of ownership. There are also special concerns that you should turn your mind to before buying a particular condominium unit.

What is Condominium Ownership?

Condominium ownership is different from other forms of home ownership. If you buy into a condominium, you become the owner of a particular apartment or townhouse. You also become an owner, along with all the other apartment or townhouse owners, of a share of the **common areas** of the condominium development such as the hallways, the elevators, the stairs, the lobby, the parking areas, the grounds, and recreational facilities. Common areas also include the exterior structure of the condominium buildings and all shared mechanical equipment such as heating, cooling, and water systems.

As an owner of the common areas you are required to pay a monthly **maintenance fee** for their repair and maintenance. The monthly maintenance fees are put into a fund out of which repairs and maintenance costs are paid. The fund is supposed to be large enough to cover ordinary maintenance and repairs. But if it is not large enough, or if something major or unforeseen happens to the common areas, you can be required to pay a **special assessment**.

There are both advantages and disadvantages to condominium ownership. A major attraction of condominium ownership is that responsibility for actually doing maintenance and repairs belongs to the condominium corporation. (That means that you won't have to worry about mowing the lawn or shovelling the snow—although you are responsible for the maintenance of the inside of your unit.) Also, some condominium developments offer facilities like tennis courts, exercise rooms, party rooms, and swimming pools. On the downside, condominiums have rules and by-laws that may limit your freedom to use your home as you wish.

Evaluating a Condominium

If you're buying a condominium you should evaluate it the way you would any other type of home. But there are additional matters to consider.

Is the Condominium Corporation Financially Sound?

As a potential unit owner, you want to be reasonably sure that your monthly maintenance fee will not change drastically, and that you will not be called upon to pay any special assessment. Asking the following questions before you decide to buy may keep you from buying into a condominium corporation that is not in good financial health.

WHAT IS THE CURRENT MAINTENANCE FEE AND IS IT REASONABLE? Find out what the current monthly maintenance fee is and make sure it is an amount you can afford. Does the fee include heat, electricity, and water, or are they extra?

Ask the condominium manager whether the level of the monthly maintenance fees throughout the condominium is high enough to cover the ongoing maintenance of the condominium and any expected repairs. Also ask whether the corporation has a fund set aside for unexpected expenses, and how much is in it. If the monthly fees are high enough and there is a fund, there is a better chance that your monthly fee won't rise too much and that you won't be required to pay a special assessment.

ARE THE OTHER OWNERS UP TO DATE IN PAYING THEIR MAINTENANCE FEES? The condominium corporation may have set exactly the right monthly fees. But if many unit owners are not paying those fees, you could end up paying higher fees after you move in. You should ask the manager if all owners are up to date in their payments, and if not, how much has not been paid. While you're at it, ask what percentage of the units are occupied by owners. Owners who live in their units are more likely to continue to make their maintenance payments.

IS THE CONDOMINIUM PROPERLY MAINTAINED? If the condominium is properly maintained, the chance of a major unexpected repair is reduced. Ask the condominium manager whether any major repairs are being planned. If so, ask whether there is enough money on hand to pay for the repair. Also ask what major repairs have recently been done.

How Well is the Condominium Managed?

The condominium manager looks after the maintenance of and repairs to the condominium. Ask other residents whether or not they are pleased with the present manager.

Features of the Unit

In addition to the things you would look for in any home, make sure that your unit will not be too noisy by checking the soundproofing between your unit and neighbouring units. Also note how close the unit is to elevators, garbage chutes, recreational facilities, and other noisy common areas.

Facilities

Find out what facilities are included in your ownership. For example:

SECURITY: What kind of security is offered and does it seem adequate for your needs?

PARKING: Is a parking spot included with your ownership, and is there enough guest parking?

RECREATIONAL FACILITIES: What facilities are available? Are they well maintained? Is use of them included in your ownership or do you have to pay an additional fee? Are non-owners also allowed to use the facilities? Are the facilities over-crowded?

Restrictions

Find out from the condominium manager what restrictions there are in the by-laws and rules of the condominium corporation. For example:

- Can you rent out your unit?
- Can you have pets?
- Can you carry on a business in your unit?
- If you have a yard, can you garden? If you have windows or a balcony, can you put out plants?

Buying a Newly Constructed Condominium

If you buy a newly constructed condominium and the condominium corporation is not registered at the closing date, you cannot become the legal owner until later. You will, however, probably have to make your down payment. You may also be required to make monthly rental payments, and you will be able to move into the building as a tenant. Once the condominium corporation is registered, you will become the legal owner—and can stop paying rent and start paying your mortgage.

SPECIAL CONSIDERATIONS FOR HOUSES UNDER CONSTRUCTION

If you are buying a house in a new development, there are a number of special concerns.

Builder's Reputation

You are buying the services of the builder as well as the land your house will be located on, so it's important to buy from a reputable builder. You probably want to choose a builder who is registered in your province's new home warranty program. Check the builder's track record for building well and responding to complaints. Try to talk to owners of houses in developments by the same builder. Call your local Home Builders' Association or your provincial new home warranty program for information—especially whether there have been complaints—about the builder.

Picturing What Your Home Will Look Like

When you buy a house in a new development, it is usually built *after* you buy it, so you have to imagine what it will look like. Sometimes the builder will have a model home for you to look at, but other times you will have to buy from floor plans and sketches. It's important to make sure that the builder agrees to build the house you think you are getting.

Your neighbours' houses will not usually be built either at the time you buy your home, so you will have to imagine what the street will look like as well as the house. You will probably pick the location of your home within the development from a site model or map. Look carefully at the model or map to see whether your street is likely to become a heavy-traffic route once the development is completed. Ask where shops, schools, and other services will be located, if it isn't clear from the model or map.

You should also go to the actual house site to check things like the view, the slope of the land, and closeness to noisy highways. If the site you chose is located near the boundaries of the development, look at what is built on the neighbouring land. If there is nothing there, ask the builder what is going to be built.

Possible Inconvenience

When you buy a home that is not yet built, there can be construction delays. You may not be able to move into your home when you planned. If you are selling your present home, you may end up having to find another place to stay until construction is finished. Once you get into your new home, you may continue to live with the dust and noise of construction for quite some time. Roads may not be paved and landscaping may not be completed until well after you move in.

New Home Warranties

All provinces in Canada have a new home warranty program. If you deal with a builder who is registered under the provincial warranty program, your home will be covered for certain problems that may arise within a specified period of time after you buy. In Ontario, all newly constructed homes are covered, but coverage is optional in the rest of Canada. If your new home is covered, you will be given warranty documents, and your lawyer will go over them with you.

If your new home is covered by a warranty, you will probably have to make a detailed inspection of the house before closing to make a note of any problems. The builder is supposed to fix them within a short time after closing. After closing you will continue to be covered for things like major structural defects, defects in work and materials, water seepage through the foundation, defects in the electrical, plumbing, and heating systems, and violations of the provincial building code. The warranty period, which depends on the province and the nature of the problem, can be from one to five years in most provinces (one to seven in Ontario).

5 MAKING AN OFFER TO PURCHASE

Once you find a house you want to own, the next step is to tell the vendor you want to buy it. You do this by making an **offer to purchase.**

Your agent will discuss with you the price you want to pay and other matters relating to your purchase of the property, and will then draw up the offer using a preprinted form. The preprinted form will be titled "agreement of purchase and sale" or, in Quebec, "promise to purchase." When the offer has been drawn up, you should have it reviewed by a lawyer before you sign it.

After you have signed the offer, your real estate agent will present it to the vendor, together with a deposit. You will have stated in the offer how long the vendor has to respond before it expires. The vendor may reject your offer, sign back a counter-offer, or accept your offer. If the vendor rejects your offer, there is no contract. You may either make another offer or walk away. If the vendor signs back a counter-offer, there is no contract. You can either accept the counter-offer, reject it, or make yet another counter-offer. If the vendor accepts your offer before it expires or you accept the vendor's counter-offer, you have a contract. The contract is called an **agreement of purchase and sale.**

THE NATURE OF THE
AGREEMENT OF PURCHASE AND SALE

An agreement of purchase and sale is a contract by which you promise to pay the vendor an agreed amount of money in return for ownership of the property, and the vendor promises to transfer to you ownership or **title** to the property. Unless you agree otherwise, that title is to be unlimited and free of claims by anyone else. The agreement of purchase and sale does not make you the owner of the property. The actual transfer of title and payment of the money take place at a later date that is called the **completion date** or **closing date.**

Even though you do not become the owner of the property until the closing date, the agreement of purchase and sale is a binding contract. This means that you have a legal obligation to pay the promised amount of money, which is called the **purchase price,** and the vendor has a legal obligation to transfer ownership to you. If either one of you decides not to go through with the deal, that person can be sued.

By law, a contract to buy and sell land has to be in writing. If you make just an oral agreement with the vendor to buy the house, you won't be able to force the vendor to transfer ownership to you.

THE CONTENTS OF YOUR OFFER

The printed form of agreement of purchase and sale used by real estate agents varies from province to province, but the contents are similar. There will be blank spaces to be filled in with the following:

- the names of the purchaser, the vendor, and the real estate agents
- a brief description of the property—its municipal address, lot measurements, and maybe its lot and plan number
- the purchase price, the deposit, and the way in which you will pay the balance of the purchase price
- any chattels to be included in the sale
- the expiry date for your offer, the date by which your lawyer's investigation of the title must be completed, and the closing date

There will also be a number of standard preprinted paragraphs, usually in very small print. Maybe it's just as well that the print is very small, because otherwise you might be tempted to try to read the paragraphs. These paragraphs are drafted by lawyers for lawyers and are very difficult to understand. The most important of these paragraphs deal with the title or ownership rights you will get when the deal closes and

- whether or not you agree to accept any limitations to your title or ownership rights

- the things your lawyer has to do to make sure you get the title or ownership rights you were promised by the vendor

- what happens if the vendor can't give you the title or ownership rights that were promised

The agreement of purchase and sale will have a place where you can insert custom-made clauses that cover matters of importance to you that are not mentioned in the standard preprinted clauses. Finally, the printed form will have a place for you to sign your offer and for the vendor to sign if your offer is accepted. Once the vendor signs the form, it becomes a contract.

Some of the things we've mentioned so far are pretty self-explanatory, like the names of the parties and real estate agents and the address of the property. But we think you need to know a bit more about some other things, so don't stop reading yet.

The Description of the Property

The dimensions of the property will be set out. You want to make sure the property is the size that you think it is. The vendor only has to sell you a property that is the size set out in the agreement.

Any **easements** will also be set out. An easement (**servitude** in Quebec) is a right that someone has to use or cross over a part of your property. For example, if there is a shared driveway, the next-door neighbour has an easement over your half of the driveway, and you have an easement over the neighbour's half. If you are supposed to be getting an easement over a neighbouring property, you want to make sure that the description says so. If the description says that the property you're buying has an easement over it, you will have to take ownership of the property subject to that easement.

The Purchase Price and the Deposit

The purchase price is what you agree to pay the vendor for the house. As we mentioned in Chapter 2, the price may be adjusted for such things as property taxes and utility payments made by the vendor.

The adjusted purchase price is the total amount you pay the vendor, and is made up of

- the deposit

- any mortgage the vendor has that you agree to assume, or any vendor take-back mortgage

- the cash you pay on closing (after deducting the deposit and any assumed mortgage)

The Deposit

When you give your offer to the vendor, it is usual to pay a deposit as a way of showing that you are serious about buying the property. Five per cent of the purchase price is common in most provinces. When a real estate agent is involved, the deposit cheque is made payable to the vendor's real estate agent. The cheque will only be cashed if your offer is accepted. The vendor's real estate agent will hold the deposit money in trust, and it will be credited toward the purchase price.

We told you before that if you back out of the purchase without a legally valid reason, you may have to compensate the vendor for any losses. Instead of suing you for the actual losses, the vendor can claim your deposit. So whatever amount of money you pay as a deposit, you stand to lose if you refuse to complete the purchase.

The vendor will want a high deposit to make it less likely that you will refuse to complete the purchase. You can ask your real estate agent how large a deposit you should make. But the real estate agent also wants to make sure that you will complete the purchase (because otherwise he or she won't receive any commission), so the agent can't be totally objective.

Your deposit, which may be many thousands of dollars, must be paid at the time your offer is accepted. It doesn't become the vendor's money until the closing date, which can be a month or more away. Until closing, it sits in the real estate agent's trust account, earning interest. If the money were sitting in your bank account, the interest would be yours. There is no reason why the real estate agent should be allowed to keep the interest, so ask your agent to put a clause into the agreement of purchase and sale that the vendor's agent will pay the interest to you.

Assumed Mortgages and Vendor Take-Back Mortgages

The vendor may have an outstanding mortgage on the house. If the mortgage is in the right amount and has a favourable interest rate, you may want to **assume** this existing mortgage instead of or in addition to arranging a new one. If you assume an existing mortgage, you will take over the vendor's mortgage payments and be given a credit against the purchase price equal to the outstanding balance of the mortgage. In other words, the amount of cash you have to pay on closing is reduced by the amount of that balance. If you wish to assume an existing mortgage, your offer will say so and set out the details of the mortgage.

Sometimes the vendor will be willing to lend you some of the purchase price by giving you a mortgage. This is called a **vendor take-back mortgage.**

The amount of any vendor take-back mortgage is deducted from what you have to pay in cash on closing. After the closing, you will make mortgage payments to the vendor. If you wish the vendor to take back a mortgage, the offer must say so and set out details of the mortgage.

Cash on Closing

On closing you are required to pay the balance of the purchase price after deducting your deposit and the amount of any assumed or vendor take-back mortgages. This money is to be paid in cash or by certified cheque. You will give the money to your lawyer for payment to the vendor.

Chattels and Fixtures

In legal jargon, there are two kinds of property: real property and personal property. Land and the house on it are real property. Personal property is property you can move like a sofa, a television, your clothing. Personal property can also be called **chattels (movables** in Quebec).

Personal property can become attached to real property. When this happens, the personal property becomes part of the real property, and then is called a **fixture.** You can go to the store and buy wooden boards, which are personal property. If you use the wooden boards to make a built-in bookcase attached to your wall, the bookcase is a fixture.

When you buy a house, fixtures are automatically included as part of the house. Sometimes a vendor will want the right to take certain fixtures out of the house. In order for the vendor to do so, the agreement of purchase and sale must specifically state what those fixtures are. Chattels on the other hand, like washers and dryers, are not included as part of what you are buying unless the agreement of purchase and sale says that they are.

It's often hard to know what is a chattel and what is a fixture. You can't always tell by looking at a bookcase whether it's attached to the wall or just standing there. If it's attached, it's a fixture and included with the house, but if it's not attached, it's a chattel and not included. So if you want something included in the purchase price, it is important for the agreement of purchase and sale to say so. If you don't, you may think it's included but the vendor does not, and is planning to remove it.

Be sure to mention

- appliances
- light fixtures and ceiling fans
- carpets, drapes, and blinds
- bookcases and shelving systems, including closet shelves

- satellite dishes
- storage sheds
- garage door openers
- window air-conditioners

Dates

There are several places in the preprinted agreement of purchase and sale for dates to be inserted.

One date is called the **irrevocable date,** which is the date that your offer to purchase the house expires. The vendor has until that date to accept your offer. If the vendor does not accept by that date, your offer automatically comes to an end. It is best to give the vendor only a short time to decide whether to accept your offer. You don't want to have to wait too long to start looking at other houses if the vendor is not going to accept your offer.

Another date is the **closing date,** which is the date on which the purchase will be completed, the day you pay your money and become the owner of the house. Choose a closing date that gives you enough time to get the money you need to pay for the house and to get ready to move. Even if you're in a hurry, give your lawyer enough time to do the necessary legal work. In addition, the registry office (where most closings take place) is busier on some days than others. If you pick a busy day for your closing, there may be delays. Ask your real estate agent for advice about choosing a date, and your lawyer will also check the date when reviewing the offer.

The agreement of purchase and sale may also state a period of time or date by which your lawyer is to complete an investigation of the vendor's title to the property. This date is often known as the **requisition date.** If your agreement is conditional on things like a satisfactory house inspection or getting a mortgage, you don't want your lawyer to have to start the title investigation until you have firmed up the deal, because investigating a title costs a lot of money. You also want to make sure that your lawyer has enough time to do a proper investigation. Your real estate agent can give you some advice about the requisition date, and your lawyer should check this date as well before you sign the offer.

Custom-Made Clauses

In addition to the standard preprinted paragraphs in an agreement of purchase and sale, there is room to add custom-made clauses.

Conditions

You may want to be able to get out of the agreement of purchase and sale, even after the vendor has signed, for certain reasons:

- You can't sell your present house.
- You can't get mortgage financing.
- The vendor's mortgagee won't allow you to assume the vendor's mortgage.
- A professional inspection of the vendor's house has turned up serious problems.

In order to be able to get out of the deal, you must add a clause that states that the agreement is **conditional** upon the happening of a certain event by a certain date. If the event does not happen by that date, the agreement is at an end and you can get your deposit back. If the event does happen by that date, the contract is binding.

MAKING YOUR OFFER CONDITIONAL ON SELLING YOUR PRESENT HOUSE: If you already own a house, you may not have sold it yet. If you sign an unconditional agreement to buy this home, you will be legally bound to buy it, even if you can't find a buyer for your old house. To protect yourself, you can make your offer to purchase conditional on being able to sell your old house within a fixed period of time. If your offer to buy is accepted and you don't sell your house before the end of that period, you don't have to go through with the deal. The vendor may not want to agree to a condition like this, especially if you're offering a lower price than the vendor would like.

MAKING YOUR OFFER CONDITIONAL ON GETTING MORTGAGE FINANCING: If you will need a mortgage to pay for your new home, you don't want to be legally bound to buy the house if you won't be able to get a mortgage. If you make your offer conditional on getting satisfactory mortgage financing, you can choose not to complete the deal if you can't get a mortgage for the amount of money you need at a reasonable interest rate.

MAKING YOUR OFFER CONDITIONAL ON BEING ABLE TO ASSUME THE VENDOR'S MORTGAGE: The vendor may have a mortgage on the house that you'd like to assume. If the mortgage documents say that the mortgagee's approval is necessary before the mortgage can be assumed, the offer must be conditional on getting that approval.

MAKING YOUR OFFER CONDITIONAL ON A SATISFACTORY HOME INSPECTION: Even though you carefully looked over the house before you decided to make your offer, we strongly recommend that you make the offer conditional on a satisfactory inspection report from a qualified home inspector. A home inspector will examine the house and report to you on its age and condition, tell you whether repairs are necessary, and give you an estimate of repair costs. Ask your real estate agent or your lawyer for the name of a reliable inspector. If the inspector finds that the house is in bad shape for its age, you may be able to refuse to go ahead with the purchase.

You can't just use a condition as an excuse to back out of the deal. You must make all reasonable efforts to satisfy the condition. If the agreement is conditional on selling your present house, you must list it for sale. If someone makes you a reasonable offer, you can't refuse it and then try to get out of the deal by saying you have not sold your house. If the agreement is conditional on your being able to get a mortgage or assume the vendor's mortgage, you must apply for the mortgage and provide all necessary information to the mortgagee. You can't simply not apply and then try to get out of the deal by saying you have no mortgage. If the agreement is conditional on a satisfactory professional home inspection, you must arrange for the inspection. You won't be able to claim that the inspection is not satisfactory unless it reveals significant problems.

Other Special Clauses

You may wish to put in a clause that gives you the right to visit the house before the closing date so that you can take measurements for carpets and drapes or have a contractor give you an estimate for work to be done after closing.

You may also wish to add a clause giving you the right to inspect the property just before closing to make sure that the property is in more or less the same condition it was in when you agreed to buy it.

If the house has a pool and you can't have it inspected because the pool isn't open for the summer, you may wish to add a warranty clause from the vendor that the pool and equipment are in good working order, and that your lawyer can hold back part of the purchase price until you can have the pool inspected. If the inspection confirms that everything is all right, the money will then be paid to the vendor.

There may be other clauses that your lawyer will suggest that you should put into your offer.

The Vendor May Not Agree to All Your Terms

What you sign is only an offer. You can put anything you like into your offer, but it's entirely up to the vendor to accept it, reject it, or sign back a counter-offer. The things that the vendor is most likely to change are the purchase price and the amount of the deposit. The vendor may also want a different closing date. The vendor may remove one or more of your special clauses. If the vendor makes any changes to your offer, you have to decide whether or not you want to accept the counter-offer.

IT'S IMPORTANT TO HAVE A LAWYER REVIEW YOUR OFFER

You might wonder why you must have your lawyer review your offer when you have an experienced real estate agent to help you draft it.

Once your offer is accepted by the vendor, you have a binding contract. You are stuck with the deal! You will have to pay a lot of money when the deal closes, and you want to be sure that you'll get what you want in return. Your lawyer reviews the offer to make sure that it includes all the right clauses so that you will get what you expect.

In a hot real estate market, you may have to move quickly to make an offer on a property before someone else snaps it up. You may think there is no time to have your lawyer review your offer, and you may be right. On the other hand you may be wrong, so call your lawyer to see if he or she can review the offer quickly. If not, ask your real estate agent to put a clause in the offer making the agreement conditional on satisfactory review by your lawyer within twenty-four to forty-eight hours. Or, finally, you can just put your offer in and hope for the best.

PRIVATE SALES

If you decide to make an offer to a vendor who is selling privately, you will not have the help of a real estate agent to draft your offer. The vendor may give you a printed form to use—the vendor may even try to fill it out for you. Your best bet is to have your lawyer draft the offer for you, but if it is you or the vendor who drafts it, it is absolutely essential to have your lawyer review it before you sign it.

THE RESPONSIBILITY TO CLOSE

Once you sign an agreement of purchase and sale, you are legally bound to pay for the property, and the vendor is legally bound to transfer ownership of the property to you and to give you possession of the house and property.

If the Purchaser Refuses to Close

On the day of closing, you have a legal obligation to pay for the house. If you refuse to close the deal without a valid reason, the vendor can claim your deposit, although he or she may have to sue to get it.

Instead of claiming the deposit, in most provinces the vendor can sue you for damages. If the vendor is successful, the damages will amount to the difference between what you were supposed to pay, and what the vendor actually receives after selling the house to someone else. You may also have to pay some of the vendor's legal fees.

If the Vendor Refuses to Close

On the day of closing, the vendor also has a legal obligation—to transfer the house to you and hand over possession. If the vendor has changed his or her mind about selling since you signed the agreement of purchase and sale, you can sue for **specific performance.** If you are successful, you will get a court order requiring the vendor to hand over the house and title on exactly the terms set out in the agreement. You may also be able to get money from the vendor by way of court-ordered **damages,** to compensate you for your trouble. The vendor will probably also have to pay some of your legal fees.

While a court action is going on, you can probably prevent the vendor from selling the house to anyone else by registering notice of your lawsuit against the title to the house.

Obviously, you didn't sign an agreement to buy a house with the intention of backing out at the last minute. Neither did the vendor. It is very unusual for a vendor to refuse to close.

Once you have a signed agreement of purchase and sale, your house-hunting is over! Now it is time to turn things over to your lawyer.

6

THE PURCHASER'S LAWYER

DO YOU NEED A LAWYER?

We'll give you the bad news right up front: you're going to need a lawyer to buy a house, and it's going to cost at least several hundred dollars and maybe as much as several thousand dollars, depending on the cost of your home and how complicated the deal is. The following discussion of the role of the purchaser's lawyer should help you understand both why you need a lawyer and why lawyers charge as much as they do.

The Role of the Lawyer in Purchasing a House

Before you decided to buy your house, you spent a lot of time and effort making sure the house suited your needs and budget. You also carefully examined the physical condition of the house and maybe even hired a professional home inspector to help you. But nothing in this process told you who actually owns the house and whether anyone other than the owner, such as a bank or mortgage company or unpaid creditor, has a claim to the house.

Before you hand money over to the vendor for the house (and you will pay tens if not hundreds of thousands of dollars), you will want to be sure that the vendor is in fact the owner of the house and has the right to sell it free of any claims by anyone else. Put into legal jargon, you want to get not only the house but a **good and marketable title** to the property. If you buy a house that has a claim against it, such as a mortgage, builder's lein or judgment, you will get not only the house but the claim too! Even though the vendor is the one who owes the money, the creditor may be able to force *you* to sell the house in order to pay the claim.

Information about ownership of and claims against land is found in land registry records and in other records kept by the government. It takes professional training to interpret these records. A lawyer has that professional training and can ensure that you are getting a good and marketable title.

A number of documents must be prepared and signed in order to transfer ownership of the house to you. The change in ownership must be registered in the land registry office, and there are taxes and fees that must be paid at the same time. Your lawyer will look after all these things for you.

The Lawyer as Insurance against Title Problems

When your lawyer finishes preparing and registering the documents that transfer ownership, he or she will certify that you have a good and marketable title to your home. This certification is really what you are paying your lawyer for. If it turns out that the lawyer was wrong about the title, you may be able to claim money from the lawyer as compensation. Lawyers are required by law to carry enough insurance to pay claims like these, which, given the cost of real estate, can be quite high.

What about Paralegals and Other Non-Lawyers?

While you may now be convinced that you need some kind of professional help in completing your house purchase, you may still be wondering why that help should come from a lawyer, as opposed to a paralegal or someone else who may seem knowledgeable about real estate and may offer a lower price.

The first reason is that, in all provinces other than British Columbia and Quebec, only lawyers are permitted by law to complete house purchases. In Quebec real estate deals are handled by notaries, and they may also be handled by notaries in British Columbia. Any other non-lawyer who looks after an entire real estate transaction is breaking the law and is subject to prosecution. The second reason is that only a lawyer's certification of title is certain to be backed up by adequate insurance if problems should arise.

WHAT DOES THE LAWYER ACTUALLY DO?

It is important to understand what a lawyer actually does in order to decide whom you want to hire and how much you want to pay. Your lawyer will

- review the agreement of purchase and sale
- search the title to the house
- review the plan of survey of the property
- advise you how to take title to the property
- prepare or review all the necessary documents
- explain the documents to you before you sign them
- close the transaction and register the documents
- notify utilities and government offices that you are now the owner
- provide you with a reporting letter and certification of title

Review of Agreement of Purchase and Sale

You may have asked your lawyer to review the terms of the agreement of purchase and sale before you signed it. If you did not, your lawyer will first become involved after receiving a copy of the signed agreement from you or your real estate agent. Either way your lawyer must review it again now.

In the agreement of purchase and sale, the vendor promised to transfer ownership of the house to you on the closing date. Unless you agreed otherwise, that ownership is to be unlimited and free of claims by anyone else. Your lawyer will review the agreement to see whether or not you agreed to accept any limitations to your ownership. Between the date the lawyer receives the signed agreement and the date of closing, it is the lawyer's job to make sure that the ownership you get on the closing date is exactly the same as the ownership the vendor promised you.

Search of Title

To make sure that you get the ownership you were promised, your lawyer must search the records for your house in the land registry office to confirm that the vendor is the owner and look for any claims against the property. He or she must also contact the utility companies (gas, electricity, water) to make sure that all charges have been paid by the current owners. Your lawyer must also confirm the amount of the municipal realty taxes, and that they have been paid. Finally, in most provinces your lawyer must make sure that the property satisfies all municipal requirements, including zoning. Let your lawyer know if there are signs that a renovation was done on the house. Then your lawyer will know to check whether or not the proper building permits were obtained when the renovation was done.

If your lawyer discovers any problem with the ownership, he or she will ask the vendor's lawyer to correct it by the closing date. If the vendor cannot correct the problem, you have the choice of going ahead with the purchase anyway or, depending on how serious the problem is, ending the deal and getting your deposit money back. Your lawyer will give you advice about the best thing to do if a problem is found.

Review of Plan of Survey

There are certain questions about your house that a lawyer will be able to answer only if there is an up-to-date plan of survey of the property. While you think you are buying a house, what you are really buying is land and any buildings that happen to be sitting on it. So you want to be certain that the house is in fact on the land you are buying. You need a plan of survey to do so. You also need a plan of survey to make sure that

- the house is totally on your land and not partly on your neighbour's land
- your neighbour's house is not on your land
- any fences are on the lot line
- the size and location of the house and any other buildings satisfy zoning requirements

A plan of survey is a scale drawing of a property, prepared by a registered land surveyor. It shows the location of all boundaries of the property, and the location and size of the house, garage, sheds, fences, driveways, and rights of way as of the date the survey was made. If any changes have been made to the size, shape, or location of any of these things since the survey was made, the survey is no longer accurate and up to date, even if it was just recently made. For example, if an addition or a deck has been built or a swimming pool has been installed, the survey will no longer be accurate. If no changes have been made since the date of the last survey, it is still accurate and up to date even if it is very old.

If the vendor has a survey, he or she will generally be required to give a copy to your lawyer. However, the survey the vendor has may not be up to date. If there is no up-to-date survey, or no survey at all, the vendor is not required to give you one. Your lawyer will then ask your permission to arrange to have one done for you. A plan of survey will cost several hundred dollars, and you will have to pay the money up front. It's your choice, but if you do not have an up-to-date plan of survey, your lawyer will not be able to provide you with a complete certification of title. If you are financing your home purchase with a mortgage from a bank, trust company, or insurance company, the mortgagee will almost certainly insist on an up-to-date survey at your expense.

Taking Title

Your lawyer will talk to you about who you want to be the **registered owner** of your home and, if there's more than one owner, what kind of ownership you want.

Who Will Be the Registered Owner?

If you are a single person and are buying the property alone, you will be the registered owner. If you are married or cohabiting with another person, or there are two or more of you buying the property, you have to decide who should be the registered owner(s).

Generally speaking, if two or more people are paying money for the purchase of the property, all of you will want to be shown as the registered owners to make sure that the property cannot be sold without your permission and that, if it is sold, you will all get a share of the money. If you are not married to each other, showing everyone as a registered owner is the only way to be sure of these two things.

Most husbands and wives who buy homes also ask that both of them be shown as the registered owners, whether or not both are paying for the house. Sometimes for business or other reasons it makes sense for only one spouse to be named as the registered owner. You should talk to your lawyer about your business and financial situation to see whether it would be wise for only one of you to be named as the registered owner.

If you are a married couple, even if you are not both named as registered owners, you may both have to give your permission before the property can be sold. This protection is not available to people who are living together but are not legally married. If you are thinking about having only one spouse named as the registered owner, ask your lawyer whether and when the property could be sold without the permission of both of you.

In most provinces, husbands and wives are entitled to a share of each other's property if they separate or divorce. So even if you are not a registered owner of the home, you may be entitled to a share of it. In some provinces, however, whether only one of you is named or both of you are named as the registered owner(s) may affect the size of the share you each get. People who are living together but are not legally married do not have an automatic right to a share in each other's property. If you are married or cohabiting, you should talk to your lawyer about how family law in your province affects your decision about who the registered owner should be.

What Kind of Ownership?

If there are going to be two or more registered owners, you can choose between two different kinds of ownership: **joint tenancy** and **tenancy-in-common**. This does not apply in Quebec, where there is no joint tenancy.

When two or more people own property in joint tenancy, each is an equal owner of the property. The most important feature of joint tenancy is the **right of survivorship,** which means that if one owner dies, that owner's interest in the property automatically passes to the surviving owner or owners, no matter what the dead owner's will says. Usually only people who are related or are cohabiting will want to own property as joint tenants. If you want to own property in joint tenancy, the deed or transfer must clearly state that title is being taken that way.

If you do not specifically state that you are taking title in joint tenancy, you will own the property as tenants-in-common. Your shares in the property do not have to be equal, and your co-owners will not automatically get your share of the property when you die. You can state in your will who will get your share when you die.

You and your lawyer should discuss which kind of ownership is best for you.

Co-ownership Agreements

If you are buying the property with another person, you should ask your lawyer whether or not you should have a co-ownership agreement to deal with such matters as

- acknowledgement of the contribution each owner made toward the purchase
- the responsibilities of each owner toward the maintenance and upkeep of the property
- what happens if one owner wants to sell the property
- how the proceeds of any sale should be divided

If you are married or cohabiting, these matters can be dealt with in a marriage contract or cohabitation agreement.

Preparation, Review, and Explanation of Documents

There is a lot of paper involved in buying a house. Both you and the vendor will have to sign documents. Some of these documents will be prepared by the vendor's lawyer and some by your lawyer. Your lawyer should explain all documents to you before you sign them.

Your lawyer will also tell you exactly how much money you will have to pay on the closing date, and explain to you how that amount was calculated. This amount will almost always be different from the amount in the agreement of purchase and sale. You already paid some money as a deposit. Then there are other items that must be taken into account that may increase or decrease the amount you pay, such as realty taxes and interest on any mortgages you are assuming. All of these are called **adjustments.** It's your lawyer's job to check that the money you pay is the correct amount. When your lawyer is satisfied that the amount is correct, he or she will ask you to bring this sum of money, in the form of a certified cheque, to the office a day or so before the closing.

Homeowner's Insurance

Your lawyer will advise you to arrange for homeowner's insurance that will come into effect as soon as you become the legal owner of the property.

Mortgages

If you are financing the purchase of your house with a mortgage from a bank, trust company, or insurance company, the mortgagee may ask your lawyer to prepare the mortgage documents, and search the title for the mortgage as well.

Closing the Transaction

On the day of closing, your lawyer will meet the vendor's lawyer to pay the final purchase amount and to receive and register the **deed** or **transfer**, which is the document that transfers title in the property from the vendor to you.

The vendor's lawyer may give your lawyer the keys to your new home at the closing. If your lawyer's office is not easy for you to get to, make an arrangement before the closing date to have the keys left with someone who is closer, such as your real estate agent. The agent will give you the keys once your lawyer confirms that the deal has closed.

In some provinces, while you get possession of your house on the closing date, the payment of the purchase amount or registration of the deed or transfer may happen at a later time.

Notification of Utilities and Government Offices

After the closing, your lawyer will notify the utilities and government offices that you are now the owner of the property and will make sure that any out-standing matters with them are cleared up.

Reporting Letter and Certification of Title

Your lawyer will then send you a **reporting letter** giving the details of the transaction along with copies of documents, including the deed, the mort-gage, if any, and the survey, if any. The most important aspect of the report-ing letter is the lawyer's certification of title.

HOW MUCH WILL THE LAWYER COST?

We hate to sound like lawyers, but it depends. Lawyers' fees vary from city to city and province to province. A lawyer's fee depends on a number of factors, including the price of the home, the complexity of the transaction, whether or not a mortgage is involved, and the level of service offered by the lawyer.

Most lawyers will charge a flat fee for a real estate transaction. Some will charge a fee based on the number of hours they actually spend on your trans-action. Some lawyers will quote a flat fee, but will reserve the right to charge you an hourly rate if unexpected title problems arise. Ask the lawyer you are thinking of hiring what fee will be charged for your particular transaction.

In addition to the lawyer's fee, which pays for the lawyer's professional services, you will have pay the lawyer's **disbursements.** These are payments made by the lawyer for such things as a plan of survey, search fees, registra-tion fees, long distance telephone charges, photocopy charges, mileage, and parking. These items, which will not vary a lot from lawyer to lawyer, can still add up to a substantial amount, so ask your lawyer for an estimate.

Some lawyers will hire someone from outside their office to perform some of their professional services, such as searching the records at the land registry office and closing the transaction. Confirm whether or not the fee the lawyer has quoted you will include such outside services. If not, ask how much extra you will be charged for them. When comparing lawyers' fees, make sure you take these charges into account.

HOW DO YOU CHOOSE A LAWYER?

Your home purchase is important to you, so you want to choose a lawyer who will do a thorough job at a reasonable price.

Get Several Recommendations

As with any other professional, the best way to choose a lawyer is to get several recommendations from people you know and trust. Ask friends or relatives who have bought a house who their lawyer was and whether they were happy with him or her. Or ask your real estate agent for a recommendation. If you have no one to ask, you can call your provincial law society for a list of real estate lawyers in your area.

Investigate the Possibilities

Once you have the names of several lawyers, you should do some investigating to decide which one is best for you.

Try to get some idea of the range of fees that each lawyer charges. The fee charged to your friend or relative may not be the same as yours, because the lawyer's fee depends on a number of factors, including the price of the house and the complexity of the transaction. You will find that there are expensive lawyers, cheap lawyers, and lawyers who are somewhere in the middle. While you do not need to hire the most expensive lawyer, it is probably not a good idea to hire the cheapest lawyer either. A lawyer who charges very low fees usually makes a profit because he or she processes a large number of transactions and may not have a great deal of time to spend with you.

Find out where the lawyer's office is. Remember that you will have to go there, perhaps several times and most likely during normal business hours. Choose a lawyer whose location is not too inconvenient.

Speak to the Lawyer

Call the lawyer's office to find out how much experience the lawyer has in the real estate area. It is not necessary to hire a real estate specialist, but you probably don't want to be your lawyer's first real estate client.

Ask the lawyer how much the fee and estimated disbursements will be for your transaction and what services are included in the fee. Ask how much contact you can expect to have with the lawyer's office. Will your contact be primarily with the lawyer or with an assistant?

Try to get a sense of the lawyer's personality and style. Is this person someone you feel you can trust and communicate with comfortably and effectively? (If the lawyer uses an assistant, you may want to meet the assistant too.) The purchase of a home should be a happy occasion, and you will be spending a significant amount of money for legal services. So don't use a lawyer who makes you feel uncomfortable or whom you do not like!

Should You Use the Same Lawyer as the Vendor?

Except in Quebec, it is not a good idea for you and the vendor to use the same lawyer, even if it results in substantial savings. What you want and what the vendor wants are not always the same, and you want your lawyer to represent your interests and your interests alone. In Quebec, it is customary for the notary to act for both parties.

☑Choosing a Lawyer Checklist

Get several recommendations

❑ Ask friends, relatives, or your real estate agent.

❑ Call your provincial law society.

Investigate the possibilities

❑ Get some idea of the range of fees the lawyer will charge.

❑ Find out the location of the lawyer's office.

Speak to the lawyer before making your decision

❑ Find out how much experience the lawyer has.

❑ Confirm what the lawyer's fee and estimated disbursements will be for your transaction.

❑ Ask what the lawyer's fee includes.

❑ Ask how much contact you can expect to have with the lawyer.

❑ Get a sense of the lawyer's personality and style: Can you work comfortably with this person?

7 MORTGAGES

There aren't many people who have enough money to pay the full cost of their new home in cash. It's difficult enough to accumulate the cash needed for a down payment, so most of us have to borrow in order to buy a home. When you borrow money to buy a house, you do it by getting a mortgage (in Quebec, a hypothec). In this chapter we will tell you what a mortgage is, the language you need to know, where to get a mortgage, and the process you will have to go through to get one.

WHAT IS A MORTGAGE?

A mortgage is a contract by which a homeowner (or purchaser) borrows money. The lender of the money is called the **mortgagee**. The borrower is called the **mortgagor**. The amount of money borrowed is called the **principal**.

A mortgage has two parts. One part is a loan like any other kind of loan: the mortgagee (usually a bank or trust company) agrees to lend the mortgagor (you) money at a given interest rate, and you agree to repay the loan with interest. The other part of the contract gives the mortgagee a claim on your house as security to make sure that you repay the loan. If you don't repay the loan, in most provinces the mortgagee can choose to sue you on your promise to repay the loan, or take your home and use it to repay the loan, usually by selling it.

SPEAKING THE MORTGAGEE'S LANGUAGE

Most people will go to a bank or trust company to get a mortgage. Some people go to a mortgage broker. Wherever you go, as soon as you walk in the door, people will start talking to you in a language that you don't understand. That's because a mortgage is a complicated legal and financial transaction. Mortgagees handle these transactions all the time and forget how complicated they are. They are also used to using legal and financial terminology and forget that the rest of us don't have any idea of what they mean.

We've already told you what a mortgage is. Now we're going to tell you about other key terms and concepts you need to be familiar with in order to understand what your mortgagee is saying.

First, Second, and Third Mortgages

If there is no mortgage on your home when you go to borrow the money you need, the mortgage you get is called a first mortgage. If you then decide to borrow more money under another mortgage, the next mortgage is called a second mortgage. The next mortgage after that is called a third mortgage. We could go on like this forever, but you've probably got the idea by now.

Each mortgage gives the mortgagee the right to take your home if you fail to repay the loan. Usually the mortgagee will sell your home and use any money that comes from the sale of the house to repay the first mortgagee first, then the second, then the third, etc.

Because a first mortgagee gets paid first and therefore has a better chance of getting all of its money back if it has to sell your house, first mortgages have lower interest rates than second and third mortgages.

The Term of Your Mortgage and the Amortization Period

Every mortgage must be repaid in full by a fixed date. The length of time you have to repay your mortgage is the term of the mortgage. Most Canadian mortgages have terms of no more than five years. But mortgages are usually for many tens of thousands of dollars. The monthly payments would be very high if you had to repay such a large loan in equal monthly instalments in full by the end of a five-year term. In order to make the monthly payments lower, mortgagees usually calculate the payments as if the loan were being repaid over a longer period of time than the actual term of the mortgage. In most mortgages, the payment is calculated as if the mortgagor had twenty-five years to repay the mortgage. This make-believe period of time is called the **amortization period** of the mortgage.

When a mortgage with a term of five years has an amortization period of (is **amortized** over) twenty-five years, the mortgagor makes four years and eleven months' worth of monthly payments as if there were twenty-five years to repay the mortgage. These payments are much lower than if the loan payments were calculated based on the actual five-year term. But the last payment is a whopper! Most people don't have enough money to make it. They renew their mortgages when the term is up and continue making monthly payments amortized over a new twenty-five-year period.

To illustrate the difference that a longer amortization period makes to your monthly payments consider this:

- A $100,000 mortgage with an interest rate of 10 per cent and a term of five years, amortized over five years, would cost $2,147.70 each month.
- The same $100,000 mortgage with an interest rate of 10 per cent and a term of five years, amortized over a period of twenty-five years, would cost $894.49 each month.

You can also choose an amortization period somewhere in between, for example fifteen years or twenty years. If your amortization period were twenty years, and you had the same $100,000 mortgage with an interest rate of 10 per cent, your monthly payments would be $969.03. Because you are making a slightly higher payment, your mortgage will be paid off five years earlier—and you will pay approximately $48,000 less in interest over the life of the mortgage. It makes sense to choose the shortest amortization period you can afford.

Blended Payments

As with any loan, you must repay not only the principal amount of the loan, you must also pay interest. Some of the payment you make each month is used to pay the interest on the loan, and the rest is used to pay down the principal. Payments which combine principal and interest in this way are called **blended payments.**

Every mortgage payment you make both pays back principal and pays interest. In most mortgages, the amount you pay every month remains the same (**equal monthly instalments**). As you make each payment, the principal of the loan is slowly (very slowly) reduced. As the principal is reduced, the amount of interest you must pay each month is also reduced, leaving more of your payment to pay down the principal amount of the loan.

At the early stages of your mortgage, almost all of your monthly payments go to pay interest on the loan. So don't be surprised to find out that, after several years, and many thousands of dollars in mortgage payments, you still owe almost as much principal on your mortgage as when you first borrowed the money. Table 1 will give you nightmares. It shows you how much of a monthly payment of $894.49 goes towards principal and how much goes towards interest if you have a $100,000 mortgage at 10 per cent repayable over 25 years.

TABLE 1: BREAKDOWN OF PRINCIPAL AND INTEREST OF BLENDED PAYMENTS

Payment	Principal Repaid	Interest Paid	Balance Remaining to Pay
First of 1st year	$78.01	$816.48	$99,921.99
Last of 1st year	85.30	809.19	99,020.75
Last of 2nd year	94.05	800.44	97,941.12
Last of 3rd year	103.69	790.80	96,750.80
Last of 4th year	114.32	780.17	95,438.49
Last of 5th year	126.03	768.46	93,991.67
Last of 10th year	205.29	689.20	84,204.74
Last of 15th year	334.40	560.09	68,262.90
Last of 20th year	544.71	349.78	42,295.31
Last payment	884.02	7.22	.00

Over the lifetime of the mortgage, you will have paid back the $100,000 principal—and you will also have paid $168,343.70 in interest.

Payment Frequency

Most mortgages are payable on a monthly basis, but some mortgagees will give you the option of making your payments on a weekly or bi-weekly basis. Paying on a weekly or bi-weekly basis may make it easier for you to budget for your payments. However, it can also affect how fast you pay off your mortgage, depending on how the weekly or bi-weekly payment is calculated. Keep in mind that there are 4.33 weeks in each month. If you just divide your monthly payment by 4.33, you won't really pay your mortgage off any faster. But if you divide your monthly payment by four and pay that amount every week, you will significantly reduce the length of time it takes to pay off the mortgage.

Here's an example. A $100,000 mortgage with an interest rate of 10 per cent, amortized over twenty-five years, has a monthly payment of $894.49. If you divide the monthly payment by four, you get a weekly payment of $223.62. If you pay that amount each week, you are in fact making monthly payments of $969.03. This is the equivalent of choosing a twenty-year amortization period—and a $48,000 saving in interest payments over the life of the mortgage.

Fixed and Variable Interest Rates

Interest rates change all the time. The interest rate for your mortgage is set at the time you apply to borrow the money. Most banks and trust companies will offer different interest rates depending on the length of the term of the mortgage. Longer term mortgages usually have higher interest rates because the lender can't accurately predict whether interest rates will go up in the future. The lender bets that they will and sets a higher rate now so that it won't lose out later if interest rates rise.

A mortgage with a **fixed interest rate** has the same rate of interest during the whole term of the mortgage.

If your mortgage has a **variable interest rate**, the mortgage interest starts at one rate but that rate will go up and down over the term of the mortgage as general interest rates go up and down. If the interest rate goes down during the term of your mortgage, less of each monthly payment goes to pay the interest, and more of each monthly payment goes to pay down the principal. If the interest rate goes up, more of each monthly payment goes to pay the interest, and less of each monthly payment goes to pay down the principal. (Enough to make you seasick, isn't it!) If the interest rate goes up so much that your monthly payment is not enough to cover the interest, your monthly payment may be increased by the mortgagee.

Different banks offer variations on the variable interest rate mortgage. Some banks allow you to set a maximum interest rate (or **cap**), or to convert to a fixed rate mortgage at any time. You may have to pay extra for these options.

Interest Calculated Semi-Annually Not in Advance

In most mortgages you'll see a term that the interest is calculated **semi-annually, not in advance**. We'll deal with the "not in advance" part first, because it's easier. Unlike rent, which is paid in advance on the first of each month, mortgage interest is paid "not in advance." When you make your June 1st rent payment, you are paying for the use of your apartment for the rest of June. When you make your June 1st mortgage payment, you are paying for the use of the money for the month of May.

Now for the "semi-annually" business. Interest can be **calculated** or **compounded** on any basis—daily, weekly, monthly, quarterly, semi-annually, annually. The more frequently the interest is compounded, the more interest you end up paying. Using the same example of the $100,000 mortgage with an interest rate of 10 per cent and amortized over twenty-five years, if the interest is calculated monthly instead of semi-annually, the monthly payment will go up from $894.49 to $908.70. Over the life of the mortgage you would pay an extra $4000 in interest.

When you're shopping around for a good interest rate, make sure you ask how the interest is calculated.

Open and Closed Mortgages

Unless your mortgage specifically says so, you cannot repay the principal amount earlier than the end of the mortgage term (even if you win the lottery). The right to make payments of principal, over and above your regular monthly payments, is called a **pre-payment privilege**. A mortgage without any prepayment privileges is called a **closed mortgage**. A mortgage with pre-payment privileges is called an **open mortgage**.

Some mortgages are more open than others. A mortgage that allows you to repay any or all of the principal amount at any time and without payment of any financial penalty is called a fully open mortgage. Such mortgages are rare and seldom seen, and you will usually have to pay a higher interest rate for them. However, most institutional mortgages allow for some *limited* pre-payment of the mortgage principal. Either the mortgage will allow relatively small pre-payments without any financial penalty to you, or it will allow you to pre-pay a larger amount together with a financial penalty.

Portable Mortgages

You may be able to choose the option of having a **portable mortgage**. If your mortgage is portable, you can transfer it to a new home that you buy.

There are two advantages to this. You won't have to pay a penalty to discharge that mortgage if you sell your house to a buyer who does not want to assume the mortgage. In addition, if interest rates have gone up, you can keep the benefit of the lower interest rate even when you move to a new home.

CHOOSING THE MORTGAGE OPTIONS THAT ARE RIGHT FOR YOU

The interest rate you will be charged depends not only on the general interest rates in effect when you borrow, but also on which of the various mortgage options you choose. You will usually get the lowest interest rate for a short-term, fixed interest rate mortgage. You will usually be quoted a higher interest rate if you want pre-payment privileges, variable interest rates, or a longer mortgage term.

The lower the interest rate, the more money you can afford to borrow. So it is tempting to go for the lowest interest rate possible. Since that usually means a short-term mortgage, remember that you will soon have to renew the mortgage, quite possibly at a higher interest rate. If the interest rates go up, so will your monthly mortgage payments. If you have borrowed the maximum you can afford, you will find yourself in trouble.

If you borrow $100,000 at an interest rate of 10 per cent, amortized over twenty-five years, your monthly payment is $894.49. If the interest rate has gone up to 12 per cent when it comes time to renew your $100,000 mortgage, the monthly payment will rise to $1053.22.

WHERE TO GET A MORTGAGE

Mortgages are available from

- banks
- trust companies
- credit unions
- caisses populaires
- life insurance companies
- mortgage brokers
- private lenders
- your RRSP

Institutional Lenders

Banks, trust companies, credit unions, caisses populaires, and insurance companies are known as institutional lenders. While all institutional lenders tend to be competitive in the interest rates and types of mortgages they offer, there are some differences.

It is tempting simply to go to your own bank branch to apply for your mortgage, but it is a better idea to shop around first to compare what the different institutional lenders have to offer. Newspapers publish current mortgage interest rates in the business or real estate sections, or you can telephone or visit several institutional lenders.

Mortgage Brokers and Private Lenders

Institutional lenders are not the only places to get a mortgage. There are individuals who have money they wish to invest, and who like the interest rates and security that a mortgage investment can give them.

Most people will get their mortgages from an institutional lender if they can. Borrowers go to private lenders when they have credit problems which make it difficult to get a mortgage from an institutional lender, or if they want to borrow more than 75 per cent of the purchase price and do not qualify with an institutional lender for a high ratio mortgage.

Private lenders are also the most common source of second or subsequent mortgages. You may need a second mortgage for any number of reasons. For example, you may need extra money over and above your down payment and first mortgage in order to buy the home of your choice. Or you may need to borrow additional money, after you have owned your home for a while, using your home as security. Second and subsequent mortgage interest rates are likely to be higher than first mortgage interest rates (whoever your lender is) because the second mortgagee's risk of losing money if you can't repay the loan is greater.

Borrowing money under a mortgage from an individual is exactly the same as getting a mortgage from an institutional lender. The trick is knowing how to find these private lenders. Your real estate agent may be able to give you the name of a private lender. Or you can go to a mortgage broker.

A mortgage broker acts as a go-between putting people who want to borrow mortgage money in touch with people or institutions who want to lend it. The broker may charge you a brokerage fee for this service, depending on your financial circumstances and credit-worthiness. Your real estate agent or lawyer can probably direct you to a mortgage broker.

Your RRSP

If you are lucky enough to have a registered retirement savings plan with as much money in it as you need to borrow as a mortgage loan, you may be able to get a mortgage from your own RRSP. You have to have a self-directed RRSP, and the mortgage has to be administered by a trust company. In addition, your RRSP must charge you a reasonable rate of interest on the mortgage. While you may not save any money on your monthly payments, at least you will be paying interest to yourself.

APPLYING FOR A MORTGAGE

Your mortgagee will have an application procedure for you to follow. The process of applying for a mortgage is designed to provide the mortgagee with enough information to decide whether or not it should risk lending you money. The mortgagee wants to make sure *first*, that you will make the mortgage payments every month; and *second*, that, if you don't make the payments, it can get enough money from the sale of your home to repay the loan.

Do You Qualify for a Conventional or High Ratio Mortgage?

One of the first things an institutional lender will decide is what type of mortgage you are eligible for, a **conventional mortgage** or a **high ratio mortgage**, because the mortgage type will determine the maximum amount you are eligible to borrow. These terms refer to the relationship between the amount of your mortgage and the amount of the purchase price of your home.

Conventional Mortgages

A conventional mortgage is a mortgage for no more than 75 per cent of the purchase price of your home. If you apply for a conventional mortgage, the maximum principal amount you can apply to borrow is three times the amount of your down payment.

High Ratio Mortgages

A high ratio mortgage is a mortgage for more than 75 per cent (up to a maximum of 90 per cent) of the purchase price. If a financial institution accepts your application for a high ratio mortgage, the maximum principal amount you can apply to borrow is nine times the amount of your down payment.

If you are a first-time home buyer, you may qualify for a high ratio mortgage of 95 per cent of the purchase price of your home. The maximum price of the house you can buy is limited under the Canada Mortgage and Housing guidelines for high ratio mortgages for first-time buyers. In the Toronto and Vancouver areas, the maximum price of a house is limited to $250,000. In other cities where house prices are not as high, the maximum price is $175,000. Everywhere else in Canada the maximum price is $125,000.

High Ratio Mortgages Cost More

If you don't repay your mortgage, the mortgagee can sell your home and use the money from the sale to pay itself back. When the amount of the loan is more than 75 per cent of the value of the house, there is a real risk that there will not be enough money from the sale to fully repay the loan. As a result of this greater risk, mortgagees generally charge higher interest rates for high ratio mortgages.

In addition, institutional mortgagees will require a homeowner who takes out a high ratio mortgage to buy **mortgage insurance**. This insurance pays the mortgagee if there is not enough money from the sale of your home to repay the mortgage. The homeowner must pay a one-time premium for this insurance. The amount of the premium will depend on the value of the house and the size of the loan. The highest premium rate charged is 2.5 per cent of the amount of the loan if the loan is for 90 per cent (95 per cent if you are a first-time buyer) of the value of the house. For example, if you buy a house worth $100,000 and need a mortgage loan of $90,000, you would pay a mortgage insurance premium of $2250.

What Is the State of Your Personal Finances?

Any mortgagee is going to be very interested in the answer to this question. Even though the mortgage gives the mortgagee the right to take your home if you don't pay, the mortgagee's first choice is to have you repay your mortgage on time as you promised. So the mortgagee will want information about you to determine the likelihood that you will do so.

The mortgagee will want to know about

- your income and expenses
- your assets and debts
- your credit rating

Your Income and Expenses

In Chapter 2, we told you to calculate your income and expenses to figure out how much of a monthly mortgage payment you can afford. Just as you don't want to borrow more money than you can afford to pay back, the mortgagee doesn't want to lend you more money than you can afford to pay back.

Mortgagees have formulas that they use to calculate how much they think you can afford to repay. These formulas are not as detailed and time-consuming as the calculations we took you through in the second chapter of this book—and if you're lucky, the mortgagee will serve you coffee while taking you through the process.

Mortgagees usually look at your *gross* income, not your net income; and while they look at your expenses, they usually only look at your debt payments. Most mortgagees do not want you to spend more than 30 to 35 per cent of your gross monthly income on your monthly mortgage payment, property taxes, and condominium maintenance fees (they call this your **gross debt service ratio**) or more than 40 per cent of your gross monthly income on these things *plus* all your other debt payments (they call this your **total debt service ratio**).

You may find that, based on its calculations, your mortgagee thinks you can afford to borrow more money than *you* think you can afford (after sweating through the calculations in Chapter 2). Think long and hard before taking on a larger mortgage than your earlier calculations have shown you can comfortably carry.

As part of its application process, the mortgagee will want to see documents that confirm the amount of your income, such as

• a letter from your employer

• income tax returns

• financial statements, if you are self-employed

Your Assets and Debts

Mortgagees are very nervous people. Wouldn't you be nervous if you were lending a person like you as much money as you are trying to borrow? So they want to make sure that, if your income turns out not to be enough to repay the mortgage, you have assets in addition to your house that you can use to repay the mortgage.

In addition to proof of your income and expenses, the mortgagee will ask you about your **net worth**, which is the difference between the value of everything that you own and the amount of everything you owe (your assets minus your debts).

The mortgagee will ask you to list all of your assets and debts and to provide details of

• bank account numbers and balances

- RRSP account numbers and balances
- stocks and bonds
- other real estate
- cars and boats
- credit card accounts and balances
- any other debts

Your Credit Rating

One good indication of the likelihood that you will repay your mortgage loan is your past history of repaying loans. This history forms the basis of your credit rating. Your credit rating is also affected by the amount of your income, your assets, and your outstanding debts.

The mortgagee will want to know your credit rating and will ask you to sign a consent to allow it to get this information from your banks, your employer, your creditors, and credit rating agencies.

What Is the Value of the Home You Are Buying?

Besides wanting to know about the state of your personal finances to find out whether you can repay the loan, the mortgagee wants to know the value of your house in case you can't. If you don't repay the mortgage loan, the mortgagee can take your house and sell it to satisfy the loan. Accordingly, the mortgagee wants to be certain that the house is worth enough to cover the loan, plus the expenses of selling the house.

While the price you pay for your house is a good indication of its value, most mortgagees, being very cautious and (as we have said) nervous creatures, will want additional proof of its value. They get this proof by having your house **appraised**. An appraisal involves an inspection by a real estate professional who decides what your house is worth by comparing it with similar houses. If your mortgagee wants an appraisal, you may have to pay for it. An appraisal costs about $100 to $200.

INSURANCE WHEN YOU GET A MORTGAGE

All mortgagees will insist that you have adequate homeowner's insurance. When you borrow from an institutional lender, the mortgagee may discuss other kinds of insurance with you as well. Some of this insurance may be required, but most of it is optional.

Mortgage Insurance

An institutional mortgagee requires a homeowner who takes out a high ratio mortgage to buy **mortgage insurance**. If you default on your mortgage loan and the mortgagee takes your house, mortgage insurance pays for the mortgagee's loss if there is not enough money from the sale of your home to repay the loan. You will have to pay a monthly premium for this insurance in addition to the regular mortgage payment.

Mortgage insurance may also be required by some institutional lenders if the home you are buying was ever insulated with urea formaldehyde foam insulation.

Other Kinds of Insurance

Often, banks and trust companies will suggest that you get various kinds of insurance that will help repay your mortgage loan if, for instance,

• you die

• you cannot work because of illness or disability

• you lose your job

Life Insurance

Your mortgagee may suggest to you that you and your house co-owners get insurance on each others' lives, which will help pay off the mortgage if one of you dies. Institutional mortgagees push something called **mortgage life insurance**. The amount of mortgage life insurance coverage decreases as the principal of your mortgage is paid down. Any life insurance policy that pays out enough to cover your mortgage would serve the same purpose, so you can shop around for the best life insurance premium rate.

Disability Insurance

Disability insurance pays you an income if you are unable to work because of illness or injury. It is possible to get mortgage disability insurance that will pay the amount of monthly mortgage payments, instead of paying you an income.

Job Loss Insurance

Sometimes it may be possible to get insurance that will make your mortgage payment if you lose your job.

The banks and trust companies don't provide any of this insurance themselves. Instead, they recommend an insurance company and will give you an application form to fill out. If you are interested in getting insurance to protect yourself against any of these misfortunes, you are not limited to the insurance company recommended by your mortgagee. You may be able to get similar protection from other companies at a better price, so you may want to speak to an insurance broker to see what other possibilities are available before you make a decision.

MORTGAGES THROUGH THE VENDOR

Until now, we have talked about mortgages that you apply for and get from a third party mortgagee. Sometimes the mortgage can be obtained through the vendor.

Assuming an Existing Mortgage

The vendor may have an outstanding mortgage on the house. If the mortgage is in the right amount and has a favourable interest rate, you may want to **assume** this existing mortgage instead of arranging a new one. If the mortgagee allows you to do so, you may take over the vendor's mortgage loan and make the vendor's mortgage payments after closing.

Vendor Take-Back Mortgage

Your down payment and what you can borrow by way of a first mortgage may not give you enough to pay the vendor what he or she wants for the house. Sometimes the vendor will be willing to lend you some of the purchase price by giving you a mortgage. This is called a **vendor take-back mortgage**. After closing, you will make mortgage payments to the vendor. If you have enough income to make this additional mortgage payment, it's a simple way of getting the extra financing you need.

AN EYE TO THE FUTURE

Thinking about mortgages is not just a one-time exercise when you first buy your house. You may revisit the subject of mortgages if you want to

- use your home as a source of personal or business financing
- refinance your existing mortgage

Your Home as a Source of Financing

Whether or not you have a mortgage outstanding on your home, you may be able to use your home as security to borrow money for other purposes. You can take out a mortgage (or a second mortgage) to

- get a lump sum of money, which you pay back by monthly mortgage payments
- secure a line of credit, which allows you to borrow money from time to time up to a maximum amount
- guarantee a loan made to your business

In addition, if you are a senior citizen and your home is not mortgaged, you may be able to take out a **reverse mortgage** on your home. Under a reverse mortgage, you stay in your home and get a monthly payment from the reverse mortgagee. The amount you receive must be repaid only when you sell your home or die. For more information, speak to your bank.

Refinancing Your Mortgage

You may want to **refinance** (renegotiate) your mortgage even though it is not yet up for renewal. Interest rates may be lower now than they were when you got your mortgage, or you may be concerned that interest rates will be higher than they are now when the time for renewal comes.

When you renegotiate your mortgage, you are paying off your current mortgage and getting a new one. Unless your mortgage contains a pre-payment privilege, you will have to pay a penalty to refinance. The penalty is usually designed to compensate the bank for the loss of interest income, which is calculated on the difference between your current mortgage interest rate and your new rate. This penalty can be thousands of dollars. It only makes sense to renegotiate and pay the penalty if you think you're going to save more than the amount of the penalty in mortgage payments over the life of your new mortgage.

Some banks offer a "blend-and-extend" option that may be better for you. Under this option, you renew your mortgage now for a longer term than the one left on your current mortgage, and the bank gives you an interest rate that averages your old rate and the new rate. This is a good choice if you think that interest rates will be even higher than the blended rate when your current mortgage comes up for renewal.

We can't negotiate your mortgage for you, but we hope that after reading this chapter, you will be better able to understand mortgages and will feel more confident when you discuss them with your mortgagee. If you need more explanation of mortgages, speak to your lawyer.

8 HOMEOWNER'S INSURANCE

WHY YOU NEED INSURANCE

Buying a home is probably the biggest investment you will ever make, and you want to make sure that your investment is protected from the moment that the house becomes yours. If anything happens to your home, you want to be able to repair it so that it doesn't lose any of its value (and, of course, so that the rain and snow don't fall on you in the living room). That's a major reason you need homeowner's insurance—to get the money you need to make repairs.

If you are borrowing money by way of a mortgage, the mortgage company has also made an investment in your home and is just as interested as you are in protecting it. In fact, they won't actually give you the mortgage money you need to buy your home unless you have homeowner's insurance in place to take effect upon transfer of the ownership to you.

THE STANDARD HOMEOWNER'S POLICY

You actually need insurance to protect you against three different kinds of misfortunes that can happen to you as a homeowner:

• Your house can be damaged or destroyed.

- Your personal possessions can be stolen, damaged, or destroyed.

- Your guests, workers, or other visitors (or their property) can be harmed while at your home.

The standard homeowner's policy is really three policies of insurance in one to protect you against each of those three kinds of misfortunes:

- **Dwelling coverage** insures your house and other structures on the property (like garages or sheds) against damage or destruction. The land itself is not insured.

- **Contents coverage** insures your personal possessions (like furniture, clothing, and jewellery) against theft, damage, or destruction.

- **Third party liability coverage** insures *you* in the event that visitors to your home are injured.

When you buy insurance, you are betting that your house will be damaged, your belongings stolen, or your guests injured (even though you are *hoping* very hard that none of these things will happen). The insurance company, on the other hand, is betting that your house, belongings, and guests will stay safe and happy. By the law of averages, the insurance company is bound to be right most of the time. Nothing happens to most of the people who buy insurance. They simply pay their insurance premiums every year. The insurance company does not have to pay any money to most of the people who pay premiums. Instead, the company invests those premiums and earns interest. The premiums and the interest are what the insurance company uses to help the few who do have something bad happen to them (and also to make a profit for the insurance company).

You can't wait until you've taken title to your home to get homeowner's insurance. In order to have insurance protection in place when you become the owner, you have to make arrangements in advance—at least several weeks before the closing date of your house purchase.

To get homeowner's insurance you must apply to an insurance company. If the insurance company accepts your application, a **policy** of insurance will be **issued**. You will have to pay for this policy by paying **premiums**. You are then said to be insured or **covered** against damage to your house, possessions, and guests. But you are not covered against damage caused in absolutely every possible way. You and your insurance company will agree in advance exactly which causes of damage you will be covered against. The ways that damage may be caused are called **perils** in insurance language.

Shop Around

There's a lot of choice out there. There are many different insurance companies and types of policies. Your choice of company and of policy will affect how much you pay for insurance and what kind of insurance coverage you will get. We suggest that you shop around before you buy insurance. Leave yourself enough time to do your comparison shopping—start at least one month before your closing date.

When you go shopping for insurance, you will soon realize that there is a lot of gobbledygook and double-talk in the insurance business. The insurance companies know this and have been trying to simplify the language of insurance. Unfortunately, the concepts involved are very complex and confusing. No matter how simply you write about them, they are still hard to understand.

Because there are so many choices available and because you're bound to feel confused at some point, it's really important to get a good insurance agent or broker to help you choose the insurance coverage that's right for you. The purpose of this chapter is to help you know what information to give to your agent or broker, know what questions to ask, and understand the answers you get.

Your agent or broker will ask you questions such as:

- Do you want standard, broad, or comprehensive insurance?
- Do you want replacement cost insurance?
- What additional riders or endorsements do you want?

The answers to these questions will affect

- what you insure
- which causes of damage you insure against
- how much your insurance will cost
- what you will get if you make a claim (and how easy or difficult it will be to get it)

Before you choose your insurance company and policy, you should think about all of these things. You want to know what your insurance company will do for you if something nasty happens, not just how much your insurance will cost. This chapter takes you through the entire insurance process.

WHAT CAN YOU INSURE?

Below is a more detailed explanation of dwelling contents, and third party liability coverage under a standard homeowner's policy.

Your House

Your house is insured under the **dwelling coverage** portion of your home-owner's policy. The dwelling coverage also covers structures such as a garage, carport or shed, and decks, swimming pools, and pool equipment.

Your land is not insured, because it can't be destroyed. Even if your house is blown away by a tornado, your land will still be there. Some things on the land which can be damaged are insured, such as landscaping (trees and shrubs, but not grass) and fences.

While the primary purpose of your dwelling coverage is to get you money to repair or replace your damaged house, this portion of your policy will also pay **additional living expenses** if you have to move out of your house while it is being repaired. Your dwelling coverage may also contain a clause that allows you to make a claim against the insurer for some of your **lost wages** if you miss work because of damage to your house.

Your Belongings

Under the **contents coverage** of your homeowner's policy, the contents of your home are insured against loss or damage. Contents are your personal property, such as your furniture and appliances, your clothing and jewellery, your television and stereo, your books and plants, your tools, a boat that you store on your premises, and so on. Your personal property is covered, to a certain extent, even when it is off your premises. For example, you are covered if someone steals your watch at work. But personal property that is not usually kept at home is not covered—for example, your horse that normally lives in a stable elsewhere. Property that is being stored temporarily in your house for people who are not members of your household is not covered either.

Illegally acquired property is not covered. Attention cross-border shoppers! This can mean both stolen property AND imported property that was not declared to Canada Customs.

Your Rear End

The **third party liability** portion of your homeowner's policy insures *you* against claims made against you by third parties up to a maximum of

$1,000,000. A **third party** is someone from outside your household. You are protected if you *accidentally* injure

- someone, either at your home or elsewhere
- someone's property, either at your home or elsewhere

You would be covered if a visitor slips on your front steps, or if you unintentionally whack your neighbour's prize rose bushes with a hoe while you are enthusiastically working on your vegetable garden. You are also protected if, while on vacation in Florida, your budding young baseball star of a son hits a home run through the plate glass window of the hotel lobby.

NOTE: Your homeowner's insurance does NOT apply to any injury you cause while you are driving a car.

If someone makes a claim against you, your insurance company must defend any lawsuit against you. This means that the insurance company will pay your legal fees and will pay the amount of any settlement or judgment. Because the insurance company is paying, it will probably choose the lawyer and will have the final say on how the matter is handled by the lawyer.

WHAT CAUSES OF DAMAGE CAN YOU INSURE AGAINST?

As we said at the beginning of this chapter, no insurance company will insure you against damage caused in absolutely every way. There are only certain **perils** that an insurance company will agree to cover you against, no matter how much money you are prepared to pay.

What Causes of Damage Can You Insure Your House and Belongings Against?

The perils that an insurance company is willing to insure you against are called **insurable perils** or **insured perils**.

Insurable or Insured Perils

The following are the only commonly insurable perils:

- fire
- lightning
- robbery, burglary, and theft

- riot
- windstorm or hail
- explosion
- water escape from (or rupture or freezing of)
    - plumbing
    - domestic appliances
    - heating systems
    - air-conditioning systems
    - sprinklers
    - pools
    - public water mains
- sudden release of smoke (excluding release of smoke from fireplaces)
- impact by aircraft or vehicle
- vandalism while the building is normally occupied
- glass breakage in a building that is normally occupied
- transportation of personal property (while it is temporarily removed from your home)
- falling objects, as long as they were not pushed by snowslide or movement of the earth (So if the earth moved for you, don't tell your insurance company!)

How many of these perils you are insured against depends on the kind of policy you buy. If you get a policy that insures you against all of these insured perils, it will state that you have **all risk** coverage. But "all risk coverage" only insures you against the risks in this list, not against all possible risks.

Additional Insurable or Insured Perils

In addition, you may be able to buy coverage against these other perils:

- earthquakes
- spills of furnace oil
- sewer backup

For these perils, you have to make special arrangements by paying a separate premium for a **rider** (also called an **endorsement** or **form**) to your policy.

Uninsurable Perils

There are certain perils that Canadian insurance companies will not insure anyone against. These include

- normal wear and tear on and normal deterioration of your property
- your own failure to maintain your property in good condition
- floods and waves
- melting snow and ice
- repeated or continuous water seepage
- leaky eavestroughs and downspouts
- sump pumps that malfunction
- freezing outside the home that causes damage
- explosion caused by vibrating pipes ("water hammer")
- direct damage from the intentional application of heat
- intentional damage by the insured
- criminal activity of the insured
- theft from a house that is not ready for occupancy
- contamination of property (by pollutants or toxins)
- war

Types of Homeowner's Policies

Homeowner's policies are categorized according to the number of perils that they insure you against. The more perils, the more expensive the policy. The three types of homeowner's policy offered in Canada are listed below, in order of least expensive to most expensive:

STANDARD COVERAGE provides coverage for your house and belongings against a package of some of the perils from the insured perils listed above. These perils are called **named perils** or **specified perils**. The package of perils is chosen by the insurance company. You should decide for yourself whether these are the only perils you want to be covered against.

BROAD COVERAGE provides coverage against *all* the perils from the insured perils listed above ("all risk coverage") on buildings, and coverage on contents against named perils only. Again, it is the insurance company that chooses the named perils in the package.

COMPREHENSIVE COVERAGE provides coverage on your house and contents against *all* the perils in the insured perils list.

A policy that insured you only against named or specified perils, instead of all perils, might cover burglary but not theft. A loss of personal property is considered burglary if there are signs of forcible entry to your home. If there are no signs of forcible entry to your home, it is considered theft.

As you can see, none of these policies provides coverage against any of the additional insurable perils. If you want to have insurance against any of those perils, you must have a rider added to your policy, which will involve the payment of an additional premium.

What Kinds of Third Party Claims Can You Insure Yourself Against?

Under your third party liability coverage, your insurance company pays claims made against you by other people. You are not covered for all types of claims made against you. You are only covered for claims for bodily harm or damage to property, and only if you harmed the other person *accidentally*.

If you are sued for something other than bodily harm or damage to property, you are not covered by the third party liability portion of your homeowner's insurance. Your homeowner's policy also does not cover you against

• any injury you cause while driving your car

• most claims arising out of your work or business

HOW MUCH INSURANCE COVERAGE SHOULD YOU HAVE?

A homeowner's insurance policy, as we have said, has three different parts: dwelling coverage, contents coverage, and third party liability coverage. The amount of coverage will be different in each part.

Dwelling Coverage

Dwelling coverage is the coverage for your house. The amount of coverage you get will depend on the value of your house and other structures on the property. Your land is not taken into account.

Insurable Value

The value of your dwelling is fixed by your insurance company and is known as the **insurable value** of your property.

If you want to insure your house for more than its insurable value, the insurance company will let you and will happily take the extra premium money you pay. But, when the time comes for you to make a claim, the insurance company won't pay you any extra. You'll get the same amount you would get if you had insured the house for exactly what it was worth.

If you want to insure your house for less than its insurable value, some insurance companies will refuse to insure you at all. Others will severely limit the perils that you are covered against. If you make a claim, you will only be paid a portion of your loss.

When you apply for insurance, your insurance broker or agent will ask you questions to help the insurance company calculate the insurable value of your property. If you have a mortgage on your home, the mortgagee will tell you how much insurance it wants you to have. Some mortgagees insist that you get coverage in the full amount of the mortgage, even if it is higher than the insurable value of the house and structures. This extra coverage is useless for both of you, but try telling that to your mortgagee!

Replacement Cost Insurance

If your house or any part of it is damaged, you want your insurance policy to pay you enough money to repair it. If your house is destroyed, you want enough money to replace it. If your house were destroyed, it would probably cost you more to replace it than it was worth before. Even if your house were damaged, the cost of repairs might be more than the house was worth.

If you want to get enough money to cover the actual cost of replacing what was damaged or destroyed, you should get **replacement cost insurance**. If you don't have replacement cost insurance, the insurance company does not have to pay you any more than your house was worth before it was damaged or destroyed. If you do have replacement cost insurance, the insurance company will pay you the full cost of replacing what was damaged or destroyed, even if the cost of doing so is higher than the actual value of the property, or even the amount for which your property is insured. However, replacement cost insurance does not guarantee that your property will be replaced. Your insurance company will not pay to replace your house, or part of it, if it would be cheaper to repair it.

An insurance company will not issue replacement cost insurance unless you get their recommended amount of coverage. Also, you must increase the amount of coverage if you make any improvements to the property which increase the value of the property.

Limits

Your insurance policy will probably set **limits** on the amount that it will pay for damage to structures on your property other than your house, like a shed or detached garage. It will probably also set limits on the amount it will pay for the replacement of trees, plants, or shrubs.

Find out from your insurance agent or broker what limits are contained in any policy he or she recommends. If you don't think the limited amounts would be enough, ask about making arrangements for additional insurance.

Contents Coverage

While the insurance company assigns a value to your house and other buildings, it is strictly up to you to decide what your contents are worth.

Replacement Cost Insurance

If your contents are damaged, you want your insurance policy to pay you enough money to repair them. If they are lost or destroyed, you want enough money to replace them.

As you know, new things cost more to buy (often a lot more) than the old things they are replacing were worth. If you want to get enough money to cover the actual cost of replacing what you have lost, you should get replacement cost insurance. However, you should be aware that your insurance company will not pay to replace an item if it's cheaper to repair it, even if you have replacement cost coverage.

Without replacement cost insurance, if your possessions are lost or destroyed, your insurance company will pay you only what they were worth immediately before the loss or destruction occurred. What your possessions were worth depends on their condition, resale value, and normal life expectancy. (Your policy may state that the value is calculated as "the cost of replacement less any depreciation or obsolescence," which means the same thing.)

Unlike replacement cost coverage on your buildings, replacement cost coverage on your contents does *not* give you the right to receive more from the insurance company than the face amount of insurance coverage you have bought. Be sure to value your belongings based on what it would cost to replace them new, and to get insurance coverage in that full amount.

Limits

For many kinds of property, your insurance company will pay only a limited amount for each stolen or damaged item—even if you buy replacement cost coverage. This is called a **limit** in your policy. If you want to be paid more than the limit for any items, you must pay extra to get a **rider** to your policy specifically identifying them. Such items typically include jewellery, furs, silverware, and stamp collections.

Each insurance company sets different limits for these various items. Ask your agent or broker what the insurance company's policy limits are so you can decide whether you need a rider. Your insurance company will require a professional valuation in writing for each item before it will issue a rider.

There are other kinds of property which are also insured only to a limited amount, but for which you cannot get additional coverage, even with a rider. These kinds of property include animals, cash, and computer software.

Third Party Liability Coverage

Insurance companies offer a standard amount of coverage for claims that may be made against you because you have injured someone or damaged their property. This amount is $1,000,000.

One million dollars may seem like a lot of money, but if someone is badly hurt, the cost of care for the rest of his or her life can easily be *several* million dollars. You can buy **excess liability insurance** if you want to increase the amount of your third party liability coverage above $1,000,000.

HOW DO YOU GET INSURANCE?

If you are anything like the authors, you have spent a good part of your adult life trying to get away from insurance agents, not looking for them! Now is the time to call up that cousin, sister-in-law, or old friend from high school you've been avoiding like the plague all these years!

The Insurance Agent or Broker

There are two kinds of insurance professionals: **brokers** deal with a number of insurance companies, and **agents** represent only one insurance company. Brokers will shop around to find the company with the best deal for you. An agent can only get you insurance from the one company he or she represents. So if you choose an agent, make sure that you have made some inquiries about the company as well as about the agent.

Finding an Agent or Broker

To find an agent or broker, ask for recommendations from family and friends, from your real estate agent, or from the agent or broker who deals with your car insurance. Or, your employer or union or professional organization may have an arrangement with a particular agent, broker, or insurance company to provide insurance to you at a special discounted rate.

What the Insurance Agent or Broker Does

The role of an insurance agent or broker is to figure out your insurance needs and get you a policy that meets those needs. You will have to talk to him or her about the value of your home and contents, what perils you want to be insured against, what amount of coverage you would like to have, and what you can afford to pay by way of a premium. You want to find an agent or broker who is willing to discuss all of your concerns in detail.

You must be sure to tell the agent or broker exactly how you will be using your home, because that can affect the insurance you should get. For example, if you will be running a business from your home, or if you will be keeping other people's valuable possessions at your home, say so.

What are the Agent's or Broker's Responsibilities to You?

If you tell your agent or broker everything about what your property is worth, how you will use your property, the perils you wish protection against, and the amount of coverage you want, he or she is responsible for getting you the right kind of coverage, within the budget you set. If it is not possible to get the coverage you want, or to get it at a price you can afford, your agent or broker must tell you so.

If you end up with a policy that doesn't cover you for a situation you should have been covered for, the agent or broker may be liable to you for the amount of money the right kind of insurance would have paid you. Ask your insurance agent or broker whether he or she is insured against making mistakes. Your provincial government may require agents and brokers to have such **errors and omissions insurance**.

Choosing an Insurance Company

Helping you to choose the right insurance company is really what you are hiring an insurance broker to do. The following information is useful if you want to make the choice yourself or if you want to discuss with your broker the reason for his or her choice.

There are many different companies that provide homeowner's insurance. Premium prices are usually competitive, but each company's policy will offer slightly different coverage. You want a policy that gives the best coverage you can get without having to pay extra for riders.

Each company has its own reputation for dealing well or badly with its clients. Ask acquaintances who have made a claim how their insurance company treated them. Some companies are very helpful and understanding and settle claims quickly; others resist paying claims and sometimes have to be sued. Keep in mind that some companies can afford to provide cheaper coverage because they don't pay very many claims.

What you want is an insurance company that treats its clients well, and a policy that provides the best coverage for your particular needs, at the best price.

The Application Process

To get homeowner's insurance, you will have to fill out the insurance company's standard application form. This form contains information that helps the insurance company to decide

- whether it wants to insure you at all
- how much insurance coverage you should have
- how much it will charge

It is *very* important to be absolutely honest in filling out the application form, because any false statements may give the insurance company the right to refuse to pay if you make a claim.

Applying for Dwelling Coverage

Remember that the insurance company fixes the insurable value of your house and other structures. The application form is designed to get from you the necessary details about your house which will help to fix this value. The questions will concern the size, age, and condition of the house and other structures. The insurance company may require an inspection of your home.

If your house is in really bad condition, you may find it difficult to get insurance at all. The insurance company may consider the house too big a risk and will refuse to gamble with you that it will not be damaged or destroyed.

Applying for Contents Coverage

The insurance company fixes the insurable value of your house, but it is up to you to know what belongings you have and what they are worth.

Before making your application for contents coverage, be sure to

- value the contents of your house for what you believe it will cost you to replace them

- buy coverage in at least that amount
- check your policy to see what kinds of possessions are subject to limits
- if you have any such possessions that you think would cost more to replace than that limit, get a rider

Before you can put a dollar value on your contents, you must figure out what you own by making an inventory which involves going through your house, room by room, and noting what you have and how much it originally cost. (If you are moving into a new home, you can make this inventory while you are packing). In the Appendix you will find sample inventory lists to help you.

You make an inventory by preparing a list of the contents of each room of the house and describing each item. You can make your inventory

- in writing, and then attach photographs
- on an audio cassette, by dictating the list and description (this works well for collections of things like books or stamps)
- on a video cassette (this is best for large items like furniture, equipment, and appliances which will show up well on film)

It is a good idea to attach receipts from the purchase of expensive items to the inventory.

Store a copy of the inventory off your premises, just in case a burglar takes your inventory along with your VCR. Your safety deposit box is a good place. You should update the inventory regularly as you get rid of and buy new possessions.

Does this sound like too much work? (If you think this is too much work, wait until you see the chapter on home safety!) If you can't bring yourself to do a thorough inventory of all your possessions, at least keep an inventory of expensive items that are likely to attract thieves, such as jewellery, TVs, stereos, CD players, and computer equipment.

HOW MUCH WILL YOUR INSURANCE COST?

The amount you have to pay for your insurance will depend on different factors for each of the three different kinds of insurance policies included in your homeowner's insurance. You will be billed a single amount as a premium for all three kinds of insurance.

Dwelling Coverage

How much you have to pay for dwelling coverage will depend on

- how many perils you choose to be insured against (this is determined when you decide among standard, broad, and comprehensive policies, and when you buy a rider for any additional insured perils)
- the value of your home
- whether or not you choose to have replacement cost insurance
- what **rating** is given to your home by the insurance company

We have already told you about all of these things except how your home is rated. Your insurance company will give your home either a **standard rating** or a **preferred rating**.

Ratings

A preferred rating is given to houses less than ten years old and to older houses that have been updated to the standards of a new house. A standard rating is given to a house more than ten years old, unless you can show it has been updated. The insurance company is concerned about wiring, plumbing, the heating system, and the roof. It may have an inspection done to find out if an older house should be given a standard rating or qualifies for a preferred rating.

Whatever your home's rating, the insurance company may give you a discount on your premium. For example, a discount will usually be given if fire alarms have been installed. Most insurers also offer a "claims-free" bonus to an insured who has not made a claim for three years or more.

Renovations

If you are carrying out extensive renovations on your home, the insurance company may insist that you pay a higher premium during the renovation process because the risk of damage or destruction is greater during this time.

Contents Coverage

How much you have to pay for contents coverage will depend on

- the number of perils you choose to be insured against (as with dwelling insurance, this is determined when you decide among standard, broad, and comprehensive policies, and if you buy a rider for additional insured perils)
- the value of your contents
- whether or not you choose to have replacement cost insurance
- what riders, if any, you buy for extra coverage on valuable items

If you are getting a discount on your dwelling coverage for having fire alarms or burglar alarms, the discount will also apply to your contents coverage. You may also be eligible for a "claims-free" bonus if you have not made a claim under your contents coverage for three years or more.

Third Party Liability Coverage

Remember that all homeowner's policies provide $1,000,000 of third party liability coverage. So the amount of coverage is not an issue in determining the cost of the premium. The premium will depend on things like the size of your property, any dangers that might be on it (such as a swimming pool), and whether there have been any claims against you in the past.

If you want coverage for more than $1,000,000, excess liability coverage can cost an extra $70 to $300 for an additional $1,000,000 in coverage. Depending on the insurance company, you may have to buy a separate policy. Some companies don't offer excess liability insurance at all.

Payment Options

Your homeowner's insurance policy is made up of three different kinds of coverage, and the premium amount for each kind of coverage is determined separately. However, you will be billed a single amount to pay for the whole policy.

Some insurance companies offer different options for paying the billed amount, such as monthly payments instead of a yearly payment. If you choose to make several payments instead of a single one, you will probably be charged some kind of service fee, and you may have to agree to automatic withdrawals from your bank account.

HOW DO YOU MAKE A CLAIM?

If your home is damaged or destroyed or your contents damaged, destroyed, or stolen, you will want to make a claim under your insurance policy for compensation. As with so many things in life, this won't be as easy as you would like it to be. A little bit of knowledge should help you find your way through what can be a complicated and frustrating process.

Consider the following questions before you make a claim:

- Whose losses are covered under the policy?
- Is it worth my while to make a claim?
- What must I do to get my claim processed?

• How much money will be paid out, and who will get it?

Whose Losses Are Covered under the Policy?

Whose losses are covered depends on what has been lost, taken, damaged, or destroyed.

Damage to Buildings

STRUCTURES: As the owner of your home, you are the person who took out the insurance. The insurance policy is therefore in your name, and you are called the **named insured**. If the building itself is damaged or destroyed, you are the person who suffered a loss and are entitled to compensation to help repair or replace the damaged or destroyed structures. If your property is mortgaged, the mortgagee is also a named insured.

ADDITIONAL LIVING EXPENSES: If your house is so badly damaged that you cannot continue to live there, your insurance will pay reasonable living expenses not only for you, the named insured, but also for members of your household.

LOST WAGES: Your policy may allow you to make a claim for wages lost because of damage to your house. In that case, coverage is limited to the wages lost by the named insured and his or her wife or husband. If you are fortunate enough to have a child who has a job (but not fortunate enough for the child to have moved out), that child's lost wages are *not* covered.

Contents

Your belongings, and the belongings of members of your family who are living in the same household as you, are covered under your contents insurance. Your family includes anyone under the age of twenty-one who is in your care. If you are cohabiting with someone, but not legally married, that person's belongings are not necessarily covered. You must have cohabited for one year if you have a child, and otherwise for three years.

If anyone else's personal property is damaged or destroyed at your house, their loss is not covered under your contents insurance. It is covered, if at all, under your third party liability coverage.

Third Party Liability Insurance

If someone is accidentally injured on your property or their personal possessions are damaged, that person cannot make a claim under your insurance policy. Your third party liability does not cover the third party directly. It covers you and certain members of your household if the third party makes a claim against any of you. It pays on your behalf any compensation you are liable to pay to that third party.

The members of your household who are also protected from third party claims under your liability insurance are the same people who are insured under contents coverage.

Is It Worth Your While to Make a Claim?

Before you make a claim to your insurance company, there are two things to consider:

- A deductible may apply, and if your claim is not large, you may not actually collect anything from the insurance company.
- When you make a claim under your homeowner's insurance policy, your premium may go up—the same way your car insurance premium rises when you make a claim.

Deductibles

Most insurance policies require the insured to pay a certain amount of each claim. This amount is called the **deductible**, and it ranges from about $200 to $500. If your premium is low, you will probably have a high deductible; if your premium is high, you will probably have a low deductible.

For example, if you have a claim for $425 and a deductible of $500, your insurance company will pay nothing on the claim. If you have a claim for $1500 and a deductible of $200, your insurance company will pay $1300 on the claim.

Check with your insurance company about the amount of the deductible for the kind of claim you want to make. There is usually no deductible if you are making a claim under a rider.

If you will receive very little once the deductible is taken into account, you may not want to bother making a claim.

Increase in Insurance Premium

Speak to your insurance company or agent before you make a claim to find out how much your premium is likely to rise if you do make that claim. Whatever the increase, it will usually last for at least three years. In some cases, you may gain something from the insurance company now but lose it all back by paying increased premiums.

What Must You Do to Get Your Claim Processed?

While the claims process may vary from insurance company to insurance company, there are certain standard steps that are usually followed.

Usual Steps

Calculate what the money value of your loss may be, and contact your agent or insurance company to find out how much your deductible will be and what the effect of a claim will be on your premium.

If you decide to make a claim, the claims department of your insurance company will tell you what particular steps they want you to follow. One of these steps may be to call the police if criminal activity is involved or suspected.

For any insurance company, you will have to prove that you have suffered a loss and that you should be paid a certain amount of money in compensation as a result. The insurance company may ask you to complete a **proof of loss** form. This will involve listing the items taken or damaged, noting the date they were bought and their cost at the time. This is the time that you will be glad you made an inventory of your contents.

Proving Your Loss

If you are making a claim for an item that was damaged, you may have to provide a written estimate of the cost to repair the item. If the item was destroyed or stolen, you may have to provide an estimate of the cost to replace it. Get the written estimate from the place where you plan to buy the replacement or have the repair made. Your insurance company may direct you to stores or repair people they are used to dealing with, if you don't know anyone.

You should take care in completing the proof of loss form, because the information you provide will become the basis for what the insurance company will pay you. You will be asked to

- list all items you intend to make a claim for
- give the make, model, and serial number of any items that have them
- state the date and place of purchase, if you can
- give the replacement cost for destroyed or stolen items (use the price of a comparable item if the identical item can no longer be found)

Insurance Adjusters

If the loss involves the building itself, or contents worth a large sum of money, the insurance company may not simply accept your estimate of the damage and may send an **insurance adjuster** to inspect damaged property.

Independent Evidence of Loss

Keep in mind that the insurance company wants to pay as little as possible. The evidence you gather yourself may establish a higher loss than evidence gathered by the insurance company. If you have independent information about the value of your loss, you will be in a better position to judge the fairness of the compensation that the insurance company offers you. And if you think the compensation is not adequate, you will be in a position to negotiate for more.

There are a number of things you can do to support your claim if you think that the insurance company may not want to pay you what your loss is worth. It's up to you how much of this you choose to do. Your eagerness will probably depend on how much money is involved and your past experience with insurance companies.

- Photograph or video the damaged property. Keep one copy for yourself and give one to the insurance company.

- Get independent replacement cost or repair estimates even if the insurance company has sent its adjuster to make an estimate.

- If you're not satisfied with what the insurance company offers you, even after you give them your own evidence, you can contact an independent insurance adjuster. An independent adjuster does not work for your insurance company but is still an insurance professional whose opinion may be accepted by your insurance company. Of course you will have to pay the adjuster. The cost will depend on the size of the claim and how complicated it is. Ask for an estimate before you hire an adjuster.

- If you're unable to reach an agreement with your insurance company, you may have to hire a lawyer. You can ask the lawyer to negotiate for you or to sue the insurance company to force them to pay you what you are entitled to.

Should You Claim First or Pay First?

This decision will depend on how badly you need to replace what you've lost or fix what is broken. If you have water gushing from a broken pipe, you probably will not want to wait for the insurance company's cheque to have it repaired. If you've lost a bracelet you wear only once a year, you can probably wait to replace it.

If you do go ahead with repairs or replacement, get invoices and send a copy to the insurance company. Make sure you keep copies for yourself too.

If you cannot live in your house, you will have to pay your own additional living expenses and be repaid later. Keep all your receipts and send copies to your insurance company.

Always tell the insurance company what you are planning to do. You need to make sure that the expense in question is one that the insurance company is willing to pay you back later.

How Much Will be Paid?

The amount you'll get from the insurance company will depend on a number of factors which we have already discussed:

- the total amount of your coverage
- the amount of any deductible
- whether or not you have replacement cost insurance
- whether your property is replaced or only repaired
- if you are entitled to have property replaced, whether you actually replace it or choose to take a cash settlement

Who Will Get the Money?

PAYMENTS IN ADVANCE: If payment is made in advance to allow you to repair or replace property, the cheque from the insurance company will probably be made out jointly to you and the person who is making the repairs or selling you the replacement article. This is the insurance company's way of keeping tabs on both you and the person you are doing business with.

REIMBURSEMENT FOR PAYMENTS ALREADY MADE: If you've already made a payment with the approval of your insurance company, the reimbursement cheque will be made payable to you.

PAYMENT OF THIRD PARTY LIABILITY CLAIMS: These payments are generally made in settlement of a lawsuit and will be paid to the third party, probably through their lawyer.

PAYMENTS TO OTHERS THAN THE NAMED INSURED: If the named insured can't or won't make a claim on behalf of anyone else covered under the policy, that other person can make the claim. For example, your teenager's stereo is stolen from his bedroom in your house. You are angry at him for never cleaning his room and refuse to make a claim. He can make the claim himself because he is insured under your contents policy as a member of your household.

CONDOMINIUM INSURANCE COVERAGE

If you own a condominium, your insurance needs will be different than if you own a house. You own the interior of your unit, and you will have to insure it. You will also need coverage for your contents and for injuries that occur inside your unit. You do *not* need to insure the building in which your condominium is located, because the building is owned by the condominium corporation, not you. The condominium corporation will have insurance on the building. It will also have third party liability insurance to cover injuries to third parties on condominium property outside your unit.

What is Covered?

Insurance companies offer policies designed for condominium owners. As with other homeowner's policies, the condominium policies are really three policies in one.

The first part of the policy covers damage to or destruction of the interior of your unit itself. This part of your policy also covers you against any special assessments made against you by the condominium corporation to pay for repairs to the condominium building (this coverage usually costs extra).

The second part of the policy covers your contents. This coverage is exactly the same as the coverage in a regular homeowner's policy.

The third part of the policy covers you against claims made against you by third parties, very much like in a regular homeowner's policy, but taking into account that your home is only your unit. The condominium corporation's insurance is intended to cover injuries on other parts of the condominium property. Some condominium unit owner policies offer coverage against a special assessment made by the corporation if the corporation's insurance is not enough to pay a claim by a third party against the corporation. This coverage usually costs extra.

How Much Coverage Do You Have?

You will have to decide how much coverage to buy for each of the three different parts of the condominium owner's policy.

Coverage for Damage to Your Unit

The basic amount of coverage will depend on the value of your unit as the unit was originally constructed. The insurance company will help you to determine the amount of coverage you require after reviewing such things as the condominium corporation's insurance coverage and the amount you paid for your unit.

If you decide to pay extra for coverage for improvements made to your unit since it was originally constructed, the amount of coverage will be based on the value of these improvements. You should consider getting this additional coverage if your unit has been upgraded with things like a new or fancier kitchen or bathroom, or built-in cabinets.

For both kinds of coverage, you must decide whether or not you wish to pay extra for replacement cost insurance. If you decide to get this kind of coverage, it will also affect the amount of coverage you must buy.

Finally, you may decide to pay extra for coverage against special assessments made because of damage to the condominium. Your insurance company will help you decide how much coverage you need, based on a review of such things as the condominium's insurance policy and your percentage share of ownership of the condominium. No matter how much coverage you buy, your policy will probably not cover a special assessment made by the condominium corporation to cover the amount of any deductible that it had to pay under its own insurance.

Coverage for Your Contents

As we said, contents coverage for condominium owners is the same as for other homeowners. Information on the amount of contents coverage can be found earlier in this chapter.

Third Party Liability Coverage

As with a regular homeowner's policy, the standard amount of this coverage is $1,000,000, but you can buy additional coverage.

If you decide to pay extra for coverage against special assessments made because of injury to third parties caused by the condominium corporation itself or on condominium property, your insurance company will help you decide on the amount of coverage you should have, based on such things as the condominium's insurance policy and your percentage share of the ownership of the condominium. Again, no matter how much coverage you buy, your policy will probably not cover a special assessment made by the condominium corporation to cover the amount of any deductible that it had to pay under its own insurance.

What Are You Insured Against?

As with a regular homeowner's policy, you choose how many perils you want to be insured against, within a range of possibilities set by the insurance company. The number of perils you choose to be insured against will affect the cost of your premiums.

You may wish to insure yourself against more perils than your condominium corporation is insured against. If the condominium corporation's structures are damaged or it is responsible for injury to a third party, its insurance will only cover the corporation for perils named in the condominium's policy. If the peril is not insured against, the condominium will have to come up with the money through a special assessment against the unit owners. Your special assessment coverage will only pay for this assessment if the cause of the damage is a peril which *you* have paid to be insured against.

9 MOVING TO YOUR NEW HOME

War is hell. Moving is worse.

Packing up everything you own, moving it to another place and then unpacking it, while you still need all the things you've either just packed or haven't unpacked yet, is a special kind of torture.

You probably haven't stopped to think about what's involved in getting yourself and all your belongings to your new home. Instead, you've no doubt spent many pleasant hours picturing what it will be like to live there. In your fantasy, all your furniture has been miraculously transported to your new home without any effort or inconvenience. Unfortunately, that's not the way it works.

Moving is chaotic, but with planning you'll at least have organized chaos instead of absolute chaos. Keep in mind too that there's more to moving than moving vans. In this chapter we tell you how to

- do some preliminary planning
- choose the right mover
- decide what the mover will do
- pack for the move
- live through moving day itself
- deal with the aftermath

Most of this chapter assumes that you're making a local move or discusses concerns that apply equally to local moves or long distance moves. There's a section at the end of the chapter about special concerns for a long distance move.

PRELIMINARY PLANNING

Preliminary planning for your move involves getting ready to look for a moving company. It also involves preparing yourself and your family for the move.

Getting Ready to Talk to Movers

Start thinking about your move early enough that you will be able to book your move at least six to eight weeks before your planned moving date.

Before you talk to any movers, you have to sit down and give some thought to certain matters. Any mover you speak to will want to know where you are moving from, where you are moving to, when you are moving, and what you want the movers to move. The moving from and to questions are easy—you know your old address and your new one. The other questions may *look* easier than they are.

When Are You Moving?

When you are moving will depend to a large extent on your closing date. If you are selling a house as well as buying a new one, you are probably doing both on the same day. You have to move out of your old house on the closing day and, unless you are storing your belongings, you'll want them moved to your new house. If you have been renting, you may choose to keep your apartment past the closing date. Doing so gives you more leeway to move gradually or to move later.

The mover will want to know not only what day you want to move but what time of day. You can ask for the **first move of the day**, which means that the movers arrive at your house at a fixed time, usually about 8:00 a.m. If you ask for the second move of the day, the mover won't be able to set a fixed time of arrival. In choosing between the two, keep in mind that you won't be able to get the keys to your new home and move your things in until your lawyer and the vendor's lawyer have finished closing your deal. This may not happen until the afternoon of the day of closing.

If you book the first move of the day and the movers finish loading the moving van quickly, you and they may end up waiting to get into the new house. You will be paying the movers by the hour, including any waiting time. On the other hand, if you book the second move of the day and you have a lot to move, you may not have to wait to get into the new house but you may still be moving in late into the night. In deciding between the two, ask your mover how long it is likely to take to load the van at your old house. If it will take a long time, you are probably better off booking the first move of the day.

What Do You Want the Movers to Move?

Keep in mind that the more the movers move, the more it will cost. The strategy then is to have them move less rather than more. There are ways to reduce the movers' load:

- Get rid of the stuff you don't need.
- Get things moved by others for free.
- Move some things yourself.

Get rid of anything you don't need by having a garage sale, by giving things to charity, or just by throwing things away. Many people hoard things they had no need for in their old house, let alone in their new home. If you are thinking about having furniture reupholstered or carpets, drapes, or furniture cleaned, schedule the work so that the items are picked up from your old house and delivered directly to your new home. Put off purchase, or at least delivery, of new furniture until you are in your new home. Finally, you may want to move some of your belongings yourself, particularly fragile or valuable items.

Preparing Yourself and Your Family

There are a number of things that you should do to get yourself and your family ready for the move.

Arranging for Insurance on Your New Home

You will need to have homeowner's insurance in place as soon as you become the owner of your new home. You should start to make arrangements several weeks before the closing date of your house purchase. We talked about insurance in Chapter 8.

Notifying People of Your Change of Address

Unless you've gone into a witness protection program or are trying to escape from your creditors, you want people to be able to find you after you move.

You want to continue receiving your magazines, and you want your friends to know where to bring their housewarming gifts.

Make a list of everyone who needs your address:

- friends and relatives
- credit card companies
- banks
- pension plans
- companies who pay you dividends
- insurance companies
- magazines and newspapers
- book and record clubs
- clubs and organizations

Notify each person on your list of your new address and your moving date. Your credit card companies and magazine publishers have change of address forms that you can send to them. For the others on your list, you can get change of address post cards from Canada Post. The post cards are free, but you have to pay the postage yourself.

In case you leave someone off your list, you should also go to the post office to arrange for Canada Post to redirect your mail to your new address. You will have to fill in a form and pay a fee of about $30.00. Your mail will be redirected for six months, and you can pay for additional six-month periods. When you receive redirected mail at your new address, be sure to notify the sender that you've moved.

If you have the newspaper delivered to your door, call the subscription office to arrange for delivery to your new address.

Once you move into your new home, you must notify the motor vehicle licensing office immediately of your change of address. You will be issued a new driver's licence and vehicle permit showing your new address.

Helping Your Children Adjust to the Move

Moving can be hard on children of any age. Younger children can be frightened and confused by a change that they don't understand. Older children may be upset at the loss of friends and the prospect of a new school. How you will help your child adjust will depend on the child's age and personality.

Whatever the age of your children, tell them about the move as soon as possible and involve them in it as much as you can. Take them to see the new house, neighbourhood, and school, or if you can't do that, show them photographs or a videotape. Let them help in planning the decorating of their new bedrooms.

Let younger children know that their furniture, clothes, and toys will be moving with them. Have them help in the packing, and don't pack favourite items until the end. Encourage older children to make arrangements to stay in touch with their friends through visits, telephone calls, letters, and E-mail.

Transferring Utility Accounts

Telephone the gas company, electric company, water department, telephone company, and cable TV company to tell them of your move. In some cases your account and service will simply be transferred to your new address. If you are moving out of the service area, your account will have to be closed, and you will have to contact the utility companies in your new neighbourhood to arrange for service. Cancel any fuel oil delivery contracts for your old house.

Making Arrangements with Your Lawyer

You will have to meet with your lawyer at least once just before closing to review and sign the necessary documents. You will also have to give your lawyer the money needed to complete your purchase—if you don't, you won't be moving. Some of this money may come from the sale of your old house, some may come from your mortgage. If your lawyer is handling the legal work involved in selling your house and preparing your mortgage, those funds will go directly to the lawyer. But there will always be some amount of money that you have to take to the lawyer yourself. Leave yourself enough time to get your hands on the money, get it into the form of a certified cheque, and deliver it.

Ordinarily, the keys to your new home will be given to your lawyer at the closing, and you will have to pick them up from him or her. If your lawyer's office is not close to either your old house or new home, it will be inconvenient for you. You should make arrangements through your lawyer to have the keys left at a more convenient location where you can pick them up after the closing.

Making an Inspection Before Closing

If your agreement of purchase and sale gives you the right to inspect the house just before closing, make arrangements with your real estate agent to do so. You want to make sure that the house is in more or less the same condition it was in when you agreed to buy it. If you see any problems, be sure to notify your lawyer immediately.

If you are buying a newly constructed home that is covered by your provincial new home warranty program, you will probably have to make a pre-closing inspection. The purpose of this inspection is to identify any problems in the house which the builder is required to fix. The builder will probably contact you to set up an appointment for this inspection. You might want to discuss the inspection with your lawyer beforehand, so that you know what to look for.

CHOOSING THE RIGHT MOVER

Before you choose a mover you should speak to three to five moving companies to get estimates and also a sense of the level of service and reliability each has to offer. Get names of moving companies from friends, your real estate agent, or the Yellow Pages.

Get Estimates

Ask each moving company for an estimate. For an accurate estimate of what *your* move will cost, the mover must come to your house and look at what you have to move. Each estimate should be in writing. In order to compare the different estimates, be sure that they all take into account the following:

- things to be moved
- packing, if any
- insurance
- any special charges
- taxes

Show the movers *everything* you want to move, including things in your attic, basement, or garage. Don't forget to tell the mover about anything stored elsewhere that you want them to pick up and take to your new home.

If you want the movers to do any packing for you, say so, and get an estimate from all the moving companies for the same items. Even if you don't want to pay for packing, you may have some items that the movers will suggest that you let them pack. If one mover makes such a suggestion, ask the others what they think.

Ask each moving company what insurance they recommend for your move and how much it will cost.

Ask each moving company if there will be any special charges, for example, for moving a piano or freezer, or because of the number of stairs at your old house or new home.

Ask each company whether they offer any discounts or promotions. Let the different companies know that you are shopping around—it may encourage them to give you a better price.

To give you a rough idea, the cost of moving the contents of an average three-bedroom bungalow (without any packing) is about $1000, going up to about $1500 in peak times (the first and last weeks of the summer months).

Check Out the Mover's Reputation

Even if someone has recommended a mover to you, you should consider checking the following:

• how long the company has been in business
• the size of the company
• how long the staff have been with the company
• whether the company is properly licensed
• whether the company can provide references from satisfied clients
• whether the local Better Business Bureau has any record of complaints about the company

Whatever the general reputation of the company, the success of your move will ultimately depend on the three or four people who show up with the truck. So try to find out if the people who will be doing your move have worked with the company for a while.

DECIDING WHAT YOU WANT THE MOVER TO DO

Once you decide which mover to use, you must decide exactly what services you want from them, and you must book the move and sign a contract. Be sure to book your move at least six or eight weeks before your moving day.

Packing and Boxes

You can arrange for the moving company to do all your packing for you. If you do, you don't have to pack anything. You don't have to live out of cartons for weeks before you move. You just go about your business until a day or two before the move, when the movers come with boxes and packing materials and pack your things. It sounds like heaven, doesn't it? Well, heaven is expensive. To have the movers pack an average three-bedroom bungalow would cost in the $800 to $1000 range (and more at peak times). If you want the movers to unpack at the other end, it would cost an additional $400 to $500. As you can see, having the movers pack and unpack would more than double the cost of a local move.

You may have certain items that the movers will recommend that you let them pack. Usually these are large or expensive items that are easily damaged, like a marble table or a large mirror. The movers will tell you that they will not accept responsibility for damage to such things unless they pack them.

If you're doing any of your own packing, you need boxes, lots of boxes. You can buy or rent boxes from the moving company. If you don't get them from the moving company, your alternatives are to buy them from a store that specializes in boxes and other moving and packing materials, or to scrounge around in grocery and liquor stores. Liquor store and grocery boxes don't cost money, but what you don't pay in cash you may have to pay in self-respect because of the begging and pleading involved to get more than two boxes at a time. You should also know that these boxes may not be sturdy enough for moving. They may also have bugs in them. Check them carefully before you bring the boxes (and the bugs) into the house.

A Few Good Men

The hourly rate your mover will charge will depend on the number of men (and they probably will be men) they send, so you will have to decide how many you want. It's not necessarily cheaper to have fewer men, because the move will take longer. If you've chosen a reputable mover, it's best to follow their advice about how many men you should have.

Storage

If you have to move out of your old house or apartment before your new home is ready for you, you will have to store your belongings. Your mover can arrange for **storage-in-transit**, which means that you pay to have your goods moved out of your old house, into a warehouse for storage for up to sixty days, and then into your new home. You will be charged a package rate that combines the moving and storage fees. If you need to store your things for more than sixty days, long-term storage arrangements must be made. If your goods will be stored in a warehouse, you may want to inspect it for cleanliness and dryness.

If overnight storage turns out to be necessary during your move, for a fee some movers will simply store your possessions in the moving van.

Insurance

The standard moving contract limits the mover's liability for damage to your belongings to less than $1.00 per pound regardless of what the actual value of the item is. So if the movers destroyed your thirty-pound stereo system, they would have to pay you less than $30.

Clearly, you need additional protection in case any of your things are lost, damaged, or destroyed in the move. You can buy insurance through your moving company which will provide greater protection. Ask your mover for a recommendation about how much insurance you should buy. But before you speak to your mover about this, contact your home insurance company to find out whether your current home or apartment contents insurance will cover your belongings during your move.

Finalizing the Contract

Your contract with the moving company will set out

- the date and time of the move
- the number of men and type of truck
- the hourly rate
- any special materials or services to be provided, like boxes or packing

Because the bulk of the cost of moving is based on the number of hours that the movers actually spend on your move, the final cost will not be set out in the contract. Only an estimated cost will be given. You will probably have to pay a deposit when you book your move, and you will have to pay the balance of the price to the moving foreman when the move is completed. The moving company will tell you how they want to be paid—usually by cash, certified cheque, or credit card.

PACKING FOR YOUR MOVE

Your things can't be moved unless they are packed. If you hire the movers to do the packing for you, a crew will swoop in and do all your packing in a day or two. If you decide to do your own packing, the crew will consist of you and, if you're lucky, a helpful spouse and cooperative children. But even with their help, don't think *you* will be able to do it all in a day or two. You don't have the expertise, you won't have the manpower, and you still have the rest of your life to contend with.

There's no way around it. Unless you want to find yourself throwing things into green garbage bags as the movers are carrying your furniture out the door (as the husband of one of the authors does), you must start packing well in advance of moving day. As time passes, more and more of your belongings will be in boxes. You have to know what you can live without and what you can't live without so that you can decide what to pack first.

By now it should be clear to you (although it never did become clear to the above-mentioned husband) that packing for a move involves planning, one might even say militarily precise planning. You want to have a plan that allows you to

• pack what you need most last
• direct the boxes to the right room in your new home
• find what you need while things are still in the boxes
• pack things so they don't get broken and are easy to find

Don't forget that everything that's packed must be unpacked. Pack in haste and repent at leisure!

Decide the Order in Which You Will Pack

Walk through your house. On a room-by-room basis, identify in each room what you can live without until after moving day. Some rooms will have lots of things you can pack early, and these are the things you will pack first. For example, you won't miss too badly

• your off-season clothes
• books, records, tapes, and CDs
• silver, crystal, and fine china
• pictures
• knick-knacks
• personal files and records
• sports equipment, games, and some children's toys
• extra linens
• tools and off-season outdoor equipment

You can pack these and seal and pile up the boxes.

As moving day gets closer, you can pack some of the items you use more regularly. Kitchens and bathrooms are filled with this kind of stuff. Don't seal the boxes, and keep them where you can get into them easily. Don't pack things you must use on a daily basis until the last moment.

You should also pack a separate box of essential items that you will want to have as soon as you reach your new home; for example:

• toilet paper
• soap
• toothpaste and toothbrushes
• paper towels

- garbage bags
- paper plates, plastic cups, and utensils
- can opener
- screwdriver and pliers
- a flashlight
- some light bulbs
- snacks and drinks

Have an Inventory Plan

Having a proper inventory plan will help you to

- direct your boxes to the right room in your new home
- find things while they're still in the boxes
- make sure that all of your boxes have arrived at your new home

As you pack each box, assign it a number. Use a magic marker to write on each box the number and the room where the box is going. Write large enough for you and the movers to be able to read easily what you've written. This way the movers will know what room to take each box to without having to ask you about every box. Write the number on the top and each side of the box, so the number is visible no matter how the boxes are piled up. If you are planning to take any boxes in your car instead of sending them on the moving van, mark them clearly "Do Not Move."

Keep a list of every box you pack. Write down the number of each box and next to each number, write the room the box is to go to and a brief description of the contents of the box. It will be several days or more before all of your boxes are unpacked. If you need something from a box, you will be able to look through your list to find what box it is in and the room the box is located in, rather than climbing over piles of boxes and rummaging through them.

As you unpack each box, check it off against your inventory list. You will know if any boxes did not get moved.

If you have a lot of furniture or a bad memory, you might want to list your furniture as well as your boxes on the inventory list. You can check off the furniture as it is moved out and in to make sure nothing has been forgotten.

How to Pack—Plan of Attack

Pick a room and start packing. When you've done all the packing you can in that room at that time, move on to another room. Don't mix things from different rooms in one box.

Boxes and Packing Materials

Make sure that your boxes are clean and sturdy. Tape the bottoms of the boxes to reinforce them. If you are assembling boxes, keep the bottom flaps flat, do not interlock them. Boxes should have either top flaps or a lid. The tops should also be sealed with tape. Use masking tape or special plastic moving tape.

Choose the right size box for what you are packing. Pack heavy items like books in small boxes. Use very large boxes only for light things like bedding and linens. Remember that some poor soul will have to lug around whatever you pack. Check that the box can hold the weight of what you've put in.

If you are packing breakable items, crumple up some paper to pad the bottom of the box and wrap each item individually. Anything really small should be packed in a small box and then placed in a larger box. If you put small things directly into a large box, you may lose them in the wrapping. Don't put heavy things on top of breakables.

If you use newspaper for wrapping, the ink can rub off. That's fine for some things, but a disaster for others. You can buy blank newsprint from your mover or from moving stores.

Special Tips

CLOTHING: Movers have special wardrobe cartons you can rent. They have built-in rods, so you can just hang your clothes in them as you would in a closet. Your mover may say that you can leave clothing in dresser drawers. Keep in mind that the drawers will be taken out of the dresser.

PLANTS: Move plants in your car if you can. They may not survive a trip in the moving van if the weather is too hot or too cold or if the van is crowded. Speak to your local nursery to see if there is anything you can do to prepare your plants for the move.

LAMPS: Remove light bulbs before packing lamps. Pack table lamps in cartons. Pack the lampshades in separate cartons. Don't use newspaper to wrap lamp-shades. Don't forget to remove and pack any ceiling or wall lights that you're taking with you.

COMPUTER EQUIPMENT: Before you pack your computer, be sure to backup any files on the hard drive. Move the computer yourself, rather than putting it on the van if you can. If you can't, keep the backup disks with you during the move. Check your owner's manual or with a computer store about pack-ing your computer for a move.

CHINA: After padding the bottom of the carton, put heavier pieces in first. Stand flat pieces on their edge; do not stack them.

BOOKS, RECORDS, AND CDs: Use small boxes, because these items are heavy. Pack books, records, and CDs on their edge; do not stack them.

APPLIANCES: Appliances with special connections, like air-conditioners, washers, dryers, dishwashers, and stoves, should be disconnected and prepared for moving by qualified service people. Refrigerators and freezers must be defrosted, emptied, and completely dry before moving.

VALUABLES AND PERSONAL ITEMS: Don't send valuable or personal items such as money, jewellery, keys, or documents on the moving van. Pack them in a suitcase and take them in your car.

MOVING DAY

For the sanity of your children and your pets (not to mention your own sanity), it is best to arrange for them to spend moving day elsewhere. If it's a school day, let your children go to school. Your move may still be going on when school is over, so arrange for a friend or relative to pick them up and look after them until you can come to pick them up. Arrange to board your pets the night before your move. Pick them up the day after moving day. Don't let your pets outside except on a leash for some time after the move, or they may try to find their way back to the old house.

If you've packed and labelled everything properly, your move should go fairly smoothly, but you will still have to be around to supervise the loading of the truck. Control your desire to run away and hide when you see the van pull up outside your house.

When the movers arrive at your door, the foreman will go through your house to get an idea of what has to be moved and to note the condition of your belongings on an inventory list. Go with him to make sure that what he writes down is accurate. (Get a copy of this inventory once it's finished.) Give him any special instructions that you might have for any particular item.

You may want to put down mats or padding on banisters and doorways to protect the house from dirt or damage during the move.

Before the truck leaves for your new home, do a last minute check of the basement, attic, garage, and all cupboards and closets to make sure nothing has been forgotten.

You can't get into your new home or get the keys until your deal has closed. Stay in touch with your lawyer's office because it will be hard for your lawyer to find you on moving day unless you have a cellular phone. As

soon as you have been notified that the deal has closed, you'll have to pick up the keys from wherever you arranged for them to be left.

When you arrive at your new home with the keys, you and the foreman should go through it so you can identify the rooms for him. This way he will know where your labelled boxes should go. Even though your boxes are labelled, you will have to be available to answer any questions the movers might have. So there's still no escape.

Before anything is moved in, put down mats and padding on banisters and doorways to protect your new home from dirt and damage.

As the movers are unloading the van, try to get a sense of whether all of your things have made it off the truck. Check off as much as you can on your inventory list, but don't expect to be able to check off each and every box. Glance over your furniture and boxes to see if there is any obvious damage. Don't worry about doing a thorough inspection—you can do that as you unpack. If you do notice that something is damaged or missing, notify the foreman.

Although you are supposed to have "vacant possession" of your new home, you may find that the vendor has left behind the odd thing—like a huge freezer in the basement that stopped working in 1972. You may want to make an arrangement with the movers to take away large items like this before they leave.

When the move is finished, the foreman will give you the final bill for payment. It should be close to the estimate you were given, but it could be significantly higher if there was a delay getting to the new house or into it. If the amount of the bill is higher than the certified cheque the mover told you to have, they will accept cash, a credit card, and sometimes a personal cheque for the balance.

If you are pleased with the job the movers have done, you may tip them if you wish. Tipping is not required, but people sometimes give the foreman $15 or $20 for the crew.

AFTER YOUR MOVE

As you unpack, check to see if anything was damaged in the move. Check the foreman's inventory to make sure that the damage wasn't there before the move. If you discover that something was damaged, notify the moving company in writing. Take a photograph of the damage. If you're making a damage claim, don't throw out any documents relating to the move. You usually have a period of several months to make a damage claim, so you don't have to worry about checking everything you own instantly.

If you think you were overcharged for your move, write to the moving company immediately. Most reputable movers want their estimates to be reasonably accurate and will be concerned if that was not the case. The mover may be able to explain to your satisfaction why your move cost more than you expected or may give you a partial refund. If you are not satisfied with what the mover does, you can complain to the national moving line that the mover is associated with, the provincial body that licenses movers, or the Better Business Bureau.

If you can't get satisfaction from the moving company about damage or overcharging, you may want to consider suing. Unless there's a significant amount of money involved, a lawsuit is probably not worth your time, money, and aggravation.

LONG DISTANCE MOVES

If you are moving to another city or province, there are additional matters to plan for.

Relocation Concerns

When you get to your new location, you will have to find a new doctor and dentist and other professionals to serve you. You can ask for recommendations from your current doctor or dentist, or from your real estate agent. Get copies of your medical and dental records before you leave town if you don't want your new doctor and dentist to have to send for them.

If you have children, speak to their school about transferring their academic records to the new school. If you have pets, get a copy of their veterinary records.

Coordinating the Move

You and the moving van may not arrive at your new location at the same time. You may have to find somewhere else to stay until your belongings arrive or your house is ready. Tell the movers where you or your representative can be contacted. If the movers can't contact you, the unloading of the van may be delayed, which will increase the cost of the move. Except for delays like this, the cost of long distance moves is calculated on the basis of weight and distance, rather than on an hourly rate.

Shipping Pets

If you are sending pets by air, you have to talk to both your veterinarian and the airline. Check with the airline well ahead of time about regulations for shipping pets. Ask when is the best time to ship your pet, whether there are direct flights available, and what kind of special cage or carrier is needed. Also ask whether there are any weather conditions, such as extremely hot or cold weather, which would prevent them from accepting your pet for shipping. Find out what arrangements you have to make for pick up and delivery of your pet.

Speak to your vet about health risks of shipping your pet, the best kind of shipping cage, and whether the pet should be tranquillized.

Cars

If you are shipping your car in the moving van, have it serviced beforehand to check that no oil or fluids are leaking which might damage other items on the van. Leave your gas tank no more than one-quarter full. Give the keys to the car to the van driver. If you are shipping the car during the winter, leave it in a heated garage for at least twenty-four hours before it is loaded onto the van to make sure that ice and snow have melted off and will not damage other items in the van.

TAX BREAKS

If you are moving for business reasons, you may be able to claim some of your moving expenses for tax purposes. Speak to your accountant or, if you dare, read your income tax guide. If your new home is 40 kilometres closer to your new place of work, you can deduct from your work-related income the following:

- transportation and storage costs
- your travelling expenses
- cost of selling your old home and buying a new one

If your employer is paying for your move, your moving expenses will not be deductible.

☑ Checklist for Moving

Eight weeks before moving day

❑ Contact movers.
❑ Decide what can be sold, given away, or thrown out.
❑ If you're not buying boxes from the mover, start collecting them from stores.

Six weeks before moving day

❑ Make a list of people to notify that you are moving—and start notifying them.

Four weeks before moving day

❑ Contact utility companies to make arrangements to transfer service to your new home.
❑ Contact insurance companies to arrange for insurance on your new home.
❑ Start packing.

Two weeks before moving day

❑ Book elevators if you are moving out of or into a high-rise.
❑ Confirm arrangements with your mover.

One week before moving day

❑ Arrange with your real estate agent for a pre-closing inspection of your new home.
❑ Make an appointment to see your lawyer.

❑ Confirm that your funds for closing are available.
❑ Arrange for service people to disconnect your major appliances.
❑ Defrost and dry out freezers.

Moving day

❑ Have a stiff drink or take a tranquillizer.

owning a
home

10 YOU'RE HOME, NOW WHAT?

Y ou're standing at the window watching the moving van pull away. Boxes are piled all around you, you're exhausted and you have every reason to be. If it's not the middle of the night, it's at least getting dark and you're probably dying for a stiff drink.

At the end of a long moving day, the job of organizing the chaos looks overwhelming. You think that you have to keep working until the kitchen is set up and a decent meal prepared for your family, the beds are made, and clothes have been hung up before they wrinkle any more. We're giving you permission not to worry about these things right now. Do the bare minimum that will let you sleep in your home tonight. Then, either go out for dinner or order in a pizza. The boxes and the mess aren't going anywhere. They'll still be there waiting for you in the morning.

You've put a lot of energy into finding your new home and moving into it. Now you're in a new stage of your life: you are a homeowner. Owning a home brings with it many special concerns and problems. In this chapter, we're going to discuss the matters you need to think about in the first days and weeks after you move in. In the next few chapters, we'll talk about some of the long-term concerns that homeowners have.

PRACTICAL MATTERS

The morning after moving day comes all too soon. Most of your time and energy over the next while is going to be spent unpacking and making your home liveable, and any time you have left over will be spent arguing with your spouse about where to hang pictures. Pressing as these matters are, there are other things that you have to turn what's left of your mind to.

Change the Locks

You should change your locks as soon as possible after you move into your new home. It seems a pity, having just received the keys to your new home, to render them useless. But you have no way of knowing that you've been given all the keys and, if you haven't, who might have one.

At the very least, you should have the tumblers changed in the locks so that the old keys won't work in them. If the existing locks don't seem adequate to you, this is a good time to upgrade them. See Chapter 12 on home security for more information about locks.

Get Connected

You should have contacted the gas company, electric company, water department, telephone company, and cable TV company before your move to arrange for service in your new home. If you didn't, do it now—if you can find a telephone. If you have moved into an area serviced by different companies than you dealt with before, you may have to fill in an application form and provide credit references.

Get Useful Information

You should prepare a list of emergency phone numbers as soon as possible after you move in. In Chapter 13 on home safety, you will find a list to fill out.

You will have to pay your mortgage and your property taxes before you know it! Call your mortgagee and your municipality to find out when and where you have to make these payments. Don't wait for your lawyer to provide you with this information in the reporting letter because the payments may be due before the letter arrives.

After your move, you're going to have garbage—lots of it. Call the municipality to find out not only what your regular garbage pick-up and recycling days are, but also whether you need to make special arrangements for pick-up of large items and hazardous waste. You may have to pay a fee to have these things taken away.

Notify People of Your Change of Address

If you haven't already done so, make a list of everyone who needs your new address and notify them. Look at Chapter 9 on moving for suggestions about people to notify.

Don't forget to contact your provincial motor vehicle office to change the address on your licence and car ownership. All provinces have short time limits for doing this after you move. If you don't make the change, you may have to pay a fine. If you have to choose between notifying your mother and notifying the motor vehicle office, choose the motor vehicle office. Your mother may forgive your neglect but the motor vehicle office won't.

If you have young children, have them memorize their new address and telephone number right away. If they carry identification, change the address and phone number. Take your children for walks to familiarize them with the new neighbourhood so they won't get lost when you're not with them.

If you have pets and have moved to a new municipality, contact the animal licensing department and arrange to have your pets re-licensed. If your pets wear identification tags with your name, address, and telephone number on it (if they don't, they should!), don't forget to replace the tags with new ones. Don't let your cat or dog outside without a leash for a few weeks after the move, until they know their new home.

Collect the Interest on Your Deposit

We told you to put a clause into your offer requiring the vendor's real estate agent to pay you interest on the deposit you paid. Now it's time to find out how much money is owed to you, and to get your hands on it. Call your own real estate agent for information about when and how you will be paid. If you run into any problems collecting the interest, call your lawyer.

Inspection and Service

If you did not have a professional home inspection done before you bought the house, have the following inspected and serviced, if necessary, before you use them for the first time:

- heating
- air-conditioning
- fireplaces
- electrical system

PROBLEMS IN YOUR NEW HOME

Most people will unpack their boxes and settle into their new home without too many problems. But sometimes, as you clear away the debris of your move, you'll be unpleasantly surprised. When you go to hang up your clothes, you may find the closets full of wire hangers—or worse, you may find that the beautiful closet organizers you thought were included in the purchase price are mysteriously gone. Later on, you may find that the air-conditioning doesn't work or that the roof leaks. What can you do when you find minor or major problems in your new home?

The Vendor's Responsibility to You

The bad news is that the vendor does not have very much responsibility to you for problems with the house. Once you become the owner of a house, you also become the owner of its problems. If things break down, even if it happens right after you move in, generally you are the person who has to pay to fix them.

The Condition of the House

The vendor has to hand over the house to you in the same condition it was in when the agreement of purchase and sale was signed, except for normal wear and tear. That doesn't mean, though, that you should be stuck with a problem that existed at that time *if the vendor deliberately concealed it from you.*

When you see the house for the first time without the vendor's furniture and pictures on the wall, you will probably see chipped paint, cracks, and little holes that you didn't notice before. If they were there when you signed the agreement, even though you did not notice them, you'll have to fix them and you won't be able to get any money from the vendor. The exception would be some major damage that the vendor purposely concealed from you, for example, a gaping hole in the wall that the vendor covered with a poster.

What if you find something more serious, like a broken pipe in a bathroom? If the pipe broke after you signed the agreement of purchase and sale, the vendor should have fixed it and in theory is responsible for fixing it now. If the pipe was already broken when you viewed the house, repairing it is your responsibility if the pipe was obviously broken and you should have been able to see it. The situation is different if the vendor hid the fact that the pipe was broken, for example, by turning off the water supply to that pipe and wallpapering over damage caused by the leak. Again, the vendor may be legally responsible for the cost of the repairs.

These possible problems show why it is so important to make a professional home inspection a condition of your agreement of purchase and sale. A good home inspector should find most of the serious problems with a house, even if the vendor has tried to hide them. If the problem happened after the agreement was signed, the home inspection report will help to prove that and to pin responsibility on the vendor.

Fixtures and Chattels

The vendor has to leave behind all chattels that were included in the agreement of purchase and sale. If the vendor agreed to sell you the washer and dryer, they have to be there when you arrive. The vendor also has to leave behind any fixtures that the agreement of purchase and sale did not say could be removed. For example, unless the agreement of purchase and sale said so, the vendor cannot pull up the wall-to-wall carpets, leaving just the tacks behind.

The vendor's responsibility to leave behind chattels is clear, because it is limited to the chattels specifically promised to you in the agreement of purchase and sale. The vendor also had to remove any chattels that weren't included in the agreement of purchase and sale and is still required to remove them if they were left in the house.

The question is more complicated when it comes to fixtures. That's because you and the vendor can have an honest difference of opinion about what was a fixture and what was not. You may think that anything that was bolted to the walls was a fixture and was to be left behind. The vendor, on the other hand, may never have intended to leave the item behind and knew that it could be easily unbolted without causing any damage to the wall or the item. This is why we told you that the agreement of purchase and sale should specifically mention any items you want left behind.

Any chattels or fixtures that were sold with the house should be in the same condition they were in at the time the agreement of purchase and sale was signed, except for normal wear and tear.

What Do You Do If There Are Problems?

We've told you what the vendor is legally responsible for, but there's a world of difference between legal responsibility and money in your hand. When you see the broken pipe in the bathroom, your first instinct may be to sue. But suing is expensive and aggravating, and the results are not guaranteed. Look upon suing as your last option, not your first.

To begin with, make a list of all your problems. Don't deal with just one problem at a time. After you have listed all the problems, collect evidence about each one:

- Get out any inspection reports.
- Speak to your real estate agent to find out what problems were disclosed by the vendor at the time of listing.
- Take pictures.
- Get estimates for repairs.

Get a sense of how much money all of the problems together are worth.

Contact the lawyer who acted for you on the purchase. Ask your lawyer whether the vendor is legally responsible for all, or any, of the problems. If your lawyer says yes, ask him or her to write a letter to the vendor's lawyer demanding payment. You may have to pay your lawyer to write this letter, although some lawyers consider a letter like this to be part of the house purchase. As a result of this letter, the vendor *may* agree to pay you some money, but if so, it probably won't be nearly as much as you think you're entitled to.

If the vendor won't pay you enough or won't pay you anything at all, your choices are either to sue or to forget the matter. What you decide will depend on the amount of money involved and your stomach for the stress and expense of a lawsuit. You can avoid some of the stress by having a lawyer handle your case, but you will have to pay legal fees. You've just had a taste of legal fees when you bought the house. Litigation is a *lot* more expensive. If the amount of money involved is only a few thousand dollars or less, you may be able to sue on your own in small claims court (call the small claims court office to find out what the monetary limit is in your province). You won't have any legal fees, but you have to put a lot of time and energy into preparing your case, and you'll have to present your case in court. When your case comes to trial, you may find that the vendor has hired a lawyer who's going to mop the floor with you. Here we'd like to share with you an old lawyers' saying that anyone who acts for himself has a fool for a client—and his lawyer's not too bright either.

This is our best advice to you: Avoid lawsuits whenever you can. Do this by being careful *before* you buy the house.

- If the vendor signed a disclosure statement, read it carefully.
- Examine the house like a hawk when you view it, and ask the vendor lots of questions if you suspect problems of any kind.
- Have the house professionally inspected for existing and potential problems.
- List in your offer the chattels and fixtures you want to buy with the house.

• Include a clause in your offer that all chattels not listed in the offer are to be removed by the vendor (legally this is unnecessary but it may remind the vendor to move the freezer out of the basement).

SPECIAL RIGHTS FOR BUYERS OF NEWLY CONSTRUCTED HOMES

If you bought your home from a builder who is registered under the provincial warranty program, your home will be covered for certain problems that may arise within a specified period of time after you buy. (A home that was registered when it was built may still be covered under the warranty, even if you bought it as a resale.)

If your new home is covered by a warranty, you probably had to make a detailed inspection of the house before closing to make a note of any problems that you saw then. The builder is supposed to fix them within a short time after closing.

After closing, you continue to be covered for things like major structural defects, defects in work and materials, water seepage through the foundation, defects in the electrical, plumbing, and heating systems, and violations of the provincial building code. The length of the warranty period, which depends on the province and the nature of the problem, can be from one to five years (one to seven years in Ontario).

If you find a problem during the warranty period, you must notify the home warranty program in writing, and possibly the builder as well. All of the warranty programs have methods in place for resolving any disputes without a lawsuit. Have a look at your warranty documents. If you have any questions about what's covered or how to make a claim, contact your lawyer or the provincial warranty program.

11 REPAIRS AND RENOVATIONS

Some people buy a house knowing it will need a lot of work because they welcome the challenge of a handyman's special. Other people buy a house because it's in move-in condition and perfect for them—they don't want to do any work at all.

If you buy a house that you plan to fix up, you know before you move in that you are going to need to deal with general contractors, plumbers, and painters. But, even if you buy a house you're not planning to lay a paint brush on, at some time something is going to break or something is going to need to be changed. So you can be sure that there are repairs (and maybe even renovations) somewhere in your future.

Whether you are building on an addition or just painting your spare bedroom, whether you are putting on a new roof or simply having your drain unplugged, there are things you need to know about the legal and practical sides of hiring workers and having them in your home. If you go about renovating the wrong way, it will seem like a nightmare. If you do it the right way, it will only seem like a bad dream.

146 The Complete Guide to Buying, Owning and Selling a Home in Canada

WHY ARE YOU DOING THIS TO YOURSELF?

You repair things because they are broken. Some things must be repaired if you want to continue to live in your home. Other things, if left unrepaired, won't drive you out of your home, but they will drive down your home's value.

Renovation and decorating are different from repairs because they are more voluntary. People renovate for various reasons. You may want more space—a bigger kitchen, another bathroom, or a family room addition. You may want to change the look of your house by taking out the wall between your living-room and dining-room or by putting in French doors to your patio. You may wish to make your home more energy efficient by installing a new furnace or putting in new windows. You may want to upgrade your home's infrastructure by replacing the plumbing or wiring.

Renovations always cost more, take longer, and are more of a disruption than you think, so there are a number of things to consider before you undertake a voluntary project. Whether you are renovating or redecorating, ask yourself the following questions:

- How can you pay for what you want to do?
- Is there a cheaper alternative to the work you think you want to do?
- Are there any obstacles that prevent you from doing what you want to do?
- Will the work you want to do increase the value of your home?
- Do you want to live through the mess and chaos?

How Can You Pay?

If you are moving into your new home with the intention of renovating or redecorating, you probably took the cost of your planned work into account when budgeting for your purchase and so already have the money set aside.

If you have been living in your house for a while, it may be that the carpets have worn and the paint has chipped, or your family has grown and you need a bigger kitchen or an extra bedroom. Some people set money aside each year so that they have a fund when they want to make changes to their home. If you have money saved, you already know how much you have. Other people need to borrow the money to pay renovation or redecorating costs.

If you need to borrow, you have to figure out how much you can afford to borrow. You can do this by reviewing your budget to see how much of a monthly loan payment you can afford. Once you know this figure, you can calculate how much money you can afford to borrow. The calculations are the same as those set out in Chapter 2, which we made you do before we let you buy a house at all.

After you know how much you can afford to borrow, the next question is: Where can you get it? There are several different ways to borrow money for home renovations:

- You can take out an additional mortgage on your home and use the money to pay for your renovations.
- You can increase the amount of your existing mortgage and use the increase to pay for your renovations.
- You can take out a personal loan (the interest rate and monthly payments are usually higher than for a mortgage).
- You can get a line of credit to pay your renovation expenses—it gives you a maximum amount you can borrow, but you borrow only as much money as you need, when you need it (the line of credit can be in the form of a personal loan, or it can be secured by a mortgage on your home).
- You can use a credit card for small jobs (the interest rate will be very high, even compared to a personal loan).

Speak to your bank or mortgagee about financing your renovations. As with your original mortgage, remember to shop around.

Is There Some Other (Cheaper) Way?

There may be a less costly way to achieve what you're trying to do.

Finding Extra Space

If you need more space, it may not be necessary to build an addition. You may be able to finish your basement to provide a family room, study, or extra bedroom.

A lot of new furniture on the market is designed specifically to make a house seem larger. Bunk bed systems allow children to share bedrooms and still have room to play and study. Hideaway beds and hideaway desks let one room do double duty as a bedroom or dining-room and home office. Closet units or closet organizers can help you find extra storage space.

Achieving Energy Efficiency

Before you undertake a major project to make your house more energy efficient, like installing a new furnace or windows, think about simpler and cheaper ways to reduce your heating costs:

- Have your furnace inspected and serviced to make sure it's working efficiently.

- Turn down your thermostat at night and when you're away from home (you can get a timer for your thermostat to turn the heat up and down automatically).
- If there are drafts coming from windows or doors, weather-strip them and caulk gaps in the frames.
- Hang heavier drapes on windows.

Cooling Your House

The installation of central air-conditioning in some houses is very expensive and difficult. As an alternative, consider installing a roof vent and ceiling fans, and supplement with individual room air-conditioners.

Improving Your Looks

If you're planning a renovation to make your home look better, you may be able to get a similar effect by simply redecorating. Instead of redoing your whole kitchen, consider painting the walls and cabinets and putting on new knobs and drawer handles. If your bathroom looks out of date, consider painting or wallpapering, re-enamelling the tub and sink, and buying a new shower curtain and towels. If your living room is dark, instead of installing new windows or a skylight, consider brightening up your colour scheme, getting rid of the heavy draperies we just told you to buy, and getting more lamps (especially lamps with halogen bulbs).

Are There Any Obstacles?

If your house is already mortgaged, you must speak to your mortgagee before you start any renovation that involves demolition of all or part of your house. Your mortgage may have a clause that allows the mortgagee to demand payment in full if you demolish any of your house.

Government regulations may be an obstacle to doing your renovation exactly the way you wanted to do it. Provincial building codes set construction standards governing structural, electrical, plumbing, heating, and fire safety requirements.

Municipal zoning by-laws restrict the size, shape, and possibly the appearance of your renovation. If the work you are planning is not allowed under the current zoning, you can apply for a special exemption from the zoning (sometimes referred to as a **variance**). Your neighbours will be given notice of your application and will be given an opportunity to object. These applications can be very expensive and take a long time.

Will You Increase the Value of Your Home?

It's not likely that you are renovating your home just to increase its value to a future purchaser. You're doing it for yourself. However, you should know that while some renovations increase the value of your home, others have no effect on its value; and still others actually decrease the value of your home. While knowing which renovations fall into which category may not affect your decision whether or not to renovate, it may affect how much you decide to spend.

The best return on your renovation dollar will come from a new kitchen or bathroom. Finishing a basement, building a wood deck, or putting in new windows will add something to the value of your home but probably not as much. A swimming pool will add nothing to the value of your home and may in fact make it harder to sell. For more information about renovations that make your home worth more on the market, speak to a real estate agent.

Any renovation that you do, no matter how little you spend, should look professional or it will lower the value of your home to a future purchaser. But while it's important to renovate to a reasonable quality, use luxury materials only if it's important to you personally. Most purchasers will not pay extra for them. Whatever kind of renovation you do, you also won't get your money back if you have over-improved for the house itself or for the neighbourhood.

Whether you have money already set aside or whether you're borrowing, there may be an additional long-term cost of renovating for you to consider. If you increase the value of your property (which is probably your sincerest wish), your property taxes may go up.

Can You Live through It?

All renovations are a pain to live through, but some are worse than others. It's not just a matter of noise, inconvenience, and dirt; sometimes it's a matter of your family's health.

Throughout your renovation, you will have to put up with workers traipsing through your home, usually starting at an ungodly hour. You must be around on a regular basis to supervise the work and to be available to make decisions and give instructions. Unless you pack fragile items away, they may be broken. Your furniture and clothes may get dust-covered unless you protect them.

Even if the ordinary level of inconvenience doesn't drive you screaming from your home, there may be particular times during your renovation that you will want to consider moving out. If you are adding on a second storey, you may have to live without a roof for a while. (Try not to make it during January, February, or March! The contractor can keep rain and snow out, but it's a lot harder to keep the heat in.) If you're putting in a new kitchen, there

will be a time when you can't cook because your old kitchen will be gone and your new one won't be installed yet. During these times you have a choice between moving out and toughing it out.

Any renovation that involves tearing down walls or cutting through cement floors will create a tremendous amount of dust. If the house was insulated with asbestos or has lead paint on the walls, the dust can be very dangerous. When floors are being refinished, there may be toxic fumes. For some people, the fumes from paint or carpet glue can be dangerous. As a matter of health and safety, you may have no choice but to move out of your house for a while.

It's important to go into a renovation with your eyes open so that you can either make arrangements to go somewhere else (even if only for part of the time) or be braced for the ordeal if you decide to stay and live through it.

PRELIMINARY PLANNING
FOR YOUR RENOVATION

If you've decided to renovate, you've got some idea of what you want to do, for example, build a family room addition or update your master bathroom. But, before you do anything at all, proper planning is essential.

Your first and most important step is to decide the maximum amount that you want to spend. There's no point in telling an architect or contractor what you want unless you also say exactly how much you have to spend on it. The plans they prepare will be useless to you if you have only half the money necessary to carry them out. To avoid disappointment, you're better off seeing only plans that fit your budget.

Next, you have to think about time, both when and how long. Do you have an absolute deadline by which the renovation has to be done—like your baby's delivery date if you are making a nursery? Do you have a particular time of year when you want the work to be done—during your vacation when you are there to supervise the workers, or during the warmer months if you are having your roof removed? Do you have a maximum length of time that you want the work to take?

Then, decide whether or not you are willing to move out of your home for any part of the work. If you can't or won't, that may limit the kinds of work you can have done to your home. Some jobs are just too disruptive or dangerous for you to stay in the house.

Finally, consider whether you're going to do the work yourself or hire professionals. You can have someone do the whole job for you, from design to completion. You may already have a design that you want someone else to build. You may want someone to do the work for you while you supervise. You may want to do some or all of the work yourself.

Before you can decide who will do the work, or before you do any more planning or preparation, you have to know what work has to be done.

WHAT IS INVOLVED IN A RENOVATION?

There's more to a renovation project than the construction work—it's just one of several stages. Someone must

- develop a design for the project, taking into account zoning and building code requirements
- find out whether a building permit or other permit or approval is required for the planned work, and if so, apply for the permit or approval
- arrange for any necessary municipal inspections
- hire contractors and workers, and select and buy materials
- pay the contractors and workers
- supervise the work

Designing the Project

However small your home improvement project, you will need some kind of design. Even if you are only having your house painted, you need to know what rooms you are painting, what colours, and how many coats of paint. If you are doing a more complicated renovation like a new bathroom, new kitchen, or an addition, designing your project will include the preparation of detailed drawings, including a floor plan, side elevations, and structural drawings.

The design stage starts with your ideal of what you want your renovation to look like and what you want it to do. Your ideal may come from pictures you've seen in a magazine or from other homes you've seen.

Next, you might develop preliminary sketches. Although they are more concerned with the look of your renovation than with technical specifications, the purpose of these sketches is to modify your ideal to take into account your budget, as well as building code requirements and zoning requirements.

Once you've settled on a design, the next stage is to prepare working drawings and specifications, which are used to get building permits and estimates for material and labour costs. If you hire someone to do the work for you, these drawings will be incorporated into the contract to define the work being done. The drawings will be used throughout the construction as a detailed guide for every step of the work.

Building Permits

Unless you're doing a small job like reshingling your roof or repainting, you may well need a building permit. A building permit is your municipality's formal permission for you to carry out your renovation. Any change to your plumbing, heating, air-conditioning, ventilation, or electrical wiring systems, or to the structure of the house will probably require either a municipal permit or municipal approval. By the way, you should know that you may need a permit to build a deck or to remove a garage.

Contact your municipal building department to find out whether or not you need a permit for the particular work you are planning to do. If a permit is required, the municipality will tell you how to apply. You will have to submit technical plans and pay a fee which can be several hundred dollars or even more.

The building department will review your plans to make sure that they comply with municipal zoning requirements, the provincial building code, and any other relevant provincial or municipal regulations. If your plans are approved, you will get your permit. For some projects you can get approval in one day, but for others, the approval process can take several months.

Getting a building permit sounds like a lot of trouble, doesn't it? But it doesn't compare to the trouble you'll get into if you do work that requires a building permit without getting one. It is illegal to start construction before getting a permit. You can be charged with an offence, you can be ordered to stop work, or you can even be ordered to tear down work you have already done.

You may think the municipality will never find out that you have done work without a permit. But after several weeks of being woken up by your contractors and looking at your dumpster, a neighbour may phone the building department to complain—at which point you'll be found out. Even if you safely make it to the end of your project, you may be found out when you try to sell your home, and the purchaser checks to see whether or not your home complies with all municipal requirements.

Building Inspections

When you do a renovation under a building permit, various municipal building inspectors will check your work at key stages of the construction to make sure that it is being carried out in accordance with the plans you submitted and the requirements of the provincial building code. It is your responsibility to know when the various inspections are required and to contact the building department to arrange for inspections at the right time.

A building inspector will probably need some notice to come out and inspect. If you don't schedule the inspection at the right time, you may have to stop the work until the inspector comes because the inspector must be able to see the area to be inspected. For example, if you put up drywall before the wiring has been inspected, the building department can make you rip out the walls so that it *can* be inspected. In addition to scheduled inspections, a building inspector can visit the site at any time.

Workers and Materials

Unless you are doing all of the actual construction work yourself, you will have to hire people to do all or some of it for you. Even if you want to do it all yourself, you may not be able to. In some provinces, certain kinds of work, usually electrical, plumbing, and heating, must be done by licensed tradespeople. Even if you are allowed to do the work yourself, your work must meet all municipal and provincial requirements and pass building inspections.

There is a wide range of building supply stores where you can get materials for your renovation. However, there may be some materials that are only available to professional home renovators or that are available to them at a better price.

Paying the Workers

If you do all the work yourself, there is no one to pay. If you hire someone who personally does the work for you, you pay that person directly. If you hire a contractor who has other people do the work, you also pay the contractor but things are a bit more complicated.

Construction, Mechanics', or Builders' Liens

Every province has laws to make sure that people who work for contractors will get paid even if the contractor doesn't pay them.

For example, you may hire a contractor to put in a new bathroom for you, for $5000. The contractor hires someone to tile the bathroom for $1000 and someone else to put in the plumbing for $2000. (These people are sometimes called **sub-contractors**.) When the work is done, you pay the contractor his $5000. What if, instead of paying the sub-contractors, the contractor pockets the whole $5000? The tiler and the plumber can sue the contractor for what they are owed. You may think that's exactly what they should do and leave you out of it.

Unfortunately for you (although fortunately for the tiler and the plumber), the law provides otherwise. Provincial statutes allow the sub-contractors not only to sue the contractor but also to make a claim directly against you and to enforce that claim by registering a **construction lien** (also known as a **mechanics' lien** or a **builders' lien**) against your home. This right exists even though you paid everything you owed under your contract with the contractor. Not only the tiler and the plumber are protected. Workers for the contractor or for sub-contractors and people who supply materials also have the same right to register a lien against your home.

Limitations on Your Liability

That's the bad news. There really is no good news, although there is a limit to the bad news. In all provinces other than Quebec, the law limits the amount you have to pay the sub-contractors (when you have already paid the contractor). In Quebec, you as the homeowner would owe the sub-contractors the full amount that the contractor was supposed to pay them. However, in the other provinces, you only owe a percentage of what the sub-contractors were supposed to be paid.

- In Manitoba, you would owe the sub-contractors 7.5 per cent of the full amount of your contract with the contractor.
- In Newfoundland, Nova Scotia, Ontario, Saskatchewan, and British Columbia, you would owe the sub-contractors 10 per cent of the full amount of your

contract with the contractor.

- In Alberta, you would owe the sub-contractors 15 per cent of the full amount of your contract with the contractor.
- In Prince Edward Island and New Brunswick, you would owe the sub-contractors 15 per cent of the full amount of your contract with the contractor for a contract of $15000 or less and 20 per cent for contracts of $15000 and over.

No matter how many sub-contractors there are and how much they are owed by the contractor, the total amount you owe to all of the sub-contractors is limited to the percentages set out above.

Holdbacks

There is a way to avoid being put in the position of having to pay twice. Instead of paying the contractor the full amount you owe at any given time, you can—and you should—hold back some of the money you owe the contractor. The amount of the **holdback** is the percentage mentioned above for your province. Every time you make a payment to the contractor, whether you pay once at the end of the contract or in instalments, you should hold back that percentage.

Back to our tiler and plumber. Let's assume that you live in British Columbia where the holdback is 10 per cent. If you are required to pay the contractor two instalments of $2500 each, you would hold back 10 per cent or $250 from each instalment.

Substantial Completion

You're probably asking yourself what you are supposed to do with the holdback once you hold it back. That's an excellent question. First of all, you hold it. Remember, we told you that sub-contractors can register a lien against your home. In each province, the sub-contractors are given only a limited period of time after **substantial performance** or **substantial completion** of the contract to register a lien.

- In Newfoundland and Quebec, the time period is 30 days.
- In British Columbia, Manitoba, and Saskatchewan, the time period is 40 days.
- In Alberta, Nova Scotia, and Ontario, the time period is 45 days.
- In New Brunswick and Prince Edward Island, the time period is 60 days.

You hold your money back for that period of time *after* substantial completion or performance of the contract. If your contract is payable in several instalments, you continue to hang on to all of the holdbacks until the end of the contract plus the lien registration period. If no liens are registered in the allowed period, at the end of the period you pay the holdback to the contractor.

If a Lien is Registered

It is very important to get legal advice if a lien has been registered against your home. If you don't do the right thing, you could end up paying twice for the same work.

When a lien has been registered, you must not release the holdback to the contractor. In some provinces, you will know if a lien has been registered because the law states that you must be given notice. In many provinces, if you receive notice of a lien, not only must you not release the holdback, you must not pay any additional money to the contractor until the matter has been settled. If you receive notice of a lien, call your lawyer.

Is it safe for you to release the holdback if the work has been completed, the lien registration period has passed, and you haven't received any notice of a lien? In some provinces you are safe if you haven't received notice of a lien, but in others you have to go to the land registry office to see if a lien has been registered on the title to your home before you release the holdback. Speak to your lawyer before you release the holdback, to find out whether a visit to the registry office is necessary.

Supervising the Work

Even a small renovation project requires a lot of supervision so that the work moves at a reasonable pace and is completed to your standards. Someone must make sure that the quality of the work is satisfactory—that the work is being completed in a **good and workmanlike manner** (the legal lingo). In addition, the work site should be relatively neat both for your sanity and for the safety of your family and the workers. Someone must decide in what order the work will be done. You may think that the sequence of the work is fixed, and it probably is if you're working in only one part of the house. But what if you're putting in a bathroom in the basement and also painting your kitchen? It makes sense to drill through the basement floor and stir up all the dust *before* you paint, rather than have the dust descend on the still-wet paint in the kitchen.

If more than one trade is involved, you have to worry about when the various tradespeople come and the order they come in. You want the electrician to do the wiring before the drywaller puts up the wall. You want the carpet laid after the painting and not before. If the electrician doesn't come on time, the whole project can come to a stop. You also have to make sure that municipal building inspections are properly scheduled.

In some renovation contracts, instalments are paid when certain stages of the work have been completed. Someone has to make sure that the stages have been satisfactorily completed before the instalments are paid.

WHO WILL DO THE WORK?

Your choice is to do all the work yourself, some of the work yourself, or none of the work yourself.

Do-It-Yourself

There are several factors to consider before you decide to do the job yourself.

* Do you have the time to do the work yourself?
* Do you have the ability to do the work yourself?
* Will it be cheaper to do it yourself than to hire professional help?
* Will you enjoy doing the work yourself?

Doing some of the work yourself may save you money and give you personal satisfaction, if you have the time and ability. (Remember that in some provinces ability is not enough—you have to be licensed to do certain work.) You may have vacation time that you can devote to your home renovation project, and you may have experience in home repairs and renovation. Even if you don't have experience, there are how-to books and magazine articles that give you step-by-step instructions on home renovation projects. Keep in mind, however, that do-it-yourself projects are often more difficult than they look in the magazines and may take longer than you think.

What you're saving by doing any of the work yourself is the cost of labour. You have to decide for yourself how much your leisure time is worth. In any event, you may pay in the cost of materials and tools what you save in labour costs. Contractors can usually buy materials for less than you can. Also, you may not have the tools you need to do the job and will either have to buy or rent them.

Ask yourself whether doing it yourself will be a positive experience for you. Do you enjoy working with your hands, or does the thought of smashing nails with a hammer frighten you? Do you love the smell of freshly sawn wood, or does sawdust make you sneeze? Living through any renovation is stressful. Doing it yourself usually means that the project (and the stress) last longer—and worse, you have nobody but yourself to blame for delays and mistakes.

Do Some of It Yourself?

Of course, doing it yourself is not an all or nothing proposition. You can choose to do part of the work and hire professionals to do the rest.

The idea of physical labour may not appeal to you, but you may want to prepare the design for your project. There are even computer software programs to help you. But unless you are familiar with municipal by-laws and building code requirements, your design should be reviewed by an experienced contractor or architect. You need plans that will pass the building department's review process before you will be issued a building permit.

You may not want to do the physical labour yourself, but you may want to supervise the work, by acting as your own general contractor. You get your own materials and hire and organize the different sub-contractors and tradespeople to carry out the work. Acting as your own general contractor can take a lot of time. If you don't know what you're doing, there may be delays and the workmanship may be shoddy.

You may want to do *some* of the physical labour yourself. It's simpler to do finishing work, like painting or wallpapering, than to do work in the middle of the project like plumbing. If you do work in the middle, you must make sure that your work is done at the right time. (Again, remember that you may need a licence to do the work yourself.)

The other extreme from doing it yourself is to have *all* the work done for you. You can have an architect do the design work for you and hire a contractor to do the building, or you can have a design-and-build company do it all for you.

Hire an Architect

You may want an architect to design your project. You choose to hire a particular architect because his or her work appeals to you. Many design-and-build firms use architects to design their projects, so you may not need to deal with an architect alone to get an architect's design.

There is another reason to use an architect's services. In addition to designing a project, an architect can help you choose a general contractor. An architect can also stay on to supervise the project, checking to see that the work is being properly completed, and advising you when the contractor is entitled to receive instalment payments. Unlike an architect who works with a design-and-build company, this architect is independent from the people who actually do the construction and can give you an objective opinion about the quality of the work.

Licensed architects are required by law to have professional liability insurance. So if you have to sue the architect because of damage to your home caused by mistakes in the design or in the supervision of your project, you know that there will be insurance money to pay your claim if you are successful.

Even when you use an architect to supervise the project, you still have to keep an eye on what's happening. You shouldn't hand over all responsibility to the architect, because you're the one who's paying the bills and you're the one who has to live with the renovation after it's done.

Hire a Contractor

If you're fixing your roof, you hire a roofing contractor. If you're painting your living-room, you hire a painting contractor. Pretty simple. But your renovation may involve several different kinds of work. If you're putting on an addition, you need someone to dig and pour the foundation, someone to frame the walls, someone to install the aluminum siding, someone to put on the roof, someone to do the plumbing, someone to put in the wiring, someone to drywall, and someone to paint. If you have all of this work to do, you hire a general contractor.

A general contractor is responsible to you for getting *all* the work involved in your project done, either personally, through employees, or by using sub-contractors. Sub-contractors are hired by the general contractor to do specific work that the contractor or the contractor's employees can't do. The general contractor is also responsible for supervising and coordinating all the different workers.

Contractors are not always required by law to carry insurance. If they have insurance, it will probably only cover injuries to people or damage to property caused by their negligence while they are working in your home. They probably won't have insurance against defects in design and workmanship that show up after the job is finished. If a contractor does not have insurance, you may find it difficult, if not impossible, to get any compensation. Many contractors carry on business as corporations, and corporations often—deliberately—have little money or property to pay your claim.

You can act as your own general contractor, hiring and supervising the different tradespeople yourself. If you have problems, there's no one person you can complain to. You have to deal with each of the trades individually.

Use a Design-and-Build Company

A design-and-build company will design your project, prepare the plans and drawings, get the necessary permits, order materials, and hire and supervise the people who do the work. A flat fee covers all services and materials from design to completion.

There are companies that specialize in one kind of project like kitchens, bathrooms, or sunrooms, and others that do general construction. In some companies, the designs come from stock plans, and in others, an architect or designer will prepare a custom design.

If the design was prepared by an architect, the architect's insurance may cover any damage to your home caused by design flaws. If no architect is involved, there is no insurance coverage for design flaws. The construction work itself may or may not be covered by insurance. As with a contractor, any insurance a design-and-build company has will probably only cover injuries to people or damage to property caused by their negligence while they are working in your home.

HOW DO YOU FIND THE HELP YOU NEED?

If you have decided not to do the entire project yourself, you will have to hire professionals to do the work. Leaving aside the question of psychiatric help, which you won't need until your project is well under way, here are the things to consider when you're hiring a contractor, an architect, or a design-and-build firm.

Contractors

You want a contractor who does high quality work for a reasonable price and who is honest and reliable.

Get Some Names

Get the names of several contractors from

- family, friends, and neighbours who have had similar work done recently
- your architect, if you are using one
- your real estate agent
- local building supply and hardware stores
- your local home builders' association

Check Them Out

You should check out two or three contractors before hiring one of them. Get on the phone to the contractors and others and ask some questions. You want a contractor who

- has been in business in your area for a number of years

- is properly licensed to do the work—get the contractor's licence number and confirm with the local licensing office
- has third party liability and property damage insurance—get the name of the insurance company and call to confirm that the insurance is in force
- can give you references from satisfied clients in your area—ask for names and telephone numbers and call the references (make sure they're not relatives of the contractor!)
- has not been the subject of complaints—check with the local Better Business Bureau and the local homebuilders' association
- is available to do the work when you want it done—has reliable access to skilled workers and tradespeople and doesn't have too many jobs on the go
- will come back after the job is done to honour any warranties given

The Contractor You Don't Want

Avoid contractors who

- call you or come to your door offering to do work at a special price
- quote a price for the work without even looking at your home
- don't have an address, only a phone number
- tell you that you don't need a written contract for the work

Interview the Contractors

Once you have the names of several contractors who sound promising, arrange to meet with them individually at your house. Ask them about any of the matters in the list above that you don't already have an answer to. Also ask if they have pictures of finished jobs.

This is a good time for you to find out who will actually be doing the work. Is it the person you're talking to or somebody else? You don't have to meet every last person who will be working at your home, but you do want to meet the person who is going to be supervising your particular job, and maybe anybody else who will be coming to your home on a daily basis. Since you'll be seeing these people a lot, you should feel comfortable with them and feel you can trust them.

Check References

The most important thing you can do is to speak to people who have had similar jobs done by the contractor. Ask if you can look at the contractor's work (even if you've already seen photographs). Whether you can or can't see it, ask lots of questions, such as:

• Was the work started and completed on time?

• Did the work come in on budget?

• Were there any disagreements between them and the contractor on price, workmanship, or materials?

• Were they satisfied with the quality of the workmanship?

• Has the work held up over time?

• Did the contractor work neatly and clean up when the job was finished?

• Did the contractor try to make the project as easy to live through as possible?

• Were they comfortable having the contractor and the contractor's workers in their house?

• Did the contractor come back when the job was finished to fix problems?

Get Estimates

Arrange to get estimates from the two or three contractors you have chosen. If you have plans prepared by an architect, the contractors will base their estimate on the specifications in the plans. Otherwise, write down a detailed description of the work you want done so that the contractors know what they're giving an estimate on, and so that they are all giving an estimate for exactly the same work. Whether you provide the contractors with plans or a written description of the work to be done, they should inspect your house before giving you an estimate.

If you haven't had plans and specifications prepared for you, you may not know in detail the exact nature of the work you will have done until you have talked to one or more contractors. The contractors may have different ideas about how to approach the job. Before you compare prices among the different contractors, you may have to talk to each one several times to help you decide on the approach you want to take. To be able to compare their estimates properly, make sure they are all quoting a price on exactly the same work.

In addition to the price, you want the estimate to set out a description of the work to be done and the materials to be used. (If the estimate is based on an architect's plans, both the work to be done and the materials to be used are specified in the plans, and the estimate can just refer to those plans.)

If there is a significant difference in the prices you are quoted, ask the various contractors to explain. Price is a very important consideration when you are choosing a contractor, but the lowest price isn't necessarily the best deal. If one contractor's estimate is much lower than the others for exactly the same work, it may mean that the contractor has underestimated the job. The contractor may have miscalculated the scope or cost of the work or may have allowed himself a very narrow profit margin. If a contractor realizes in the middle of the job that he is not going to make any money (or may even lose money), he may be tempted to walk off the job. In any event, price shouldn't be your only consideration. Also take into account what you have found out about each contractor's reliability and the quality of workmanship.

Architects

You base your choice of an architect on different considerations than you do your choice of a contractor. You want your architect to be honest and reliable and to charge reasonable fees, but your main reason for choosing a particular architect is that you like that architect's work.

An architect's main reference is the work you have seen. If you see a house or a building you admire, find out who the architect was. You can ask people you know for names of architects and addresses or pictures of projects they have done. If you don't like what you see of the architect's work, there's no point going any further.

If you are interested in a particular architect, check with your provincial association of architects to make sure he or she is properly registered. Also check with people who have had the architect do work for them to see if they were happy.

Architects charge for their work on an hourly basis or a flat fee basis. If you are using the architect to supervise your project as well as design it, the architect may instead charge a fee equal to a percentage of the total contract price.

Design-and-Build Firms

In choosing a design-and-build firm, you must take into account everything you would if you were choosing a contractor. In addition, you've got to like the designs the firm produces. It may be difficult to compare estimates from different design-and-build firms because the estimates are based on different designs and materials.

THE RENOVATION CONTRACT

The renovation contract is your agreement with the renovator about what work will be done and how much you will pay for it.

The Importance of a Written Contract

You should always have a *written* contract for any repair or renovation project. It doesn't matter whether you use an architect, contractor, or design-and-build firm, it doesn't matter how highly recommended the person is, it doesn't even matter whether you're paying in cash—*put it in writing*. Both you and the contractor or architect or firm should get a signed copy of the agreement.

A contract is simply an agreement between two parties. In a renovation contract, the basic agreement is that the renovator will do the work and that you will pay. But that's just the basic agreement. In order for your contract to be useful, it has to have a lot more detail than that. And whenever you get into details, there's room for confusion and misunderstanding. Putting the agreement into writing forces everyone to define the details, and that's when you find out whether everyone really is in agreement. When you leave out the details, you may think everyone shares the same idea but in fact, each person has a different idea of what the agreement is.

When you have a detailed written contract, you have a written record of what everyone agreed to if there's a dispute later about what work is to be done and how much it costs. You don't have to rely on your own memory or someone else's—which is good since people tend to remember what's in their interest and to forget what's not. If you end up suing your renovator, the written contract is there for the court to look at too.

No reputable architect, contractor, or design-and-build firm will be offended if you ask for a written contract. In fact, they will want the contract in writing as well.

Cash Deals

Your contractor may offer to do the work for a lower price if you pay in cash. Or you may ask the contractor if you'll get a better price if you pay cash. The obvious reason for paying cash is to let the contractor avoid paying taxes. You hope he or she will pass on some of the savings to you. Legally, it is the responsibility of the contractor to collect and pay to the government any provincial sales tax and GST on the work. It is illegal for the contractor to avoid paying taxes, and it is also illegal for you to conspire with the contractor to allow him or her to avoid paying taxes.

If you do pay cash, it doesn't mean you cannot have a written contract. There's no connection between a written contract and the contractor's intention (or lack of intention) to pay taxes. The contract doesn't get sent straight to the GST office to be compared with the contractor's GST returns. However, the contractor may say to you, "Cash deal, no written contract." If you agree to a repair or renovation without a written contract, you are giving up all the protection a written contract offers—particularly evidence of what your deal was if you have to sue the contractor. Think about whether you're saving enough money to give up that protection. Then think about whether you want to get involved with this contractor.

What Your Renovation Contract Should Contain

A contract for a major renovation is a complex legal document involving a lot of money. So you should have your renovation contract reviewed by a lawyer before you sign it. The contract should contain the following things:

- names, addresses, and telephone numbers of the contractor and the home-owner
- list of contract documents
- description of the work to be done
- extras and deletions
- description of any excluded work
- description of materials to be used
- removal of material from the worksite
- use of other contractors
- who obtains permits
- timing
- contract price and payment schedule
- quality of the work and warranties
- insurance

A contract for a more limited project like installing a roof or painting the interior of your house does not need to be as long. It may just consist of the written estimate. But it should contain at least the following:

- names, addresses, and telephone numbers of the contractor and the home-owner
- description of the work to be done
- description of the materials to be used
- timing
- contract price and payment schedule
- quality of the work and warranties

An architect's contract will probably be in a standard form prepared by the provincial architects' association. You might still wish to have your lawyer review it before you sign it.

Names, Addresses, and Telephone Numbers

It is important to identify the person or company responsible for doing your work. The name on the contract should be the same as the name of the person or company you have been dealing with. The agreement should also set out the name of an individual person who will be your contact, with a telephone number where that person can be reached. There should be an address and it should not be simply a post office box number.

List of Contract Documents

The contract should list all the documents that will make up the contract, such as:

- the written agreement itself
- drawings (which should be either listed in the contract or attached to it)
- specifications (which should be either listed or attached)
- additional documents signed by both parties during the course of the project

Description of the Work

Your contract should contain a complete and detailed description of all the work you want done. The written description of the work can take up several pages of the contract, or it can be very short if the drawings and specifications are very detailed and are attached to the contract. Either way, the description should include

- site preparation, such as tearing down walls
- structural details, such as framing, subfloors, insulation, and electrical and plumbing hook-ups
- size and location of doors, windows, and closets
- how the work will match such things as the existing roof-line, paint, trim, and flooring of your home

Extras and Deletions

You may wish to make changes to the contract as the work progresses. Any change to the contract is a new contract and has to be agreed to by both parties. You may wish to have additional work done (an **extra**) or to cancel some of the original work (a **deletion**). All changes should be in writing. This written **change order** should describe the change, set out the price for the change, and should be signed by the parties and attached to the original contract. The change orders will then form part of the contract as well.

The contract may contain a clause setting out how the price for an extra or the credit for a deletion will be calculated if changes are made.

Changes are a common reason why renovations end up costing more and taking longer than originally planned, so think twice before you ask for anything to be changed after the work has started. Sometimes, though, changes can't be avoided. Just make sure that everyone is clear about what the change is and how much it will cost. And put it in writing. Then accept the fact that making the change will probably add time to the renovation.

Description of Any Excluded Work

The contract should state any work that the contractor is *not* responsible for because you or another contractor will be doing it instead, such as:

• painting
• wallpapering
• carpeting
• landscaping

Description of the Materials

The contract should say who is to supply the materials, you or the contractor.

If the contractor is supplying the materials, they should be described in detail, including brand names and styles for furnaces, plumbing fixtures, windows, flooring, paint, etc. The contract should also state what warranties the contractor is giving for the materials supplied. Materials may come with a manufacturer's warranty, but you should be able to deal with your contractor if there's a problem, rather than having to go to the manufacturer. Just in case, make sure that the contractor gives you copies of any manufacturer's warranties.

Some contracts will say that materials costing up to a stated maximum price will be supplied by the contractor and that you get to choose them. This arrangement is commonly used for things like bathroom tiles and fixtures. The contractor will send you to a supplier. If you choose materials that cost more than the stated maximum price, you will have to pay the extra cost.

Removal of Materials

If you want the contractor to salvage anything from an area that is demolished, the contract must say so and must also say what you want done with the items. You may want the contractor to use the salvaged material else-where in the project, or you may simply wish to keep something for your own use later on.

The contract should state who is responsible for the removal of all other debris. Keep in mind that there is a cost attached to garbage removal whether you do it or the contractor does it. One way or another, you'll have to pay for the actual removal of the garbage and perhaps for a dumpster.

Use of Other Contractors

If you want a different contractor to do some of the work, the contract must say so. Your contractor may wish to charge you an administrative fee for coordinating that work with the rest of the project. If this is the case, the contract must say so, setting out what the fee will be.

Permits

Building and other permits may be required for your renovation, depending on the nature of the work involved. The contract should list the permits required (the contractor will usually be the source of this information), and whether it is your responsibility or the contractor's to get the permits.

Timing

The contract should state the date on which the work will commence, and a date by which it should be substantially completed. If the work can be bro-ken down into distinct stages, the contract may set out a completion date for each stage.

If you want to discourage your contractor from starting the work late or taking too long to complete it, put a clause into the contract that allows you to end the contract or pay the contractor less if he's late. Keep in mind, how-ever, that the dates in the contract are estimates and not guarantees. You have to accept a reasonable amount of delay in starting or finishing the job.

Whether or not the contractor is penalized for lateness, it is usual for the contract to allow the contractor extra time to finish the work without penalty for any of the following reasons:

- changes you make to the work you want done
- unforeseen problems with the structure or systems (electrical, heating, plumbing, air-conditioning, etc.) of your home
- reasons beyond the contractor's control, such as:
    - union disputes

- unavailability of materials
- fire and natural disasters
- court orders
- delays caused by work you were responsible to do

The contract should set out the days of the week and hours that you want the contractor to work. If you don't want him or her to work evenings and weekends, or to start too early in the morning, put it in the contract.

Contract Price and Payment Schedule

THE CONTRACT PRICE: The contract price should be the same as the estimate that the contractor gave you.

DEPOSITS: For a small job, a deposit may or may not be requested when you sign the contract. The entire contract price is often payable when the job is finished. On a larger project, it is not unusual for the contractor to ask you for a deposit at the time the contract is signed. The deposit should be no more than 5 to 15 per cent of the total contract price. If the contractor must order custom-made products for your job, the contract will probable require you to pay the contractor for them when they are ordered. The contractor may also ask you to pay more of the contract price when the work begins, and this amount should not be more than 20 to 25 per cent of the total price.

INSTALMENT PAYMENTS: The balance of the contract price may be payable on completion, or if the project has distinct stages, the contractor may ask you to make **progress payments** after specific work has been finished. It is reasonable for you to agree to progress payments of this kind, but do *not* agree to progress payments that are linked simply to dates and not to completed work.

If your contract is being paid in instalments rather than when the job is finished, you have to take care in calculating how much you should pay as you go along. On the one hand, you want the contractor to have enough money to cover expenses—and maybe even make some of his profit—as the work proceeds. On the other hand, you don't want the contractor to have so much money that it's to his or her financial advantage to walk away from the job without doing another lick of work.

PAYMENTS ON COMPLETION: If payments are tied to the completion of specific work, don't make the payments unless the work has been completed—and to your satisfaction. This goes double (if not triple or more) for the final payment; otherwise, you may never see your contractor again. Having an architect supervise your project comes in handy here. The architect will certify that the work has been satisfactorily completed.

AND DON'T FORGET: Whenever you make any payments under your contract, always be sure to get a receipt. And don't forget to hang onto the lien holdback!

Quality of Work and Warranties

In the contract, the contractor should agree to

- be **diligent** in doing the work and to complete the work in a **good and workmanlike manner**
- complete the work in compliance with all provincial and municipal requirements, such as the provincial building code and municipal regulations and inspections
- protect your home from construction damage and to complete the work with as little inconvenience to you as possible (which is still a lot of inconvenience)
- keep the project site safe and in reasonable order at all times
- restore your home to a reasonable state of order and cleanliness at the end of the job

The contractor should give a minimum one-year warranty on workmanship and materials. Unfortunately, the warranty is worthless unless the contractor will actually come back to honour it. That's why it's important to check a contractor's past performance in this area before you decide to use that contractor.

Insurance

THE CONTRACTOR'S INSURANCE: The contract should require the contractor to provide proof of the following insurance:

- workers' compensation coverage as required by provincial law
- third party liability coverage of at least $2 million

YOUR INSURANCE: The contract may require you to have certain insurance as well, usually fire, comprehensive, and third party liability. This is the kind of coverage already provided by your homeowner's insurance. But the renovation contract may require you to have more than the usual amount of third party liability coverage.

The contract may require you to notify your insurance company of the renovation, but even if it doesn't, you should speak to your insurance company before any work starts on your renovation to make sure that

- you have the coverage required of you by the contract
- your insurance will remain in force during the renovation
- your coverage is adjusted to take into account the increased value of your home when the renovation is finished

TIPS FOR SURVIVING YOUR RENOVATION

There are things you can do both before, and during your renovation to make it easier on you.

Advance Preparation

Your renovation will go more smoothly if you prepare in advance:

- Remove everything that can be removed from the work area.
- Protect anything that can't be removed from the work area.
- Expect dust everywhere in the house, and protect your belongings accordingly.
- Decide where you want to put the dumpster (it will look nice behind your peonies).
- Decide where you want the workers to
    - keep their tools
    - come in and out of your home
    - eat
    - pee
- Tell your neighbours about the renovation before work starts—it may help to reduce complaints about noise, dirt, and your dumpster.

As the Work Progresses

If you want your project to come in on time and on budget and not be *too* nerve-racking, here are some of the things you should do:

- Find out who is the supervisor on your project—you should direct any questions or comments about the work to the supervisor and not to the workers themselves.
- Speak to the supervisor on a daily basis about how the project is going.

- Bring any problems you notice to the supervisor's or contractor's attention immediately.
- Be visible so that everyone knows you're keeping an eye on things, but don't follow the workers around obsessively.
- Keep your children away from the work area.
- Keep an eye on pets, especially cats—we know of several who ended up (temporarily) behind the new drywall.
- Get out for a while if the noise and dirt start to drive you crazy.
- Try to be present whenever an inspector is scheduled to visit.
- Be pleasant to the workers so that they'll *want* to do a good job for you.
- Don't make changes.
- If you do make changes, put them in writing.

WHEN PROBLEMS ARISE

It goes without saying that there will be problems with your renovation. When you're trying to schedule a lot of different tradespeople who are working on other projects at the same time, there are bound to be some delays and mix-ups. There may even be problems worse than delays and mix-ups.

The Problems

Here are some of the problems you may run into:

- Your contractor never shows up in the first place.
- Your contractor abandons the job.
- Your contractor *doesn't* abandon the job, but you'd like to abandon the contractor because of delays or rotten workmanship.
- Your contractor charges you for changes that were not ordered in writing—or that were not ordered at all.
- A subcontractor, labourer, or supplier files a lien against your home.
- The contractor refuses to finish the job after you've paid in full.
- The contractor refuses to honour the warranty.

The Solutions

The best solution to almost all these problems is to avoid them in the first place by choosing your contractor carefully, drawing up a detailed written contract, and being sensible about how much you pay and when you pay it.

The Contractor Who Doesn't Show Up

If your contractor doesn't show up when the work is supposed to start, call and find out when he or she is coming. If the delay drags on, write a letter saying that if the contractor hasn't shown up by a specified date, you will consider the contract abandoned—you will want your deposit back and will hire someone else. This letter may be just the encouragement your contractor needs. If it isn't, you may have to sue to get your deposit back.

The Contractor Who Abandons

If your contractor abandons the job, and it's clear he's never coming back, there's really nothing you can do to make him come back. If you set up your payment schedule properly, you'll only have paid for work that has actually been done. While you're left with a half-finished job, you should also be left with about half your money—which you will use to have the job finished by another contractor. Even so, it will probably cost you more than you have left over from the first contract to have the job finished, especially if the work that *was* done was badly done.

You can think about suing. But generally a contractor who abandons a job is in such deep financial trouble that he won't care about another lawsuit (and won't have any money to pay, either).

The Contractor You'd Like to Abandon

If you realize part-way through the job that the workmanship is poor, start by speaking to the contractor. If the contractor disagrees, you can call in the building inspector or some other third party for an objective opinion. (Be careful about calling in the building inspector—if the workmanship is bad enough, you may end up with a **work order** from the municipality forcing *you* to fix it, whether the contractor agrees or not.) The contractor may have a change of mind and be willing to fix the work if a third party agrees with you. Or you can report the contractor to his or her licensing body, or the local home builders' association, or the Better Business Bureau.

If you want to get rid of the contractor, have your lawyer write a letter to him or her stating that you consider the contractor to be in breach of the contract, ordering the contractor off the job, and saying that you consider your damages to be equal to whatever you haven't yet paid the contractor (if not more—more is better). The contractor may end up suing you, but at least the next time you see him, it will be in court and not in your kitchen. Again, you'll have to find someone else to finish the job, and it will probably end up costing you more than you set aside for the original contract.

If you're not happy with the work, don't pay. You may technically be breaching your contract, but you'd rather be sued for money you owe than have to sue the contractor to get back money you've paid for work that hasn't been done right. Walk through the project before you pay at any stage to see whether you're satisfied with the work.

Your contractor may have several jobs on the go, and you only see him one or two days a week. If you're thinking of getting rid of the contractor because it's taking too long to finish the job, get an estimate from someone else on how much it will cost to finish the job. If it's no more than the unpaid balance of the contract, write a letter to the contractor (or have your lawyer write the letter), giving a fixed number of days to complete the work. Say that if the contractor does not finish the work within that time, you will find someone else to do so, and you will subtract the cost from what's still owed to the contractor.

Charges for Changes

If the contractor presents you with a bill for changes that were not in writing, what do you do? If the contract says that all changes had to be in writing, legally you can refuse to pay for changes that were not. If you, in fact, asked for the changes and they were done, legally speaking you may or may not have an obligation to pay, but morally speaking you should pay something even if you dispute the amount. If you didn't ask for the changes, don't pay for them.

Liens

If a lien is filed against your home, do not pay the holdback to the contractor. Call a lawyer. Your liability should be limited to the amount of the holdback.

The Contractor Who Won't Come Back to Finish

You paid the contractor in full even though there were a few little things still left to be done. And the contractor never came back. Didn't we tell you not to pay until the job was finished! There's nothing you can do to force the contractor to come back. You can vent your feelings by complaining to the provincial or municipal licensing agencies, the provincial consumer protection branch, the Better Business Bureau, and the local home builders' association. You can sue for the cost of the unfinished work, but it's probably not worth your while if it's only a small amount of work.

The Contractor Who Won't Honour the Warranty

Some time after the work is finished—and paid for—problems may arise. How you handle the situation will depend on whether or not the problems are urgent. If the problems are not urgent, make a list of them as you notice them.

Call the contractor when you have collected several problems, instead of calling each time you find a problem. If it's a major problem or one that needs attention fast (like no heat, or crackling noises when you turn on a light switch), call the contractor immediately. With luck, your contractor will honour the warranty in the contract and send someone to fix the problems.

If the contractor does not honour the warranty, it's up to you to decide whether you want the work done. Then you'll have to find someone else to do it. And then you'll have to decide whether or not to sue the contractor for the cost of the work.

12 HOME SECURITY

There are hundreds of burglaries across Canada every day. If you take reasonable precautions, you can reduce the chance of your home being targeted by burglars. The things you do to prevent break-ins don't have to be fancy or expensive. It's more effective to make your house look like a bad bet to burglars than it is to install a burglar alarm. You can do that by getting rid of places outside your house where a burglar can hide and work in peace, and by getting neighbours to keep an eye on each other's property.

If you do decide to turn your home into a burglar-proof fortress, don't make it so difficult for burglars to get in that it's also impossible for *you* to get out if there's a fire.

Whether you are at home or away, you can reduce the chance of your home being broken into. These should be your main goals:

- You **don't** want to attract the attention of potential burglars to your home.
- You **do** want your neighbours to pay attention to your home.
- You **don't** want to make it easy for burglars to enter your home.
- You **do** want to make it difficult for burglars to dispose of your belongings.

NEIGHBOURHOOD WATCH

The best protection against break-ins is neighbours who keep an eye on each other's houses. You should get to know who your neighbours are, when they come and go, and when suspicious-looking people are walking, driving, and parking around your home. You want neighbours who do the same. Exchange phone numbers with neighbours whose houses can be seen from yours. Have an agreement to report suspicious activity directly to your neighbours or to the police.

You can make these arrangements informally or you may join a community organization such as **Neighbourhood Watch** or **Block Watch**—or you can be the one to set it up for your neighbourhood. To find out about joining or starting up a Neighbourhood Watch, contact your local police department.

OUTSIDE

You want your home to look nice, but if security is your concern, you don't want your home to be so nice-looking that it attracts the attention of potential burglars. Don't go out of your way to have the best-looking house on the block, with the most expensive car in the driveway. That can lead potential burglars to believe that you also have the best stereo, computer equipment, jewellery, etc.

Be Visible

Make sure that your doors and windows are visible from the street or from neighbouring houses by trimming back or cutting down tall shrubs around entrances and windows. You don't want to give a burglar privacy to break into your house, or an intruder a place to hide when you're opening your door.

If you are going to fence your property, remember that a privacy fence not only blocks your neighbour's view of your house, it also blocks their view of your burglars. On the other hand, although a burglar may be able to get into your property over a high fence, he'll have a bit of trouble getting your sound system and television out over the fence. If you fence your property, check that the gate is solidly hinged and keep it locked.

Burglary Tools

Don't leave tools in your yard or unlocked garage. A burglar will really appreciate it if you set out a ladder, hammer, axe, metal-cutter, or saw to help him enter your home. Cut back any tree limbs that come close to a second-storey window and could be used as a ladder to the window.

Lights

At night, light your entrances and ground-floor windows so that burglars won't have a safe, dark place to work. These lights can be motion-sensor lights, which are triggered by anyone prowling around your yard, or they can be light-sensor lights, which come on at dusk and turn off automatically at dawn. Install exterior lights high up, beyond normal reach, or put vandal-proof light covers on them so they cannot easily be unscrewed or broken.

Don't get completely carried away with lighting up your house, or you will attract attention to it and make burglars think you must have something to protect. To avoid annoying your neighbours, make sure your lights don't shine brightly into their houses.

WHEN YOU'RE AWAY

You don't have to be gone for a week to be at risk for a break-in. If someone is watching your house with the intention of breaking into it, they may make their move while you're at the convenience store or walking your dog, or even working in your garden. Lock all doors and windows every time the house will be empty, even for a few minutes. If you have an alarm system, turn it on. Take particular precautions around Christmas, when burglars know that houses are full of presents and homeowners are likely to be out partying.

Telephone Calls

Sometimes a potential burglar will find out the phone number of a house he has his eye on and will call periodically to see if anyone's home. If you start receiving phone calls from someone who hangs up as soon as you answer, be suspicious that your house has been targeted. (Of course, it could be nothing to worry about—just your spouse having an affair.) With the availability of caller identification features on phones, this practice has fallen off.

Dogs and Warning Signs

Let potential burglars know that breaking into your house is not worth the effort. Get a big dog that barks at strangers. If you don't have a dog, you can still post a "Beware of the Dog" sign (although a burglar who has been watch-ing your house won't be fooled). If you have an alarm system, post stickers that say so. Even if you don't have an alarm, you can still post stickers that say that you do.

Lights and Timers

When you're out, leave lights on inside (but not always the same lights), and leave a radio playing (tuned to an all-news station, or a station that has talk rather than music). Also, leave some lights on outside.

If you are going to be gone for more than a day or two, put several inside lights and the radio on automatic timers. Set the timers so that lights go on and off in different parts of your house at different times. Have the bedroom lights come on after the living area lights have turned off, and have the bedroom lights turn off at usual bedtimes to make it more difficult for a potential burglar watching to be sure that you are away. (If you are using lamps with a shade, take the shade off to reduce the risk of fire.)

You should also notify your immediate neighbours and ask them to keep an eye on your home. But be cautious about telling too many other people about your absence. Your teenager or the local delivery boy may have acquaintances who might take advantage of this information.

Outdoor Maintenance

When you're away, ask a neighbour to pick up your newspaper and mail daily. If you expect to be away for more than several days, stop delivery of your newspapers. Make sure that your grass is mowed regularly, or your driveway snowplowed and your walks shovelled after each snowfall. Have an agreement with a neighbour that you will do these things for each other if either is away, or hire a neighbour's child to do them, or contract with a gardening and snowplowing company to look after your premises. In snowy weather, ask a relative or neighbour to drive into your driveway to leave tire marks when you are away.

DOORS AND WINDOWS

To reduce the chance of a break-in, pay special attention to your doors and windows.

Doors and Locks

When most people think about protecting the entrances to their home, they think about installing proper locks. However, any locksmith will tell you that a lock is only as strong as the door and frame to which it is attached. Entrance doors and door frames should be solid wood, metal, or laminated wood core construction. Door hinges should be on the inside, not the outside, and they should be attached with heavy-duty screws that go right through to the framing stud.

Pay particular attention to doors leading from the garage to the house. A person who succeeds in getting into your garage will have lots of time and privacy to work on these doors. Lock your garage door as well as your house doors to reduce the risk of this happening.

Don't rely on locks that are part of the doorknob because they can easily be forced or removed. You should install **single-cylinder deadbolt locks** on exterior doors, including doors from the garage into the house.

Double-cylinder deadbolt locks must be unlocked by a key from the inside as well as the outside. These locks are often used when there is a glass panel in or beside the door to prevent someone from breaking the glass and simply reaching in to unlock the door. The down side to this type of lock is that it may be difficult to get out the door in the event of a fire or other emergency. Keep a key near the door (but out of reach from the outside) and make sure that all members of your household know where the key is located. Instead of installing a double-cylinder deadbolt, you can install break-resistant plexiglass, or you can protect existing glass with metal grillwork.

Keys

If you keep a spare key somewhere outside the house (just in case you lock yourself out), here are some places NOT to keep it, because they are places that burglars know all about: under the door mat, in a planter, above a ledge or door frame, in the mailbox. Take in all hidden spare keys before you go away on a trip.

Do not carry identification on a key ring. If someone gets hold of your house or car keys, there's no reason to let them know exactly what door the keys fit. Just be sure to have your locks changed immediately if your keys are stolen or lost.

Peepholes

Install a wide-angle peephole in your front door so you can see who is there without having to open the door. If you have a mail slot that opens directly into your house, make sure that it does not open wide enough for someone to reach in and unlock the door.

Sliding Doors

Sliding glass doors can be jimmied off their tracks. To prevent this, put a wooden broom handle or hockey-stick handle in the floor track when the door is closed. The stick should be exactly the length of the track for a snug fit. Or have a metal "patio bar" installed half-way up the door (they're available at the hardware store).

Windows

Secure windows that slide to one side the same way you secure sliding doors, with a broom handle or other piece of wood in the track. Double-hung windows (windows whose lower or upper panel, or both, can be raised and lowered) are usually fastened by a crescent latch, but crescent latches can be opened from the outside by slipping a knife between the sashes. Secure double-hung windows by putting on a better lock.

If you mount an air-conditioner in a window, it should be bolted to the window frame so that it cannot be lifted out. Keep the window from being opened further by blocking either a sliding window or a double-hung window with a length of wood.

You may want to make basement windows burglar-proof by replacing the glass with plexiglass or by putting up security bars. Be sure that it will still be easy to get *out* through the basement windows if there is a fire.

ALARM SYSTEMS

Alarm systems make your home a less attractive target to a potential burglar. This is recognized by home insurance companies, which usually offer lower premiums to homeowners with approved alarm systems. If you are considering installing an alarm system, find out from your insurance company what kind of system they'll give you a discount for.

The least expensive alarm systems simply set off a siren if someone enters your house through a wired door or window. Then it's up to you to get help. The more expensive ones are connected through your telephone line to a friend or relative's phone, or to the alarm company's own switchboard. (If you have this kind of alarm, check whether your alarm is designed to go off if someone cuts your telephone cable.) It may be possible in your area to have your alarm connected to the local police station—but considering that there are far more false alarms than true alarms, you may not wish to have a direct connection with the police. If you have a history of false alarms with the police, they may not respond to a true alarm. If you pay a service fee for your alarm to be connected to a company switchboard, an operator at the company will notify police that your alarm has gone off. Usually the operator will first call your home to find out if the alarm is a false one. You may have to provide the operator with an identification number to prove that it's the homeowner and not the burglar answering the phone.

To find out what kinds of alarms are available, ask in your local hardware store, call some alarm companies, or call your local police department. If you choose a system that is connected to an alarm company's switchboard, make sure that the company is well-established and reliable. If they go out of business, your alarm will go out of business too.

An alarm system only works if it's turned on. Turn it on every time your house is going to be empty, even if it's only for a few minutes.

PROTECTING YOUR VALUABLES

There are two steps to protecting your valuables. The first is to keep them in a safe place. The second is to identify them permanently to increase the chance that you'll get them back if they were stolen.

Safekeeping

Expensive jewellery is best left in a safety deposit box at the bank. If you do so, you can arrange to pay for insurance on these items only when they are out of the safety deposit box. Contact your insurance agent about this possibility. It is also a good idea not to keep large amounts of cash in your home.

If you want to keep cash and jewellery in your house, consider installing a burglar-proof and fire-proof safe in your home. For a lot less money and less security, you can buy a safe that fits into a hole cut in the baseboard and looks like an electrical outlet. You can also buy containers for hiding valuables that are disguised as beer or soft drink cans or other kinds of cans, or you can buy hollowed-out books. If you decide to try this method of hiding things, remember that quite a lot of people have accidentally thrown out what they thought was a can . . . and then found out that it was really their jewellery collection.

If you simply want to hide your valuables, here are some places that *burglars will be sure to look:* in the refrigerator and the freezer, under your bed or your mattress, under the bathroom or kitchen sink, in, under, and behind drawers. It is a good idea to leave some costume jewellery in your jewellery box to make a burglar think that he has found everything you have. If you really use your imagination to hide valuables, be careful that you are not so creative that *you* can't find them later.

Identification

Burglars are usually more interested in selling what they've stolen than in using it themselves. If a thief knows he will have trouble selling your possessions, he's less likely to spend time stealing them. **Operation Identification** is a national program set up through police departments to identify personal property so that it's hard to sell if it has been stolen, and so that burglars know before they break in that your property is identified.

Contact your local police department or your insurance agent to find out about Operation Identification. Identifying your belongings involves engraving a personal identification number on them and placing an Operation Identification sticker in your window to let potential burglars know that you have done so. The police may loan you an engraving pencil or tell you where you can borrow or buy one (hardware stores carry them).

The engraving pencil will not work on some things such as jewellery, silver, china, fur coats, paintings, and papers (for example, stock certificates or bonds). Paintings and paper can be marked using a non-toxic invisible marking pen. Fur coats can be marked by lifting up the lining at the bottom of the back and writing your last name and/or your personal identification number in BIG letters across the skins of the back of the coat. Use an indelible pen if the fur is dark or an ordinary ball-point pen if the fur is light (an identifying number or name on the lining is of no use because the lining can be removed).

IN THE EVENT OF A BURGLARY

If you come home and find that a door or window has been forced open, leave the house immediately. Call the police from a neighbour's house or from a cellular phone. The burglar may still be in your house and may attack you in order to escape or to prevent being identified. Do not clean up your house until the police have looked it over for evidence, but do look around outside to see if there are any suspicious vehicles or people. If there are, note licence numbers and descriptions.

If your house is broken into once, it may be broken into a second time shortly afterwards. That's because the burglar expects you to have contents insurance and to replace everything that was stolen. Do a general security check of your premises. Take a burglary as a hint to upgrade your locks, doors, and alarm system, and to identify all your possessions (new and old) with your personal identification number. You will be pleased to know that many homeowner's insurance policies will help pay for new locks after a burglary.

☑Home Security Checklist

Neighbourhood Watch

❑ Join or organize a Neighbourhood Watch in your community.
❑ Arrange with neighbours to keep an eye on each other's houses.

Outside

❑ Make sure your doors and windows are visible from the street or neighbouring homes.

❏ Don't leave tools that a burglar might find useful in your yard or unlocked garage.

❏ At night, light your entrances and ground-floor windows.

When you're away, make it look like you're still home

❏ Make arrangements with your neighbours to keep an eye on each other's homes.

❏ Use timers or sensors to turn on inside and outside lights at night and turn them off during the day (or ask a trusted neighbour to turn lights on and off for you).

❏ Leave a radio playing, tuned to an all-talk station.

❏ Stop delivery of newspapers.

❏ Have a neighbour pick up your mail.

❏ Have your walks or driveway shovelled of snow in the winter, and your grass mowed in the summer.

❏ Have a neighbour park in your driveway from time to time.

Doors and windows

❏ Entrance doors and their frames should be of solid construction, with hinges on the inside.

❏ Install deadbolt locks.

❏ Keep your doors locked, including doors leading from the garage to the house.

❏ Don't leave a spare key in an obvious place such as the mailbox, under the door mat, above the door frame, or in a planter.

❏ To prevent sliding glass doors and windows from being jimmied open, insert a stick snugly in the track.

❏ Consider installing an alarm system.

❏ Display a sticker stating that you have an alarm system (whether you do or not!).

Protecting your valuables

❏ Keep cash or valuable jewellery in a bank or home vault.

❏ Don't hide your valuables in obvious places such as in, under, or behind drawers, under the bed or mattress, in the refrigerator or freezer, or under the bathroom or kitchen sink.

❏ If you've chosen a hiding place that is not obvious, don't forget where it is!

❏ Make your belongings harder to sell, and therefore less attractive to a thief, by identifying them permanently.

In the Event of a Break-in

❑ If you're in the house, get out. If you're out, don't go in. For your personal safety, it is best not to confront a burglar.

❑ Thieves often return, so review your home security to avoid a second break-in.

☑ "To Do" List

❑ Get acquainted with immediate neighbours you don't already know.

❑ Light up your ground floor entrances.

❑ Install deadbolt locks on exterior doors.

❑ Put a wooden stick in the track of any sliding glass doors or windows.

❑ Install a peephole in exterior doors.

❑ Make sure any outside hiding place for your keys is a safe one.

❑ Permanently identify your valuables and put an "Operation Identification" sticker in your windows.

❑ Find a secret place to hide your valuables.

Things Not To Do

• Don't burglar-proof your home so well that you can't get out if there's a fire.

• Don't leave your house unlocked or windows open while you are out.

• Don't enter your house when there are signs of a break-in.

• Don't confront a burglar or intruder in your home.

13 HOME SAFETY AND ACCIDENT PREVENTION

WARNING: This is a chapter full of warnings. The first warning is that read-

ing too much about safety at one time can be harmful to your mental health. If you read this chapter in one sitting, you may wish to take to your bed and pull the covers over your head. But if you do, make sure that you haven't left the car running in the garage or oil heating on the stove.

Another warning: Being safe involves a lot of cleaning. Worried already? This is just the beginning. Read on.

Safety is an area of major concern to homeowners, even though it is unpleasant to think about. This chapter is organized to allow you to face all or part of your fears, as you choose. Under each major heading, we have provided a checklist of the most urgent safety concerns. Following each checklist is a more detailed discussion.

FIRE SAFETY

There are stories in the news almost daily about the loss of life and property caused by home fires. Many people's greatest terror is of a fire breaking out in their home. But most fires are preventable, and, even if a fire does break out, proper fire planning can at least prevent loss of life. The following checklist sets out the key fire safety and planning matters of which every homeowner should be aware.

☑Fire Safety Checklist

Smoke Alarms

❑ Place a smoke alarm on each floor.
❑ Test smoke alarms and the batteries once a month.
❑ Clean smoke alarms once a month.

Plan Ahead

❑ Plan an escape route.
❑ Plan two ways out of every bedroom—door and window.
❑ Plan a meeting place outside the house.

In the Event of Fire

❑ Getting out is more important than fighting the fire or calling the fire department.
❑ Stay near the ground where the air is best.
❑ Stop, drop, and roll if on fire.
❑ Call the fire department from outside the house.

Fire Prevention: Electrical

Live within the capacity of your home's electrical system or have it upgraded

❑ Don't make permanent use of extension cords or "octopuses."
❑ Don't use oversized fuses.
❑ If fuses or circuit breakers blow repeatedly, have the circuit checked by an electrician.

Unless your home has just been built, have the wiring checked by an electrician

❑ to determine whether or not you have aluminum wiring
❑ to see whether original wiring and any possible changes are safe

Have the wiring checked by an electrician if

❑ electrical outlets or switches are unusually warm
❑ you have had trouble with mice or squirrels in your home

Use appliances correctly

❑ Don't run electrical cords under carpeting.
❑ Don't use higher than 60-watt bulb unless the light fixture says so.

Fire Prevention: Heating

Furnaces

❑ Have your furnace professionally inspected and cleaned once a year.
❑ Keep flammable materials away from the furnace.
❑ If you smell gas from your gas furnace, open the windows or leave the house. Call the gas company.

Space Heaters

❑ Space heaters are very dangerous. Treat them as you would a live fire.
❑ Never use a kerosene, propane, or butane heater indoors.

Fireplaces

❑ If you use your fireplace, have it professionally inspected and cleaned once a year.
❑ Use a fireplace screen or glass fireplace door to keep sparks away from carpeting and wood floors.
❑ Don't start a fire with gasoline, lighter fluid, or any other flammable substance.
❑ To prevent build-up of flammable substances in your chimney, burn seasoned hardwood rather than softwood or firelogs.
❑ Never leave a fire unattended.

❑ Don't dispose of ashes until they are cold.

Fire Prevention: Cooking

❑ Keep a class ABC fire extinguisher, or a class B fire extinguisher (designed to put out grease fires) in the kitchen.
❑ Don't leave food, especially grease or fat, cooking unattended.
❑ Keep the entire stove and oven area clean of grease.
❑ If you have a grease fire, do not throw water on it. Use your fire extinguisher, baking soda, or salt; if the fire is small enough, smother it with a pot lid.
❑ If your microwave sparks or the door does not seal tightly, have it professionally checked before using it.
❑ If a fire starts in your oven or your microwave, don't open the door—that will simply give the fire more oxygen.

Fire Prevention: Flammable Materials

❑ Careless smoking is a major cause of house fires. If you must smoke in the house, take these precautions:
  • Don't smoke in bed.
  • Don't smoke anywhere if you are drowsy.
  • Set out and use ashtrays.
  • Empty ashtrays into a toilet or metal container, not into wastepaper baskets.
❑ Keep matches and cigarette lighters out of the reach of children.
❑ Do not use flammable products (container will have flammable sign) near open flames or heat sources such as stoves, furnaces, fireplaces, cigarettes, pilot lights.
❑ Christmas trees are flammable. Don't leave them unattended with the lights on.

Here's more detailed information about the items mentioned in the fire safety checklist.

Smoke Alarms

Every home should have one smoke alarm on each floor. In fact, some municipalities require you to do so. Check with your local fire department to find out if the law requires you to install a smoke alarm.

Types of Alarms

There are two types of smoke alarms. An ionization alarm can detect fire in its first stage before there is any smoke visible. A photoelectric alarm can detect a fire in its second stage, the smouldering stage, when smoke has appeared but there are not yet flames. The third stage of a fire is the flame stage, and the fourth stage of a fire is the heat stage. If you do have a fire, you want to know about it before the third or fourth stages.

Smoke alarms can be powered by battery or by electricity. A battery-powered alarm can be installed fairly easily by the homeowner, but an alarm powered by electricity should be installed by an electrician. If you choose an electricity-powered alarm, make sure it is not wired to a circuit that can be turned on and off by a switch. Also, make sure the alarm has an auxiliary battery in case of a power failure.

Where to Install

Where should you place a smoke alarm? On the ceiling, first of all, because smoke rises. Because they can be triggered accidentally by such things as shower steam or burning toast, alarms should not be too close to either a bathroom or a kitchen. You wouldn't want to frighten your teenage son who is taking his first shower in months, or discourage your spouse who has decided to make you breakfast (of burnt toast) in bed. An alarm should be placed near the bedrooms or sleeping areas of your home. If there is a municipal requirement for the installation of smoke alarms, it will probably also specify where in the house they must be placed.

Maintenance and Testing

Read the manufacturer's instructions for information about testing and maintenance of your particular alarm. Test your smoke alarm once a month by putting a source of smoke, such as a candle or incense, near the alarm until it sounds. The "Tester Button" usually only tests battery charge. Test your batteries once a month too. Replace batteries when they become low. Use *only* the exact batteries recommended by the manufacturer. Even if the batteries are not low, replace them once a year. DO NOT use rechargeable batteries in a smoke alarm because they can fail without giving any warning. Vacuum dust from the alarm's smoke chamber and protective cover once a month (more often if someone in your house smokes).

If your alarm isn't working, replace it!

Plan Ahead

Plan an Escape Route

Plan one from every area of your home, and then try it to see if it works. Be sure everyone knows two ways out of their bedroom—a door and a window. You may have to smash it open, so keep something near each window that can be used to smash it if necessary. "If necessary" is a subtle point you will have to impress upon your children lest they be tempted to test out this piece of equipment during one of your fire drills. If you have bars on any windows, they must be easily removable from the inside. If you have a door or window lock that must be opened from the inside with a key, always keep a key hanging near the lock—but not where someone outside can get it by smashing a window.

Know the Escape Route

Make sure everyone—children, babysitters, and guests included—knows the escape routes and knows that no one is to go back inside for pets, toys, or valuables.

Arrange a Meeting Place

Arrange a place outside the house where everyone is to gather in the event of a fire. That way, you will know exactly who is safe and who is missing.

In the Event of Fire

Get Out!

Getting out of a burning house is the first priority. If a fire breaks out, unless it's very small, concentrate on getting everyone out of the house, NOT on trying to put the fire out, on getting dressed, or on saving your favourite possessions. Don't even stop to call the fire department. Call from a neighbour's house once everyone is out.

Use These Survival Techniques:

CRAWL on your knees to the nearest exit, since the air near the floor is safer to breathe because smoke and dangerous gases rise.

FEEL THE DOOR before leaving a room. **Do not open a hot door** because there is probably fire on the other side. Close doors behind you as you get out to slow the spread of the fire.

IF YOU HAVE TO ESCAPE THROUGH A WINDOW, SHUT THE DOOR to the room before you open the window, or the air coming through the window may fan the fire.

STOP, DROP, AND ROLL. Have everyone in your house learn the **"stop, drop, and roll"** technique to smother flames if someone's clothes catch on fire. **Stop** instantly—running will fan the flames. **Drop** to the floor and cover your face with your hands. **Roll** on a rug, blanket, or coat to put the fire out. If you are outside, you can use dirt or snow to put the fire out.

Contact the Fire Department

Make sure everyone in your family knows how to contact the fire department. In many, but not all, areas of Canada, this is done by dialling 911. Check the number you must use by looking in the front pages of your telephone book under Emergency Numbers.

Fire Prevention: Electrical

Live within Your Electrical Means

Don't exceed the electrical capacity of your home. Do not plug multiple electrical appliances into one outlet, using "octopus" type plugs. Make only temporary use of extension cords: they can cause appliances to overheat.

Do not use oversized fuses in your fuse box. A 15-amp fuse is the one usually required for regular domestic circuits. If your fuses blow repeatedly, have an electrician investigate to find out if you are overloading your system. If you cannot convince the members of your family that they cannot watch television, play computer games, listen to the stereo, and dry their hair all at the same time, your system may need upgrading.

Have Your Wiring Checked by a Professional Electrician if:

YOUR HOME IS NOT NEWLY BUILT. The electrician will be able to determine whether you have aluminum wiring, and whether the original wiring and any changes made to it by previous owners are safe.

ELECTRICAL OUTLETS OR SWITCHES ARE UNUSUALLY WARM. A hot outlet or switch may be a sign of faulty wiring. Stop using the outlet or switch until it has been inspected.

YOU HAVE ALUMINUM WIRING (found in older homes). Corroded aluminum wiring can get very hot, and aluminum wiring that is under compression can cause sparks.

YOU HAVE HAD TROUBLE WITH MICE OR SQUIRRELS IN YOUR HOME. Visiting rodents may have gnawed off the protective covering on your wires, which may result in a low heat-source fire that your fuse box or breaker may not detect quickly.

Use Appliances Correctly

If you have pot lights in your ceiling, keep insulation and anything else that may burn away from them. Do not use a light bulb of higher wattage than recommended in a lamp (you can usually find the recommended wattage on a label on the lamp or shade). If in doubt, do not use a bulb higher than 60 watts.

Do not run electrical cords underneath carpets. If your appliances have frayed or brittle electric cords, replace the cords. If you have an "instant-on" television, unplug it if it is not going to be used for an extended period. Don't unplug any appliance by pulling on the electric cord; always pull out by the plug.

Make sure that all your electrical appliances and electrical cords carry the CSA seal (Canadian Standards Association) or the ULC seal (Underwriters' Laboratories of Canada).

If an appliance sparks, smokes, or has flames coming out of it, turn it off and unplug it, or shut off power to that circuit. Do not put water on electrical equipment that is on fire until it has been unplugged.

Fire Prevention: Heating

Furnaces

Have your furnace professionally inspected once a year by a heating contractor. Between inspections, keep an eye on your furnace yourself. Have it serviced immediately if you notice loose parts, rust, leakage, or any other sign that the furnace is starting to fall apart. Also, change the filters regularly.

Keep the area around your furnace clean and free of dust and lint, which can catch fire if they get close to the furnace. Periodically vacuum out the furnace vents and filters on each floor of your house.

If you have an oil furnace and your oil tank is old, have it professionally checked for pinholes that may be about to leak.

If you have a natural gas furnace and you think you smell gas, open the windows immediately, or leave the house. Call the gas company's emergency number or call the fire department. Another thing to remember with a gas furnace is to keep the outdoor natural gas regulator clear of ice and snow, which can cause the fuel flow to become uncontrolled.

Space Heaters

Use only electrical space heaters indoors. Never use kerosene, butane, or propane heaters indoors. You should treat even an electrical space heater as you would a live fire: don't put it near anything that might catch fire, like furniture or draperies. Newer electrical heaters have a switch designed to turn the heater off automatically if it falls over. It is best not to leave an electrical heater unattended, especially if it does not have an automatic shut-off switch. Do not leave children alone with an electrical heater that is turned on.

Fireplaces and Chimneys

INSPECT: Before you use your fireplace for the first time, have the fireplace and chimney cleaned and inspected by a professional chimney sweep. In addition to cleaning the fireplace and chimney flues, the chimney sweep should check that your chimney has a liner. If you live in an older house, it may not. Chimney liners reduce the build-up of flammable creosote, which can cause a chimney fire, and they prevent small holes in the chimney mortar from leading to fire in the walls. New homes should have chimney liners because in most areas builders are required by law to install them. Even though owners of older homes may not be required to install a chimney liner, you should have one installed.

The chimney sweep should check that your chimney is tall enough that sparks will not blow onto the roof or back through open windows. You may want to install a spark screen or spark arrester around the chimney cap. You may also want to install a rain cap on your chimney to prevent rain and snow from entering and causing the masonry to crumble.

Have a professional chimney sweep clean and inspect your chimney flues once a year. The spring is a good time, after you've been using the fireplace during the winter. Or have it done in the fall before you start using the chimney again.

You may think that the lovely smell of wood smoke is the nicest thing about a fire. Unfortunately, wood smoke contains toxic chemicals and allergens and should be going up the chimney, not into your room. If your room smells of wood smoke while you are using your fireplace, have your chimney inspected immediately—don't wait for spring. You should also periodically touch the wall in front of the chimney to check for excessive heat. If it is very hot, have your chimney inspected immediately.

BURN THE RIGHT KIND OF WOOD: Do not burn wood that is green or wet; the wood should have been split and seasoned for six months to a year. It is preferable to burn hardwood logs (such as maple, yellow birch, oak, or elm), not softwood (such as cedar or pine). If you burn green wood, wet wood, or softwoods, you can get a build-up of creosote in the flue which can cause a chimney fire. You should also avoid burning only treated logs in your fireplace. If you use treated logs, do so only occasionally and alternate with natural firewood. If you don't, you can end up with a build-up of paraffin in your chimney, which is also flammable. Also avoid burning painted wood, pressure-treated wood, magazines, cardboard, and coloured paper such as comics. While burning these things will not cause a fire, they do give off toxic fumes.

Do not use lighter fluid or gasoline to get your fire started. Instead use newspaper and small pieces of kindling.

PROTECT AGAINST SPARKS: To protect against sparks and embers setting fire to your rug, floor, or furniture, use a fireplace screen or have glass fireplace doors installed. You should also have at least eighteen inches of protective tile, brick, or cement between the fireplace itself and wooden floors or carpets. If you don't, use a hearth rug made of 100 per cent pure virgin wool, which is naturally fire-resistant up to very high temperatures. Check for the woolmark symbol, as the wool must not be reprocessed. Alternatively, you can treat the carpet you already have with a flame-retardant spray, available at most hardware stores. Keep fireplace implements (tongs, poker, shovel) and heat-proof gloves beside the fireplace and use them to return hot embers that have fallen out to the fireplace. Keep a fire extinguisher (a class ABC extinguisher or a class A extinguisher designed to put out wood and paper fires) handy—just in case.

Make sure a responsible person (if you can find one!) is always in the room when a fire is burning. Don't leave the house or go to bed while there are still flames or burning embers. Do not clean out the fireplace until the ashes are cold, and then put the ashes in a metal container outside the house.

Wood-burning Stoves

A wood-burning stove should be properly designed and installed only by a qualified installer.

Have the chimney, flue pipes, and stove inspected regularly for creosote and soot build-up, as well as for ash. Check the colour of the smoke from the chimney; it should be either white or invisible. If it is blue or grey, or any other colour, this is a warning that the stove is improperly vented, or that a fire is smouldering, or that you are burning poor quality wood. (It does not mean that the College of Cardinals has not yet chosen a new Pope.)

As with a fireplace, do not burn softwood or green or wet wood. They can produce creosote that can cause a flash fire in your chimney. Use wood, preferably hardwood, that has been dried and seasoned for six months to a year.

Fire Prevention: Cooking

House fires very often start in the kitchen. You can use this as an excuse not to cook dinner ever again. But if it's cook or starve, take the reasonable precautions that follow.

Fire Extinguishers

Keep a dry chemical fire extinguisher (either an all-purpose class ABC extinguisher, or a class B extinguisher designed to put out grease fires) in the kitchen, in an easily accessible place: it should be kept near an exit rather than near the stove. If it is too close to the stove, you may not be able to reach it if there is a stove fire. Make sure it is always in working order. The fire extinguisher should have a ULC seal (Underwriters' Laboratories of Canada). Know how to use the fire extinguisher—remember to **PASS**: Pull the pin, Aim low, Squeeze the handle, Sweep from side to side. Don't attempt to fight the fire yourself unless it is very small. If you cannot put the fire out right away or if it is large when you first see it, get everyone out of the house and call the fire department.

You must inspect your fire extinguisher periodically to ensure that the pressure is right, the nozzle is not blocked, and the seal is not broken. The fire extinguisher will contain instructions from the manufacturer saying how often you should inspect. You should also take your fire extinguisher for inspection and maintenance to a servicing agency recommended by the manufacturer. Your instruction manual will tell you how often to do this. If you have used or damaged your fire extinguisher, take it to a servicing agency immediately.

Stove and Oven Fires

Grease is a common cause of kitchen fires. Keep your stove and oven clean of grease (there's that cleaning stuff again), and don't forget to clean grease-traps, vents, and hood filters over the stove too. Any grease in the area will ignite if a fire starts.

STOVES: Do not leave oil or fat, or any food for that matter, on the stove to heat or cook unattended—even for one minute while you answer the phone or investigate why one of your children is strangling the other. Do not even leave a pan of fat or oil on a cold burner. Someone may accidentally turn on the burner. (We bet you're thinking right now who that someone in your house might be!)

If a grease fire breaks out in a pot or pan, you can smother the fire by covering the pan with a large lid. If you see smoke coming out of a covered pot, do not remove the lid because doing so may cause flames to leap out of the pot. Leave the cover on the pot and take the pot off the burner. Do not throw water or flour on a grease fire. The flames will spread rather than die out. Use your fire extinguisher (we told you that you'd need it) or else throw baking soda or salt on the fire.

OVENS: Do not store anything in your oven. (What are you saving old pizza boxes for, anyway?) Do not use your oven for science experiments or arts and crafts projects, except for products specifically designed for use in a home oven. Do not use your oven as a dryer (especially not for your hair, or for clothing you are wearing at the time).

Do not keep flammable materials near the stove and oven. (What are you trying to do? Start a fire?) Find someplace else to keep cleaning supplies, grocery bags, magazines and cookbooks, aprons, potholders and towels, or your collection of wooden spoons. Don't hang curtains on a window near the stove. Instead use venetian blinds or shutters.

If a fire starts in your oven, turn off the oven, but do not open the door—that will only give it more oxygen to burn. (This is the same principle as the pot lid.) If you leave the door closed, the fire is more likely to die out on its own.

Microwave Oven Fires

Proper installation of your microwave can prevent some microwave fires. Make sure that your microwave is properly grounded by using a three-pronged plug. Do not block the air vents of your microwave. Put the oven in a place where it has air space on top and on all sides.

Keep the oven clean of grease (more cleaning!), because you can end up with a grease fire in a microwave oven too. Do not put anything metal in the microwave, including metal bowls, metal-edged or metal-decorated bowls, metal cutlery, aluminum foil, and twist-ties. Metal will cause sparking (also known as arcing) in the oven. If you have a lot of sparking in your microwave, even though you've remembered not to put any metal in, or if the door does not seal tightly, have the microwave professionally inspected and repaired before using it again.

Don't use your oven as a dryer or to heat anything other than food, unless it's a product specifically designed for use in the microwave.

If a fire does start in your microwave, do not open the door until the flames are gone. As with a conventional oven, opening the door will simply give the fire more oxygen to burn. Instead, keep the door closed and unplug the unit.

Fire Prevention: Flammable Materials

Smoking and Matches

Smoking is not only bad for your health in the long run, it can be an immediate danger to you and those who live with you if you are careless. You should consider banning **all** smoking in your home. This decision is not only good for the health and safety of your household, but it may save you money on your insurance premiums. Ask your insurance agent if there is a reduced premium for non-smoking households. And, as a bonus, a no-smoking rule will cut down on your cleaning—you won't have to vacuum your smoke alarm as frequently!

If you must smoke in your home, never smoke in bed. Do not smoke anywhere if you are drowsy. If you fall asleep with a lighted cigarette, a sofa or chair can catch fire as easily as a bed. Set out lots of deep ashtrays and empty them regularly. Do not empty ashtrays into wastepaper baskets; empty them into a toilet or a metal container.

Do not smoke while you are using, or have just been using, flammable materials. Even such seemingly harmless products as hair spray, nail polish, or nail polish remover may ignite.

Keep matches and cigarette lighters out of the reach of children. Train your children to hand over to an adult any matches or cigarette lighters that they may find.

If there is a power failure, do not use matches or a lighter to find your way around in the dark. Use a flashlight. Keep a flashlight on each floor in an easy-to-find location (easy to find in the dark, that is), for this purpose. There are rechargeable flashlights on the market which are designed to stay plugged into an outlet. Some of them light up when there is a power failure.

Other Flammables

Most flammable materials are marked by this sign:
Examples of flammable materials are:

- hair spray
- nail polish
- nail polish remover
- cleaning fluid
- aerosol spray cans
- varnish
- paint
- paint stripper

- sealants
- gasoline
- lighter fluid

STORING FLAMMABLES: Do not store any flammable products near any heat source, including the furnace and stove.

There are certain flammable materials that you should not store inside your home at all, such as gasoline, kerosene, or stove oil. The same holds true for rags that you have used to soak up paint, solvents, oil, fuel, glue, or any product that contains linseed oil. They may suddenly burst into flame. (This is known as spontaneous combustion.) Store them outside, if you feel you must keep and cherish them or take them to a hazardous waste recycling depot.

Do not store trash and paper, or other materials that may burn, in your basement or attic. While these things are not particularly flammable by themselves, they will act as fuel for a fire that has already started.

WASHERS AND DRYERS: Clean out the lint-collector in your clothes dryer every time you use the dryer, because the heat in the dryer can ignite it. Also, check every now and then that the dryer exhaust pipe has no lint in it.

Do not dry foam rubber in the dryer. Do not use your washer or dryer to clean rags soaked in flammable liquids. And since we already told you not to store them in your house dirty, why don't you just throw them away?

CHRISTMAS TREES: Christmas trees, while beautiful, can constitute a fire hazard. Set up your Christmas tree well away from any heat source, including heat vents and incandescent light bulbs. Keep your tree well watered so that it doesn't dry out. Not only will your tree look better longer, but it will not turn into firewood while still in your home. Do not turn on your Christmas tree lights and then leave the room—either stay to enjoy them, or turn them off.

Precautions with Natural Gas Appliances

If you have natural gas appliances that require lighting with a match, light the match and put it by the gas valve before you turn on the gas to avoid a gas build-up that might explode. If you have appliances that have a pilot light, you should be aware that the fumes from flammable materials (see the list above) can be ignited by the pilot light. Turn off all the pilot lights if you are using these materials, keep the area well ventilated, and do not re-light the pilot lights until all fumes are gone. This is especially important in basements.

CARBON MONOXIDE SAFETY

Carbon monoxide has been called the silent killer. Carbon monoxide is a colourless, odourless gas caused by burning when there is not enough oxygen present. It can be produced by cars and by appliances that run on natural gas, oil, or propane, including furnaces. High levels of carbon monoxide will cause convulsions, respiratory failure, coma—and death.

☑ Carbon Monoxide Safety Checklist

Prevention of carbon monoxide build-up

❑ Have your furnace professionally inspected and cleaned once a year.
❑ Don't leaving your car running in the garage.
❑ Don't use outdoor barbecues inside the house.
❑ Don't use a propane, kerosene, or butane heater inside the house.
❑ Let some air into your house!
❑ Consider buying a carbon monoxide detector.

If you suspect carbon monoxide poisoning

❑ Get fresh air immediately: open the windows, or better yet, go outside.
❑ Seek medical treatment.

Prevention of Carbon Monoxide Build-up

To prevent a build-up of carbon monoxide in your house:

• Let some air into your house, especially if it's tightly sealed to conserve heat in the winter.

• If your garage is attached to your house, open the garage door before starting your car, and don't leave the car running in the garage.

• Never use any outdoor barbecue or grill (charcoal or propane) indoors.

• Never store a propane cylinder indoors, even if you are storing your propane barbecue indoors.

• Never use a propane, butane, or kerosene heater in your house, even for a very short period of time.

• Have your furnace and chimney checked by a heating-system professional once a year.

- Check that your fireplace has its own outside air source
- Have your fireplace chimneys inspected once a year. A blocked chimney can cause a build-up of carbon monoxide.
- Do not smother a fire in a fireplace or wood stove.
- If you have a propane refrigerator, make sure it is vented directly outdoors. If it is not vented outdoors, move it outdoors immediately. Even if it is vented outdoors, have it checked regularly by a certified propane fitter.

Carbon Monoxide Detectors

Carbon monoxide (CO) detectors are available at hardware stores and cost about $50 and up. They do not need to be professionally installed. They either plug in or run on batteries. They are similar to smoke alarms and will sound when carbon monoxide reaches an unsafe level in your house. Be sure to buy one that carries one of these approval seals: CGA (Canadian Gas Association), UL (Underwriters Laboratories Inc.), or ULC (Underwriters Laboratories of Canada). A CSA (Canadian Standards Association) seal alone is not sufficient because it only indicates that the device has been tested for electrical safety, not for its efficiency in detecting carbon monoxide. Install your carbon monoxide detector near bedrooms or sleeping areas.

Carbon Monoxide Poisoning

As we said before, high levels of carbon monoxide will cause convulsions, respiratory failure, coma, and death. The symptoms of lower-level carbon monoxide poisoning are similar to those of the flu and can include a headache or tightness across the front of the head, weakness, dizziness, nausea, watering eyes, and loss of muscle control.

If you suspect carbon monoxide poisoning, get the victim into fresh air immediately. Open the windows, or better yet, get the victim outside. Then seek medical treatment.

ACCIDENT PREVENTION

Most accidents in the home can be prevented by doing the things your mother always told you to do, like watch where you're going and clean up after yourself. When you prevent accidents, you are not only protecting yourself and your family from injury, you are also protecting yourself from potential legal liability to any other person who might be hurt on your property.

The following checklist sets out the key steps to make your home safer. You will find more information on safety in the home after the checklist. If you do these things, your mother will be proud of you.

☑Accident Prevention Checklist

❑ Make sure your address is clearly visible from the street so that emergency vehicles can locate your house.

❑ Have a list of emergency telephone numbers close to your kitchen telephone.

❑ Keep your house well-enough lit, especially stairways, so that people can see where they are going.

❑ Don't leave things that people can trip over or slip on, such as toys, electrical cords, loose rugs, bathroom and kitchen spills, or ice. In the winter, sprinkle salt, sand, or ashes at icy entrances.

❑ Provide sturdy support rails on stairways and in bathtubs and showers.

❑ Prevent scalding by setting your water heater at 130 degrees F (55 degrees C) or less.

❑ Install ground fault circuit interrupters in bathrooms and laundry rooms to prevent electrical shock.

❑ If you have a swimming pool or hot tub and young children or pets, consider an extra fence to enclose it separately.

❑ Consider installing specialized safety equipment for children, the elderly, or the disabled.

What follows is a guided tour of your home, and the accidents that might happen unless you take steps to prevent them. Come on in (if you dare).

Entrance

In case you are not successful in preventing all accidents, it is a good idea to make sure your address is clearly visible from the street at all times so that emergency vehicles will have no trouble locating it. Use dark numbers against a light wall, or light numbers against a dark wall. Illuminate the numbers with a light on a light sensor so that it comes on automatically at dusk. While we're on the subject of emergency telephone calls, keep a list of emergency telephone numbers near the main telephone so that no time is wasted looking these numbers up if there is an accident at your home.

You don't want people to slip or trip at your door. There are a number of things you can do to make your entrances safe. The area around the door should be well lit so that people can see where they are going. Keep the steps and porch in good repair. Sagging or missing boards should be replaced, and any serious cracks or unevenness in the concrete repaired quickly. Keep the entrance way clear of snow and ice. (Can you believe this? You even have to clean outside!) It is a good idea to keep a container of sand, ashes, or salt near the entrance so that you can sprinkle icy areas before someone slips. Wet leaves can be almost as dangerous as ice, so rake leaves away from your entrance.

Make sure there are protective railings on all steps, porches, and decks, and that they are in good repair. Railings are not only a good idea, they may be required by the municipality depending on the number of steps.

Living Areas

If people make it safely through your entrance way, try not to put them into danger once they are inside. Highly polished floors of any kind (wood, tile, or marble for example) are slippery, especially when wet. Consider covering these surfaces with a rug with non-skid backing. But beware! Having protected your family and guests from slipping, you may be setting them up to trip instead.

To prevent people tripping or slipping on scatter mats or area rugs, hold the mats in place with non-skid backings or double-sided carpet tape. Tidy up toys and other articles left lying around on the floor, so people don't trip over them either. Also, run electrical and telephone cords along the wall, not across the room where people might stumble over them.

To keep people from walking into sliding glass doors, which are hard to see if they're clean (finally, a situation where cleaning doesn't pay!), stick decals on them at adult and child eye-level.

Kitchen

Set-up

When you set up your kitchen, think about safety. If you are buying a stove, choose the one that has the safest controls for your family. If the controls are located at the front or side rather than on the back panel, you won't have to reach over the burners to get to them, but they may be within easy reach of young children. If you are buying an electric kettle, toaster, or iron, choose one that has an automatic shut-off.

In arranging your cabinets, try not to place things you will need all the time on shelves out of easy reach. (For the 5-foot 2-inch authors of this book, this is anything above the first shelf.) Make sure your kitchen has a stable stool with four legs to allow the height-challenged to reach high

shelves. Consider the risks of placing goodies out of the reach of your children. If you know that they will get to the goodies no matter where you put them, don't keep them where your children can injure themselves on the way, over the stove for example.

Maintenance

Once your kitchen is safely set up, make sure that you work safely in it. This involves (you guessed it) more cleaning. If you spill something on the floor, clean it up right away before you or somebody else slips in it. Do not leave cooking food or heating kettles on the stove unattended. Turn the handles of pots and pans in towards the centre of the stove, rather than out, so that you or your children do not accidentally knock them over. When you're cooking, don't wear clothes that hang loosely, especially in the sleeves, because they can get caught on pot handles or even catch on fire. Always make sure all burners and the oven are turned off when you've finished cooking.

Don't let the cord of any electrical appliance, especially a kettle, dangle over the counter so that the appliance can be pulled down. If a plugged-in electrical appliance falls into the water, do not put your hand into the water! Unplug the appliance immediately or cut off power to the circuit.

Stairs and Hallways

Stairs should have a solid handrail in good repair and should be well lit with a light switch at the top and at the bottom of the staircase. Do not use stair coverings that make it difficult to see where each step ends, such as flowered or striped carpets or checkerboard tile. Repair or replace stair coverings that are loose or that have holes in them.

Put night lights in the hall and the bathroom, so that no one trips or runs into something when they're prowling around in the dark.

Bathroom

Slipping

Slipping is a common cause of injury in the bathroom. Most bathroom tile is slippery, and the more highly polished it is, the more slippery it is. Put a rubber-backed bath mat next to the bathtub, and clean up spills of water, soap, or lotions on the bathroom floor right away. Install horizontal or angled grab bars in the bathtub or shower stall, and put down a rubber mat or rubber safety-strips on the bathtub or shower floor.

Scalding

Scalding is another common bathroom injury. The risk of scalding can be reduced by turning down the thermostat on your water heater to 55 degrees C (130 degrees F), or even less if there are young children or elderly people in the household. You can get a second-degree burn from two seconds of contact with water that is 65 degrees C (150 degrees F). Whatever temperature your thermostat is set at, it is wise to test the temperature of the water with your forearm before getting in or putting in a child.

Electrical Shock

Having safely escaped injury by slipping or scalding, you probably would also like to avoid injury by electrical shock. Don't plug in your hair dryer or electric razor if your hands are wet—and especially don't do this if all of you is wet, for instance if you are still in the bathtub. The shock you get may be your last.

Have an electrician install a ground fault circuit interrupter. This device will not prevent a shock altogether, but it will interrupt the power fast enough to prevent a fatal shock. If your plugged-in hair dryer or razor or any other electrical appliance falls into the water, do not put your hand into the water. Unplug the appliance immediately.

Basement

If you have a basement that you use only for storage, it is very easy to take an "out of sight, out of mind" attitude towards it. Keep in mind, however, that you will have to venture down those stairs some time, and that you should follow the same safety guidelines there as you do in the rest of your house. Your basement stairs should be solid, with a sturdy handrail, and well lit. Store your possessions so that you don't fall on them and they don't fall on you.

Outdoors

Inspection

Inspect the garden and outside of your home several times a year, and following any major storms, to make sure there are no objects likely to fall, such as bricks, shingles, eavestroughing, shutters, antennas and satellite dishes, wires, and tree branches.

Ladders

If you use a ladder during your inspection, be very careful! Lean it against a solid wall or tree (instead of against your next-door neighbour who's giving you a hand), with the feet on solid ground. Place the feet of the ladder a distance of one quarter of the ladder's length away from the wall. Make sure that the ladder is not touching overhead electric wires.

If you have a wooden ladder, check to see that it won't give way as you climb. Before you use the ladder, lay it on the ground and walk along the rungs to test that each rung will support your weight. Don't stand on the top rung of a ladder, and don't lose your balance trying to get at something that's just a bit out of reach. If you don't have a good head for heights, or you get dizzy sometimes, stay off the ladder completely.

Swimming Pools and Hot Tubs

If you have a backyard swimming pool or hot tub, check with your municipality, because you will almost certainly be required to install a locked fence of a minimum height around your entire yard. Consider fencing the pool or hot tub area separately, following those municipal standards. If you have young children, this arrangement will provide a separate play space in the yard. In addition, you may not have to meet those municipal standards for the fencing around the rest of your yard. No matter how you fence your pool or hot tub, keep the gates locked at all times.

A pool is a year-round source of danger. Even when the pool is closed for the season, it still contains water. Most winter pool covers will not prevent someone from falling into the water, they will just prevent others from seeing that person. (There are pool covers designed to be walked on safely, but they require special installation and are very expensive.) Keep life-saving equipment and a telephone close to your pool, summer and winter, in case of an emergency.

Decks

If you have an outdoor deck, inspect it regularly. Loose or rotting boards should be replaced, as should rickety railings. Don't forget to check the supporting timbers under the deck. Even pressure-treated wood or cedar will eventually rot and have to be replaced. The lifespan of the average deck is between ten and twenty years.

Garden Tools

Even outside, it is important to pick up after yourself. There's just no escape from cleaning, is there? Don't leave hoses, rakes, clippers, or other gardening tools where they can cause injury.

Special Tips for Parents of Young Children

There is specialized safety equipment designed for the protection of young children. These include

- window guards to prevent windows from opening far enough for a child to get through and fall
- safety latches for cupboard and other doors
- child-proof covers for electrical outlets
- child-proof barriers for the top and bottom of staircases

While this list is by no means complete, here are some additional tips for making your house safer for your little ones:

- Make sure that the vertical banister supports on stairs are not spaced so widely apart that a child's head can get caught between them.
- Keep all medications, household cleaning supplies, and anything else you do not want your child to eat in high or locked cupboards.
- Don't put heavy objects such as plant pots, aquariums, or televisions on stands that are not stable and sturdy.

• To reduce the risk of accidental strangulation, shorten venetian blind and drapery cords so they cannot be reached by young children.

PREVENTING WATER DAMAGE

Although every spring brings news coverage of rivers flooding residential districts, most water damage to homes is caused by clogging or freezing of pipes.

Freezing

Inside Pipes

If the temperature drops below freezing inside your home for an extended period, your pipes may freeze and burst. If you are going to be away in the winter, make sure that you arrange for someone to come in daily to check that the temperature in your house remains above freezing. If you don't do this, your homeowner's insurance policy will probably not cover damage due to freezing if you have been away for more than four days. If the inside temperature does drop, prevent pipes from freezing by turning on your taps just enough to keep a little water flowing out, because running water is not as likely to freeze.

Outside Taps

If you have outside taps, the water pipes leading from the inside to those taps may freeze unless the tap is shut off and properly drained. Before the arrival of cold weather, turn off the inside tap controlling the flow to each outside tap. Then, because water may still be left in the pipe, open the outside tap and leave it open to allow room for expansion if the water freezes.

Clogging

To prevent your pipes from clogging, don't let food or fat go down your kitchen drain, unless it is equipped with a garbage disposal system, and don't let hair go down your bathroom drains. If you do have a clog, use a plunger. Use caustic chemical drain cleaners with care because some of them (for example, those containing lye) may eat through your pipes as well as through the clog. Don't try to clear a clog by sticking wire down the drain because you may make a hole in the pipe. If you can't clear the clog with a plunger or a drain cleaner (use one or the other, not both), it is best to call a plumber.

Know where the main water shut-off valve is and mark it clearly so that anyone can turn it off if pipes flood. Keep a pair of pliers nearby in case the valve is stuck. If a toilet is overflowing or a sink faucet gushing, there are usually shut-off valves at each sink and toilet also.

Shut off the electric power supply before entering a flooded room, or there is a chance you may be electrocuted. If the main circuit controls are located in the room that is flooded, call your local electric company to switch off the power.

"TO DO" LISTS

As you probably noticed, home safety takes a lot of work. Many of the home safety steps set out in this chapter need to be taken only once, soon after you've moved into your new home. For the other ongoing tasks, get into the habit of following a home safety timetable. Taking safety precautions will seem less overwhelming if you choose a particular day of the month to do routine safety maintenance and if you spread your annual safety checks out over the whole year (instead of over one nightmarish weekend). To help you, the following "To Do" lists organize tasks by how important they are and how often they need to be done.

☑To Do Immediately

❑ Install smoke alarms.
❑ Plan a fire escape route.
❑ Buy a fire extinguisher (all-purpose class ABC, or class B for grease fires).
❑ Have your electrical wiring inspected if you live in an older home and did not have the wiring looked at when you moved in—or if you have had any problems with electricity in your home.
❑ Look around the house to make sure that no heat source has flammable materials near it.
❑ Put a list of emergency telephone numbers near your main telephone.
❑ Make sure your house number can be seen easily from the street by day or night.
❑ Turn down the thermostat on your water heater to 55 degrees C (130 degrees F).
❑ Install ground fault circuit interrupters in bathrooms and the laundry room.
❑ Keep life-saving equipment and a telephone near your swimming pool all year round.

☑To Do Monthly

❑ Test smoke alarms and batteries.
❑ Clean smoke alarms.

❑ Inspect your fire extinguishers.

❑ Replace furnace filters during heating season.

❑ Vacuum up the dust around your furnace during heating season.

☑ To Do Once a Year

Fall

❑ Turn off inside valves for outside water taps and leave outside taps open.

❑ Have your furnace professionally inspected.

❑ Have your fireplace and chimney professionally inspected and cleaned.

❑ Vacuum furnace vents on each floor of the house.

Winter

❑ Prepare containers of sand, salt, or ashes to set out near each entrance to your home.

❑ Keep your Christmas tree watered.

Spring

❑ Inspect the outside of your home for damage to bricks, roofing, and eavestroughing.

❑ Inspect your garden for trees or branches that may fall.

Summer

❑ Take a break.

☑ Things Not to Do—Ever!

❑ Do not throw water on a grease fire.

❑ Do not throw water on a fire involving a plugged-in electrical appliance.

❑ Do not use oversized fuses.

❑ Do not open an oven door if there is a fire in the oven.

❑ Do not smoke in bed or when you are sleepy.

❑ Do not use flammable materials around any flame, including cigarettes and pilot lights.

❑ Do not try to start a fire with gasoline, lighter fluid, or other flammable substance.

❑ Do not use an outdoor barbecue indoors.

❑ Do not use a propane, kerosene, or butane heater indoors.

❑ Do not leave a car running in the garage.

❑ Do not use an electrical appliance when you are wet.

❑ Do not put your hand into water in which a plugged-in electrical appliance has fallen.

❑ Do not leave water or spills on bathroom, kitchen, or entrance floors.

Well, you made it safely to the end of the chapter! Take a five-minute break until your panic attack passes. Then get started on your home safety improvement plan—and don't forget your cleaning!

EMERGENCY PHONE NUMBERS

If an emergency arises in your household, you don't want to waste time looking up phone numbers. Fill out this list of emergency phone numbers right away. Securely attach one copy next to each telephone in the house. Keep a copy with your cellular phone too.

Emergency Phone Numbers List

Fire Department
Police
Ambulance

Poison Control Centre
Natural Gas Company
Family Doctor
Pediatrician
Emergency Veterinary Services

Family Member #1 to Contact
Family Member #2 to Contact
Family Member #3 to Contact

Nearest Neighbour #1
Nearest Neighbour #2
Nearest Neighbour #3

Municipal Water Emergencies
24-hour Plumber
Hydro Company
Taxi
Stress Counsellor/Travel Agent

14 VISITORS WELCOME AND UNWELCOME

Y ou've moved in, unpacked, renovated, made your home safe and secure, and now you are ready to receive guests. Before you mail out your house-warming party invitations, you should know that you will have responsibilities to your guests, to the mail carrier who delivers their replies, and to the caterer who will bring in the food. You may also have responsibilities to the guy who crashes your party and the burglar who tries to steal your house-warming gifts.

WHO CAN COME ONTO YOUR PROPERTY?

There are people you want on your property and others you don't. You need to know whom you can keep off your property (and how).

Welcome Guests

If you invite someone to your home, that person has a right to come onto your property and into your home, and then has the right to stay there until you say it's time to leave. Once you've told your guest to leave, he or she must do so as soon as possible and must take the most direct route out. A guest who does not leave when ordered becomes a trespasser, and you have the right to remove him or her—by force, if necessary. (Clearly, this is not an etiquette book that you're reading—Emily Post would not approve of taking this approach with your guests.) Don't go overboard in the force department. You can't injure your now-unwanted guest, you can only push or carry your guest off the premises. (If you think you may have to resort to carrying your guests out the door, it would be wise not to serve them a heavy dinner.)

People with a Right to Be There

There are people who have a legal right to be on your land (but not in your house) even though you do not specifically invite them.

There may be telephone, cable TV, or electrical wires that run across your neighbours' land and yours to provide service to the homes in your area. The utility companies probably have an **easement** over your property (and your neighbours') which allows the companies to have their wires there. Their easement also allows employees of the utility companies to come onto your land to service the wires. These employees don't need your permission each time they come onto your land.

If someone nearby is having a land survey done and the land surveyors have to come onto your property to complete the survey, they can do so without your permission.

In the case of an emergency, police, firefighters, and other emergency workers have the right to come onto your land (and even into your house) if it's necessary to save property or lives or to pursue an escaping criminal. If it's not an emergency, these people need your permission, a search warrant, or court order to come into your home.

People with a Reason to Be There

There are people who arrive at your door unexpectedly but who have perfectly legitimate reasons to be there—people like the Girl Guide selling cookies, the political canvasser, and the door-to-door salesperson. While these people have no right to enter your home without your permission, they do have the right to make their way to your door. If you tell them to leave, they must get off your property as soon as possible and by the most direct route. If they don't, they become **trespassers**, and you can remove them by force. If you have to use force, use only the minimum amount of force necessary to get them off your property.

People with No Good Reason to Be There

Some people may come onto your property for reasons that have nothing to do with you at all—they're not trying to sell you anything or deliver anything to you. They come onto your property for their own purposes—to take a shortcut, to pick your flowers, or to snowmobile in your field. These people have no legal right to be there. They are trespassers from the moment they set foot on your property, even if they did not use force to enter and are not threatening you in any way. You can remove these people by force, but only after you have told them to leave and they haven't left immediately. Even if you've posted a "No Trespassing" sign to keep such people out, you must tell them to leave before you use force to remove them. Use only the minimum amount of force necessary to get them off your property.

The rules are different if someone uses force to get onto your property or has come there to commit a crime. You don't need to tell a burglar to leave before using force to get rid of him. If the person is only after your property and is not threatening you or any other person, you may only use as much force as necessary to remove the intruder. You may not unnecessarily injure the intruder—your guard dog may bite him, and you may hit him if necessary, but you shouldn't beat him to a pulp or shoot him.

If the intruder is threatening you or any other person, you have the right to use force, not only to get the intruder off your property, but to protect yourselves. You should not use any more force than is reasonably necessary to defend yourselves, but the law allows you to use a greater amount of force to protect lives than to protect property. If you have good reason to think that your life is in danger, you can even kill the intruder.

Even though the law may give you the right to use force to get people off your property, you should only do it as a last resort. Your first choice should always be to call the police.

WHAT CAN YOU DO TO KEEP PEOPLE OUT?

There are limits to what you can do to keep people off your property. You can put up signs that say "No Trespassing" (to keep everyone out) or "No Soliciting" (to keep salespeople out). These signs will discourage some people but not everyone. You can fence your property. You can keep a dog on your property.

You can't deliberately harm people in trying to keep them off. You cannot set a deadly trap, such as a gun that would automatically go off at someone who climbed your fence or broke into your home. And your fence or dog must be designed to keep people out rather than to trap them there once they're inside.

WHAT CAN YOU DO IF SOMEONE GETS IN?

What you do if someone gets onto your property or into your home depends on whether or not the situation is an emergency.

If It's an Emergency

If you have an intruder in your home or on your property, call the police if you feel at all threatened by the person's presence. Some kinds of trespass are criminal offences, for example, trespassing at night, or standing on your property and looking through your windows at any time.

If It's Not an Emergency

It is a provincial offence for someone to trespass at your home in Alberta, British Columbia, Manitoba, Nova Scotia, Ontario, and Prince Edward Island. If someone trespasses on your property repeatedly, or if someone trespasses and damages your property, you might want to lay a charge against that person if you know who it is. Contact the police to find out how to lay the charge (the police may do it for you). If the trespasser is convicted of the offence, he or she may have to pay a fine. In British Columbia, Nova Scotia,

Ontario, and Prince Edward Island, a convicted trespasser may also be ordered to compensate you for any damage done to your property.

You also have the right to sue someone who trespasses on your property. (Again, you have to identify the trespasser first.) A court may award you compensation for actual damage caused to your property and for the interference with your enjoyment of your property. If the trespass is ongoing, a court may give you an **injunction** which orders the person to stop trespassing. Unless the damage caused is major or the trespasser is a neighbour who is trying to get a claim of some kind over your property, it is probably not worth the time, money, and aggravation to start a lawsuit. If you have an ongoing trespass, you should ask your lawyer for advice.

HOW DO YOU TREAT THE PEOPLE WHO COME IN?

What about the people who do come onto your property, whether you invited them or not? How you treat these people is more than a matter of etiquette and courtesy—it's a matter of law. This area of law is called **occupier's liability**. It is a very complex and confusing area of the law (are there any other kinds?), especially since it's slightly different in every province.

You're more responsible to some kinds of visitors than to others, and we could tell you about the fine distinctions between classes of visitors that lawyers and judges love to make. But it's best to treat everyone (except maybe an intruder) with the highest level of care that the law requires of you. When someone comes to your door, you can't tell what class of visitor he or she belongs to, and even if you could, you're just going to have one standard of safety in your home anyway. The legal distinctions between visitors only come into play when you're standing in a courtroom defending a lawsuit started by somebody who was injured on your property.

So, What Is Your Responsibility?

You have some responsibility for the safety of everyone who comes on your property—even a trespasser. (You have less responsibility to a trespasser—but more about that later.)

As a homeowner, you hope that nobody will be hurt on your property. And if someone is, you hope like hell that you can't be successfully sued. The way to avoid both injury and lawsuit is to treat everyone who comes on your property with the highest level of care that the law requires. This is what the level of care is:

> *You must take reasonable care to make sure that anyone on your property will be reasonably safe.*

That's not particularly helpful, is it? The law is intentionally vague so that there's room to compensate people who are injured, through no fault of their own, on other people's property. A judge may have to choose between protecting you (who have insurance) and helping the injured person who has bills to pay. Assuming neither you nor the injured person did anything wrong, what would you choose if you were the judge?

If you take reasonable steps to make your home and property safe for yourself and your family, you reduce the chance of anyone being injured there. We gave you advice on how to make and keep your home safe in Chapter 13 on home safety. If you make your home safe and someone is hurt anyway, in theory, you should be protected from liability. Keep in mind though that nothing can prevent a person injured on your property from suing you. And if a lawsuit gets as far as a trial, the judge may want to help the injured person by awarding him or her **damages** that you (or your insurance company) will have to pay.

Here are some examples of situations where homeowners have had to pay damages when someone was injured. In each case the homeowner did not take reasonable care to make sure that people were safe on the premises. The homeowners failed to

- remove snow and ice from steps
- repair a stairway railing
- warn that a floor was freshly waxed and slippery

(Because you read and took to heart Chapter 13 on home safety, we know that *you* would never be this careless.)

You can be ordered to pay damages if someone is injured because you didn't fix dangerous conditions that you knew about (or you didn't at least warn your visitors about them). You could even be ordered to pay damages if you didn't know about the danger *but you should have known* about the danger. A homeowner is required to inspect the premises to find out if something needs fixing—and then to fix it.

What If the Person Is on Your Property without Your Permission?

Lots of people come onto your property without your specific permission. For most of them—for example, the mail carrier, the Girl Guide selling cookies, and the political candidate who's asking for your vote—you have the same responsibility to keep them reasonably safe that you have towards invited guests.

Your responsibility is different to trespassers. There are special rules that apply to burglars and to people like snowmobilers, dirt-bike riders, and skateboarders who use your property without your permission. While you don't have to keep them reasonably safe, you can't deliberately harm them more than is necessary to remove them from your property. You also can't create a danger with the intention of harming anyone who might trespass. You can't put up obstacles or traps designed to injure these people if they get onto your property.

What about Children?

If you have something on your property which you know is likely to attract children yet could be dangerous, such as a swimming pool or playground equipment, you either have to take effective steps to keep children off your property or you must make sure that children will be safe if they get on your property—even if they get onto your property by trespassing.

It is not enough for you to post warning or "No Trespassing" signs. You have to put up a fence capable of keeping the children out. When it comes to swimming pools, most municipalities have by-laws requiring them to be surrounded by locked fences of a minimum height. If you don't have a child-proof fence and you have playground equipment, you have to make sure that your equipment is reasonably designed and maintained to prevent injuries to children.

YOUR DUTY AS A HOST

What if you have a party and serve your guests alcohol, and one of your guests causes a car accident on the way home? Will you be liable to the guest or anyone your guest injures?

In some places in the United States, the answer is yes. Homeowners have been ordered to pay damages to people who have been injured by the drunken guest. No court in Canada has yet held a homeowner responsible in a similar case. To make sure that you're not the first homeowner held liable, don't let your guests drive home if you have any doubt at all about their ability to drive. Call them a cab, have a sober guest drive them, or let them sleep at your home.

ANIMAL VISITORS

Some unwanted visitors have more than two legs. What you can do to try to keep them out or to get rid of them depends on whether the animals are domestic or wild. What will work is another matter altogether.

Your Neighbour's Animals

If fate is good to you, you will never have your neighbours' dogs and cats digging up your garden or using your children's sandbox as a toilet. Fate only smiles on some people, and unfortunately, controlling your neighbours' animals is really a matter of controlling your neighbours.

If you find a dog or cat in your yard or on your lawn, it may be that the animal has escaped from its owner and is lost. The owner will probably be delighted if you return the pet. If you don't know who the owner is, you can call the Humane Society or your municipality's animal control department to pick the animal up and take it to the local shelter, or you can take the animal there yourself.

But a neighbour may let his dog or cat wander loose around the neighbourhood even though many municipalities in the country prohibit this. What can you do if your home is on the animal's daily route?

- If you can figure out whose dog or cat it is, you can consider talking to the animal's owner. However polite you try to be, confronting a neighbour with a complaint about his or her pet is likely to be awkward.

- You can call the municipal animal control department. They may come and pick the animal up, they may speak to the animal's owner, or they may do nothing. Even if you make the call anonymously, your neighbour may suspect that it was you (especially if you previously complained to your neighbour directly).

- You can fence your property. If you weren't planning on having a fence for any other reason, this is a very expensive solution. Fences work better at keeping out dogs than cats.

- There are various chemical sprays on the market that are designed to discourage dogs and cats from coming onto your property without harming the animal. You have to keep reapplying the sprays and they're not very effective. Ask at your hardware store about animal-repellent sprays.

- You can shout at the animal and chase it every time you see it. You can even spray the animal with your garden hose (this works quite well with cats). After the animal encounters your wrath a few times, it may finally get the idea that it should visit elsewhere.

- Try not to attract the animals to your property. Don't leave your garbage outside in garbage bags. Keep it in your garage or in an animal-proof container.

- If the animal is using your property as a toilet, consider collecting the droppings (if you have the stomach for it) and dumping them on the pet owner's lawn, either singly or in a batch. (If you catch a dog in the act and it's being walked on a leash at the time, try politely offering its owner a plastic bag for clean up purposes.) Many municipalities have "stoop and scoop" by-laws that require dog owners to clean up after their dogs. Contact the by-law department of your municipality to ask them if they have such a by-law and how it's enforced.

- Unless you want regular visits, don't feed neighbourhood animals.

As much as you may want to, you cannot harm or kill the animal. Not only is it illegal but, in trying to kill the animal, you may injure a child or your own pet.

Wild Animals

You don't have to go to the country to find wild animals in their natural habitat. There are probably more wild animals of certain kinds living in Canadian towns and cities than in the woods and fields. Stop thinking about how to get rid of your animal neighbours permanently—the most you can do is to get them out of your house and keep them from getting back in. And if they're just in your garden or the ravine behind your home, you probably can't get rid of them. All you can do is prevent them from moving inside with you. Other than that, you'll have to learn to live in peace with them.

Keep your distance from wild animals, even when they're sharing an address with you. Any wild animal that is cornered or feels threatened may attack. Furthermore, rabies exists everywhere in Canada (except the Pacific coast of British Columbia) and is always fatal without early treatment. Make sure your pets are vaccinated against rabies. And if you are bitten or scratched by a wild animal, speak to your physician.

Don't Let Wild Animals into Your Home in the First Place

It is easier to keep wild animals out of your home than to get rid of them once they've decided to move in. While, for the most part, outdoor animals prefer to live outdoors, there are certain times of the year when your home will seem particularly attractive to them. Field mice like to move inside for the winter, and squirrels and raccoons look for indoor accommodations during the spring nesting season. To keep raccoons, skunks, and squirrels from taking up residence in your attic, crawl space, chimney, or under your deck or porch, you should do the following:

- Cap chimneys.
- Screen open vents with rust-proof screening.
- Repair holes or cracks in the foundation or siding of your house immediately.
- Repair holes in your roof and eaves immediately.
- Enclose the bottom of your porch or deck so that animals can't get underneath.
- Keep your garage and shed closed at all times, and check that there are no holes or weak spots where an animal can get in.
- Keep trees near your house trimmed back, and take down your unused TV tower so that raccoons can't jump onto your roof.

- Keep your garbage in raccoon-proof containers—use metal or heavy plastic containers with a cover that cannot be easily removed (a twist-top cover, or one secured by a bungee cord), and store the containers in a rack, or tied into an upright position so that raccoons can't tip them over.

- Store your garbage in your garage or in a shed and make sure the doors and windows are closed tight.

- Do not put your garbage out the night before collection since raccoons prefer to dine on your garbage at night.

- Ask neighbours to make their garbage raccoon-proof too.

- Maintain your lawn properly so that it doesn't get grubs (a favourite food of raccoons and skunks).

Evict Them If They Get In

If, in spite of your best efforts, animals do move into your home, get rid of them either yourself or with the help of a wildlife removal service. Once you do get rid of them, unless you want to get rid of them again and again, you should identify all potential entrance points and animal-proof them.

If you think that the animal living in your house might be a mother with dependent babies, don't try to evict the family until the babies are old enough to leave on their own (nesting season is late winter to early summer). This is not just soft-heartedness. If the babies are not old enough to leave on their own, they probably won't leave at all. If you evict the mother and the babies starve to death, you will then have to deal with the smell of—well, you get the picture.

If you want to try to evict the animal yourself, locate the entry to the animal's nest. Then, when the animal has left on an errand, do these three things all together:

- Put a transistor radio in the nest or near the entry, tune it to a talk station, and turn the volume up high.

- Put a commercial animal repellent (or you can use cayenne pepper) in the nest or entry way.

- Point a bright flood light or spot light at the entry.

Most animals will not want to live under these conditions for long. To find out if your animal has left, roll up some paper into a ball and put it in the entry way (don't plug the entry with the paper, though). Check the entry daily. If the ball has been pushed out, it means that the animal has left but it doesn't necessarily mean the animal has left permanently. Put the ball back into the entry and check it again the next day. Continue checking and putting the ball back until the ball hasn't been moved for two full days. Then, you can be fairly sure that the animal has left the nest.

Once the animal has left, put on a pair of rubber gloves and clean out the nest. (This is another reason to use an animal removal service—they'll do it for you.) Take away the repellent, the radio, and the bright lights. To make sure the animal does not get back in, seal up the entry to the nest with thick wire mesh that animals can't chew through. If you don't like the look of the mesh, you can cover it with whatever material goes best with the rest of the wall or the porch (brick, wood, etc.). While you're at it, check your house for other likely entrances and seal them up too. If you use a wildlife removal service, they will help you identify and seal up possible entrances.

If the nest was in a chimney, have a chimney sweep inspect and clean out the chimney before you cap it. If the nest was in your walls or attic (especially if your houseguests were squirrels), have an electrician check your wiring.

Pests

If the wildlife with which you are sharing your home are of the insect or vermin variety, you have our permission to use deadly force to get rid of them. Depending on the nature of the pest, the seriousness of the infestation, and your own bloodlust, you can call an exterminator or take on the beasts yourself. Your local hardware store will be able to recommend the appropriate pest removal products.

If you have an infestation of carpenter ants, termites, or rats, you should call your municipality, which may help you to get rid of them.

Pests

In this section we'll tell you about various pests and

- why you don't want them around
- where to look for them
- how to avoid them in the first place

ants (the kind that don't chew wood)

- They can carry disease.
- Inspect your kitchen counter; they may be marching into your sugar bowl.
- Clean up food crumbs and spills; keep food (especially sweet food) in sealed containers; close off possible outside entry points, such as cracks and holes around doors and windows.

carpenter ants

• They tunnel in wood and can cause structural damage to your home; they can carry disease; they bite.
• Inspect damp areas of your home for chewed wood that looks like sawdust; look for black ants 6 to 13 mm long.
• Keep your home well ventilated and dry; do not store firewood inside your home; do not leave lumber, logs, or other wood lying around your property; keep food in sealed containers, and clean up crumbs and spills immediately.

carpet beetles

• They eat wool, fur, and animal hair.
• Inspect clothing and carpets regularly for holes; inspect furs and brushes made of animal hair for uneven surfaces; keep an eye out for oval black beetles 3 to 5 mm long.
• Keep your home clean and free of other pests since beetles also feed on dead insects.

clothes moths

• They eat wool and fur.
• Inspect clothing and carpets regularly for holes; inspect furs for loose and clipped hairs; have a fit if you find a beige or golden moth, or a larvae tube, among your woollen clothes or on your carpet.
• Clean clothing, furs, and carpets regularly; inspect used furniture or clothing before you bring them into your house; if you're away from home, inspect any bureau or closet before you put your clothes into it.

cockroaches

• They spread disease (and your mother-in-law will think less of you).
• Inspect cupboards for dead cockroaches or for black ground-pepper-like droppings; even if you've never seen a cockroach before, you will instinctively recognize it when you see your first. Remember this ancient wisdom: there is no such thing as one cockroach.
• Keeping your kitchen and the rest of your house clean will help to reduce a cockroach infestation if one gets started—but a cockroach can live very happily on a drop of water and the glue in the spine of a book, so try to keep them out by inspecting food, including produce, packages, and boxes that have held food, as you bring it into your home.

fleas

• They transmit disease; their bite can cause an allergic reaction.
• Watch pets for scratching and examine their skin for ground-pepper-like flea droppings (if your pet has a bad case of fleas, you may even see a flea—but

fleas spend most of their time away from their host); watch yourself for itchy red bites; put on a pair of white socks and walk around your carpets (you'll see the fleas jumping if they're in your carpet).
* Keep pets from starting a flea infestation by using flea-collars, flea-pills, or flea shampoos (speak to your veterinarian); do not allow stray or wild animals to sleep in or near your home.

flies

* They carry disease.
* They'll be buzzing around your kitchen.
* Keep doors and windows shut or screened; keep garbage and food debris in closed containers, and empty the containers to your outdoor garbage cans often.

mice

* They spread disease and parasites.
* Inspect for droppings near food and for gnawed holes in food bags and boxes.
* Keep possible food sources (human food, pet food, birdseed, etc.) in sealed jars or tins, and keep garbage in sealed containers; close up or block with steel wool all possible outside mouse entry points, particularly spaces around doors and around outside water taps—a mouse can get through a very small hole or crack.

rats

* They spread disease and can gnaw through electrical wires and wood—and they bite.
* Inspect for droppings, gnaw marks, and greasy marks on walls.
* Keep possible food sources (human food, pet food, birdseed, etc.) in sealed jars or tins, and keep garbage in sealed containers; close up possible outside rat entry points (they need more room to get in than mice do); keep your house free of possible nesting sites, like rubbish in your basement or attic.

spiders

* They're actually beneficial since they eat other insects (the two poisonous North American species, the Black Widow and the Brown Recluse, are rarely seen in Canada), but there are limits to the number and size of spiders most people are willing to put up with.
* If you are afraid of spiders, you don't have to look for them—they'll find you; otherwise look around windows, lighting fixtures, and ceiling corners.
* Vacuum, dust, and "disturb" your house regularly; keep your house free of other insects; clean your basement and crawl spaces; get rid of wood piles and litter, which are attractive nesting sites, and cut high grass around your home.

termites

- They chew wood.
- Inspect for runways or tunnels over the surface of wood; inspect for chewed wood that looks like sawdust; check for infested wood by probing beams with a sharp instrument (the wood will be spongy or almost hollow).
- Keep your home well ventilated and dry; do not store firewood inside your home; do not leave lumber, logs, or other wood lying around your property; remove dead trees and rotting decks and porches.

wasps and hornets

- Wasps and hornets sting (and may cause a fatal allergic reaction in some individuals), and if you disturb their nest they can swarm and sting in great numbers (which can be fatal even if you have no allergies); they also hang around parties and won't leave when asked.
- They can build their nests in the ground or in rock gardens, under or behind steps, under the eaves of a building, in cracks in a house's siding or foundations—you will notice large numbers of wasps entering and leaving; they can also build nests in trees (the nest looks like it's made from greyish mummy wrappings).
- If you have fruit trees, clean up fallen fruit immediately; clean up any garbage that would attract wasps or hornets (especially any sweet food or drinks); seal off holes and cracks in the exterior of your house or in your deck or garden where wasps or hornets might want to build a nest.

This is not a complete list of pests. You may be visited by other insects, such as sowbugs, silverfish, and earwigs, none of which will cause you much harm. (Despite their threatening appearance and their unpleasant habit of dropping onto your head when you least expect it, earwigs are not harmful to humans—only to garden plants.) If you have these or any other pests, ask at your hardware store for a product that will rid you of them, or call an exterminator.

Now that you've got rid of your unwanted visitors, it's time to get out of the house—and do battle with your neighbours. In the next chapter, we'll talk about problems you may have with the people who live next door and nearby.

15 NIGHTMARES WITH THE NEIGHBOURS

When you were choosing your house, we told you to pay close attention to the neighbourhood and your neighbours. We told you to look for people who are quiet and who take good care of their homes. People like this may or may not turn out to be your best friends, but at least they probably won't annoy you.

If you did not choose your neighbours wisely (or if the lovely people next door move and are replaced by the neighbours from hell), there are more ways than you can imagine for them to make your life miserable—as you will see.

When you have problems with your neighbours, there are different options available for dealing with them, ranging from a friendly chat to a lawsuit to a fistfight. Whatever option you choose, we want to warn you from the outset that it may not be easy. Even where the situation and your rights are clear, and you are being reasonable and civilized, the reaction you get from your neighbour may not be what you hope for. It is only human nature for people to become defensive (and even nasty) when confronted with a complaint about themselves.

Sometimes, no matter what you do, you won't be able to make the problem go away. In fact, trying to solve the problem may create other problems with your neighbour. In any situation, you will have to weigh your options. When we set out options for you to consider, keep in mind the following:

- Whether we mention it or not, doing nothing is always an option.
- If you contact a lawyer, it doesn't necessarily mean starting a lawsuit—a lawyer will first try to solve the problem without litigation.
- If you win a lawsuit and the court orders your neighbour to pay you money, it's up to you to collect the money—officials like the sheriff will help you, but don't think that the judge just hands you a wad of cash at the end of the trial.
- Whatever you decide to do, you're going to have to continue to live with your neighbour—unless one of you moves.

NUISANCES AND ANNOYANCES

How can your neighbours annoy you? Let us count the ways. Your neighbours can

- hold loud parties
- yell at each other on their driveway
- own a dog that barks and howls all day and all night
- keep chickens and a rooster who crows (and not only at sunrise)
- have young children who seem to be screaming all the time
- have older children who believe they are disc jockeys broadcasting to the neighbourhood
- run an air-conditioner that clanks, whines, and thumps
- tear up their driveway with a jackhammer

Or your neighbours may be quiet but they

- cook smelly fish on their barbecue every weekend
- sit on their back porch smoking cigars whose stink wafts over onto *your* back porch
- have seventy-two cats and never change the cat litter

Then again, your neighbours may be quiet and odour-free but they

- store two or three wrecked cars in their backyard (and one on their front drive)
- let their grass and weeds grow five feet tall
- haven't painted or repaired the outside of their house within living memory
- *have* painted their house—bright fuchsia with lime-green trim

• have an army of flamingoes and garden gnomes on their front lawn in assorted colours and sizes

We hope that none of this sounds familiar to you. But if it does, what can you do?

Call the Police

If your neighbour's conduct is not only annoying but also dangerous or illegal, call the police. If the police think that the situation is serious, they will act. If they don't think it's serious enough for them to act, ask them what you ought to do. They may have some useful suggestions. The police may also respond to complaints about noise, especially at night, and about domestic arguments.

Get Help for Your Neighbour

Whatever your neighbour is doing that's annoying you may really be a symptom of a larger problem that your neighbour is having. The lady with the seventy-two cats may not be able to take care of herself, much less the seventy-two cats. The neighbour who hasn't painted his house may not have enough money for food, let alone property repairs. The neighbours' children may be screaming or their dog may be howling because they're being beaten.

If you have a neighbour who seems unable to look after herself, you can call the department of social services or the medical officer of health. They'll investigate the situation and may get your neighbour whatever help is needed. If you have a neighbour who is having financial problems, you (or you and a group of neighbours) can offer to help with repairs and maintenance. If you suspect that your neighbours are abusing their children, you should contact the local Children's Aid Society. If you suspect animal abuse, call the local Humane Society.

Speak to Your Neighbour

If your neighbour's conduct is annoying but not dangerous or illegal, size up the situation before you act. First of all, consider that the conduct is probably not aimed at you. Your neighbour has his own reasons for doing what he's doing and they probably don't include trying to raise your blood pressure to 250. It may be that your neighbour doesn't even realize that what he's doing is bothering you and would stop if he knew.

If you think that a politely phrased complaint might stop the conduct, you may want to speak to your neighbour. But first take a few deep breaths to calm yourself down. It's not a good idea to confront your neighbour when you're fuming. Your neighbour is more likely to get angry too than to fix the problem. You might also remember that you're probably not a candidate for sainthood yourself—you probably make noise occasionally that disturbs the neighbours. Tell your neighbour what the problem is but act as though he or she has no idea that whatever it is might be bothering anyone. Then suggest how the problem could be solved.

For example, if your neighbour is having a loud outdoor party, do not storm into his backyard shouting "Shut up you @#$%&* idiots!" Instead, telephone your neighbour (if you have the phone number) or, if you can't phone, go over and find your neighbour and speak to him privately. He probably already knows that the party is loud so say something like, "This looks like a really good party, and everyone seems to be having fun. I'm sure you don't realize that we can hear you all the way to my house. Could you turn down the music or move the music inside?" With luck, your neighbour will turn down the music—or he may invite you to the party. But he may just tell you to get lost. Unfortunately, no matter how pleasant you are when you make a complaint, you don't know how your neighbour is going to react.

Sometimes it works better if you ask someone else to act as a go-between. It may be easier for both you and your neighbour. For example, a neighbour that you don't know well may have a dog that is left outside and barks to get in. Instead of speaking to the neighbour yourself, you might ask another neighbour who is friendly with the dog-owner to mention that she knows that the dog's barking is bothering you.

In some situations, you can communicate with your neighbour without using words. If the neighbour's children play noisily in their yard or on the street, bring out your radio and turn up the volume to drown them out. Your neighbour may get the message. Similarly, loud coughing and choking fits in response to the cigar smoke may help your neighbour realize that the smoke isn't staying on his property.

Make an Official (although maybe anonymous) Complaint

Your neighbour's annoying behaviour may be a breach of a municipal by-law or a provincial law. Most municipalities have by-laws prohibiting excessive noise and foul smells and establishing property standards. Most provinces have laws (which are usually enforced by the municipality) requiring property owners to control certain weeds. Some provinces also have laws prohibiting property owners from polluting air, water, or soil.

If talking to your neighbour has done no good, or if you have (on reflection) decided to bypass that stage altogether, call the municipal by-law enforcement department. Tell the by-law enforcement officer what your neighbour is doing and ask if there's a by-law against it. If there is a by-law, ask how it is enforced. The municipality may send someone to investigate the matter and to speak to your neighbour, and then may lay a charge under the by-law if the neighbour's conduct continues. However, in some munici-palities, it is up to you to lay a charge under the by-law and then to prose-cute it. If your neighbour is convicted of a by-law offence, he will have to pay a fine and may be ordered to stop the conduct.

If you're concerned about pollution coming from your neighbour's property, contact your provincial ministry of the environment.

If you think you may have to make a complaint and you want to do it anonymously when the time comes, it's not a good idea to speak to your neighbours first. They'll know it was you who turned them in. Actually, somehow or other, neighbours always seem to know who turned them in.

Start a Lawsuit

If your neighbour's conduct has not only annoyed you but has caused actual harm to you or your property, or has significantly interfered with your use of your land, you may wish to start a lawsuit to get compensation for the harm. The court can also grant you an **injunction** ordering your neighbour to stop the annoying conduct. This area of law is called **nuisance**.

Lawsuits are time-consuming and expensive. You should only consider litigation if you can't live in your house because of your neighbour's conduct or if you have lost a great deal of money because of it.

Just Live with It

You may decide that doing anything at all will only make matters worse because your neighbour is a total lunatic. Or you may find that you have no legal right to stop your neighbour's conduct. There are some things that the law won't help you stop. In either case, you have to learn to live with the conduct—or move.

If the annoying conduct is one-time only, or very occasional, you will probably not find by-law enforcement or a lawsuit effective. If a call to the police or a word with your neighbour won't bring you relief, you probably have to put up with it for the moment.

PROBLEMS WITH YOUR IMMEDIATE NEIGHBOURS

People can come from all over the neighbourhood to annoy you, but your immediate neighbours have special ways to drive you crazy. Only they share a boundary with you. The boundary or property line is the invisible dividing line between your land and the land belonging to the people on either side of you or behind you. Unless you and your neighbours have a legal right to

be on each other's property, you're supposed to stay off each other's property. You and your immediate neighbours may have disputes about staying off or getting onto each other's land. Common disputes involve

- the location of the property line
- fences on the property line
- trees
- shared driveways
- unauthorized use of your land

The Location of the Property Line

If there are no boundary fences between you and your neighbours, you can't tell by simply looking at the ground where your property line is located. Even if there *are* fences, you can't tell just by looking at them whether they're actually located on the property line.

Property line questions can arise between neighbours when for example:

- You want to put up a boundary fence for the first time or check whether an existing fence is on the boundary.

• You suspect your neighbour has taken over part of your yard.

If you want to put up a fence between your property and your neighbour's, you must locate the property line on the ground so that you know where to build the fence. If you don't have a survey of your property, you will need to have one made. Tell the surveyor that you intend to put up a fence and ask for survey stakes to be placed in the ground to mark the boundary. Even if you already have a survey, you will need a surveyor to come to your property to mark the boundary with survey stakes. If there is already a fence in place between the properties and you are happy with its location, you can simply build the new fence in the same location as the old one. If you are not certain that the old fence is on the boundary line (and you care enough to go to the expense), you'll have to call in the surveyor.

You may think that your neighbour is acting as though part of your yard belongs to him or her, for example, by planting a rose garden or by putting up a shed that you strongly suspect is located in your backyard. Before you confront your neighbour with your suspicions, make sure you're right by having a surveyor check the property line. If you are right, ask the surveyor to mark the boundary by placing survey stakes at the property line. Then have a chat with your neighbour. Your neighbour may have used your yard without realizing it, but even if it was an innocent mistake, the reaction you get may not be an apology.

If your neighbour doesn't retreat behind his or her property line, you have several options:

• You can put up a small or large fence or plant shrubs to mark the boundary, and treat whatever is on your side as your own—by keeping it or tearing it out.

• If a structure has been placed partly on your property, you can move it back to your neighbour's property, as long as you can do so without damaging the structure—this would work for swing sets, picnic tables, or a small shed.

• If a more permanent structure like a deck, garage, or fence has been built partly on your property, don't try to tear any of it down before you speak to a lawyer.

Fences on the Property Line

You or your neighbour may want to put up a new fence on your property line or repair or replace one that is already there. You may want a fence to keep your dog in, or your neighbour may have to put up a fence to enclose a swimming pool. The question is: Who should pay? If it's your neighbour's idea, you probably think that he should pay, and if it's your idea, she probably thinks that you should pay. It's not that simple.

Either owner has a right to build a boundary fence. More important, in most provinces, no matter who wants the fence and no matter what the reason for wanting it, both property owners have to share the cost of building, replacing, or repairing a fence put up on the boundary between properties.

If you want to put up a fence, speak to your neighbour. Your neighbour may surprise you by being willing to share in the expense, and you can cooperate in choosing the style of fence and the contractor.

If your neighbour is reluctant, do not despair. In almost every province there is a method in place for appointing someone to look into the matter and to decide questions about the type of fence, its location, and how much each of you should contribute. In some places, you and your neighbour will choose the person, and in other places, the municipality will choose the person who will decide these questions.

Before you discuss the fence with your neighbour any further, go away and do some homework. First of all, call your municipality to find out how fence disputes are dealt with in your area. Next, call some contractors to get estimates for different kinds of fences, from the cheapest to the kind you really want. Then, knowing what the law is and what a fence will cost, speak to your neighbour again. Once your neighbour knows his or her legal responsibility, he or she may be willing, although not necessarily eager, to share in the cost of the fence.

If your neighbour still won't agree to contribute, contact your municipality again to ask how to arrange to have your dispute resolved. A person may be appointed to investigate and make a decision in the matter. Once the decision is made, your neighbour will probably go along with it.

If your neighbour *still* does not cooperate, you will have to build and pay for the fence and then try to collect the amount ordered in the decision from him or her. Contact your lawyer or the municipality for advice.

Trees

How can something as lovely as a tree cause trouble between you and your neighbour? Well . . .

- A tree right on the boundary between neighbours may need to be trimmed or cut down.
- One neighbour's tree branches can hang over into the other neighbour's yard.
- One neighbour's tree roots may spread into the other neighbour's yard.
- You may have a problem with a tree that belongs to the municipality.

Trees planted on the boundary between neighbours belong to both neighbours equally. Both must agree before either one can trim the tree or cut it down. But if the tree is likely to injure you or cause damage to your property (for example, if it is rotting and about to fall down, or its roots are damaging your foundation), you can act without your neighbour's permission. However, you can only do what is necessary to solve the problem. If your neighbour trims or cuts down a boundary tree without your permission (if your permission was required), your only remedy is to sue your neighbour for damages to compensate you for losing the tree. In most cases, the damages involved will not justify the expense of a lawsuit.

If a branch from a neighbour's tree hangs over your property and injures you or causes damage to your property, your neighbour is legally responsible for the damage. If you see a tree branch that you're worried may cause you damage, you can ask your neighbour to have it removed. If your neighbour doesn't want to remove the branch, he may change his mind if you point out that he will be responsible for any damage it causes, for example, if it comes crashing through your roof during a storm. If you don't want to talk to your neighbour or if your neighbour refuses to do anything, you have the right to cut the branch off. You can only cut off the part of the branch that is hanging over your property, and you can't go on your neighbour's property to do the cutting.

If roots from a neighbour's tree are invading your property (or your pipes, weeping tile, or basement), you have the right to cut the roots out. You can only cut out the roots that are actually on your property, and you can't cut out the roots in such a way that you kill the tree if there's a way of removing the roots *without* killing the tree. Your neighbour may be legally responsible for damage caused by the tree roots.

The neighbouring tree whose branches or roots are causing you trouble may belong to the municipality. Call the municipality and ask them to remove the offending branches or roots. You'll probably find that your municipal neighbour is more reasonable than your human neighbours. However, the municipality may not be legally responsible to pay for any damage that the branches or roots have caused to you or your property (check this out with your lawyer).

Trees on your lawn which you think belong to you may in fact belong to the municipality. You can't trim or cut down a municipal tree. In some municipalities, you may not even be able to cut down your own trees because of by-laws that protect mature trees. Check with the municipality before you get out the saw.

Shared Driveways

Sometimes neighbouring houses share a driveway just wide enough for one car, with the property line running right down the middle of the drive. You have an **easement** over your neighbour's half of the driveway, and your neighbour has an easement over your half. The easement gives each of you the right to drive from the street to the garage or parking space on your own property.

Neither neighbour can block the driveway, either permanently or temporarily. This means that you can't build a fence on the property line. You can't park your car in the driveway either, unless you and your neighbour specifically agree to this. If your neighbour does block the driveway, you can remove the obstacle as long as you act reasonably and do only a minimum amount of damage. If removing the obstacle would cause a lot of damage, don't do it yourself. Speak to a lawyer because you may have to sue to get the obstacle removed.

You cannot force your neighbour to maintain or repair his or her half of the driveway—and your neighbour can't force you to maintain or repair your half either. If the driveway needs maintenance or repair, you have the right to go onto your neighbour's half to do the work (and vice versa). If the driveway needs to be resurfaced or if the snow needs to be shovelled, speak to your neighbour about getting the work done. If the neighbour won't agree and you want it done anyway, you'll just have to do it (and pay for it) yourself.

Unauthorized Use of Your Land

Adverse Possession

We talked about what to do if your neighbour takes over part of your yard. You may want to take steps against your neighbour simply to get the use of your own property back. In some parts of the country, there is another reason to take action—if you let your neighbour continue to use part of your land for a long enough time, you can lose ownership of that part of the land. The right to become the owner of another person's land in this way is called **adverse possession**. For someone to become the owner of your land by adverse possession, that person must be the only person using your land, must use it openly, and must use it without your permission for a continuous period of at least ten to twenty years (the time period varies from province to province).

If, for example, your neighbour puts up a fence that encloses part of your property on his side of the fence, he will become the owner of that part of your property after the end of the time period unless you do something. You can prevent him from becoming the owner of the property by

- removing the part of the fence that's on your property (and putting a new one up on the property line)
- suing your neighbour for trespass

Before you do anything, speak to your lawyer.

Whether or not it is possible for someone to become the owner of your land by adverse possession depends on the system under which ownership of your land is registered. There are two systems in Canada: the **registry** system and the **land titles** (or **Torrens**) system, and the right to become an owner by adverse possession exists in the registry system but not in the land titles (Torrens) system. If you live in Alberta, British Columbia, or Saskatchewan, all the land is registered under the land titles (Torrens) system. If you live in Nova Scotia, Newfoundland, Prince Edward Island, or Quebec, all the land is registered under the registry system. In Manitoba, New Brunswick, and Ontario, your land could be registered under either system. When you speak to your lawyer about getting the use of your own property back from your neighbour, ask whether or not you need to be concerned about adverse possession.

Prescriptive Easements

We told you several times about easements. If your land is registered in the registry system and a person uses your land as if there were an easement over it for a long enough period of time (usually twenty years), that person will eventually get a legal right to that easement by **prescription**. This is more of a concern in rural or cottage areas (where someone crosses over your land on a regular basis to get on and off their land) than it is in urban areas. If someone is crossing your land on a regular basis, speak to your lawyer. Even if you are not concerned about your neighbour getting a permanent right to cross your land, you may simply want to stop him from crossing it all the time.

THE CONSTRUCTION ZONE

If your neighbour decides to renovate, you can be annoyed by the design of the renovation or by the construction process itself.

Objecting to the Design

As long as the design for your neighbour's renovation complies with municipal zoning and other by-laws, you have no say in what the renovation looks like. If, however, the proposed renovation does not comply, your neighbour will have to apply for an exemption from the by-law. Once she makes an application for the exemption, close neighbours will be given notice and an opportunity to oppose the application. If you get notice of an application, look carefully at the details of the proposed renovation. If the renovation will have an unwanted effect on you, you should follow the procedure set out in the notice of application for opposing it. You may also want to speak to your lawyer about opposing the application.

You may want to try to work out your objection privately with your neighbour. Even so, it's important to file your notice of opposition within the required time so that you don't lose your legal right to protest if you and your neighbour can't come to an agreement. When you're discussing your objections with your neighbour, find out what the alternative designs are. It may be that she could legally do something without your permission that you would hate even more—and that that's what she *will* do if your objection succeeds.

If you don't receive any official notice before your neighbour starts construction, it usually means that she didn't need an exemption in order to do the work. But it could also mean that she is building without official permission from the municipality. If you don't see a building permit displayed in an obvious place, you might wish to call the municipal building department to find out whether or not a permit has been issued. It's a wise idea to check, because if your neighbour is proceeding without a permit, she may also be proceeding with a design that is contrary to the by-laws.

Objecting to the Construction

Even if your neighbour's building permits and permissions are all in order, you may object to aspects of the construction process, such as:

- construction noise or dirt
- damage caused to your property
- an unsafe construction site

Construction noise and dirt are like any other kind of noise and dirt. You can speak to your neighbour or call the municipal by-law enforcement department. (You may be surprised at how early in the morning construction work is allowed to start.)

The construction workers may tear up your grass by driving their minibulldozer across your lawn, or they may excavate so close to the property line that your driveway collapses. If your property is damaged by the construction, your neighbour is responsible for repairing the damage caused or paying for it to be repaired. Speak to your neighbour. He may be as appalled about his contractor's conduct as you are. If you can't come to an agreement with your neighbour about how the damage will be repaired, you may have to sue him for compensation.

In the course of renovating or re-landscaping, your neighbour may have changed the drainage patterns on his property so that run-off from rain or melting ice floods your property. Your neighbour will be responsible for the damage if you can prove that he changed the drainage patterns and that the change caused the flooding. Contact your municipality because the change may be contrary to a by-law. You may also have to hire your own engineer to examine the site.

IF THE TABLES ARE TURNED

You, of course, are a responsible and thoughtful neighbour and you always take care not to disturb your neighbours by mowing the lawn at 6 a.m. on Sunday morning, having smoky barbecues, and decorating the outside of your home in bad taste. And when you do something that might annoy your neighbours, like hold a noisy party, you let them know about it in advance and thank them afterwards for putting up with it.

However, if a neighbour should happen to come to you with a complaint about *your* annoying conduct, try to be reasonable about the complaint. Don't take it as a personal attack on you. Listen to what your neighbour is saying and, if there's a valid reason for the complaint, see what you can do to make your neighbour happy without making yourself unhappy.

16

MONEY TROUBLES

When you run into serious financial trouble, everything is affected—including your home. Even though we hope that you are never in the position of having to use the information in this chapter, it's a good idea to know exactly what effect money troubles can have on you as a homeowner.

In this chapter we discuss such pleasant topics as:

- mortgage foreclosure and sale
- separation and divorce
- lawsuits
- insolvency and bankruptcy
- taxes
- expropriation

Yes, this is yet another chapter that will make you want to crawl into bed and hide under the covers.

MORTGAGE FORECLOSURE AND SALE

As we told you in Chapter 7, a mortgage is a loan agreement. We also told you that the mortgage agreement gives the mortgagee a claim on your house as security to make sure that you repay the loan. If you don't repay the loan, in most provinces the mortgagee not only has the right to sue you on your promise to repay, it also has the right to take your house.

Now we're going to tell you in more detail what can happen if you don't repay your mortgage loan. Not everything we talk about can or will happen in every province. Ask your lawyer what is likely to happen to you.

Default

Failure to make your mortgage payments on time is a **default** under your mortgage. It is also a default under your mortgage if you don't pay your property taxes, if you don't have insurance on your house, or if you don't keep the house in good repair. If you demolish all or part of your house, it can be a default under your mortgage too—even if it's part of a renovation. The default most mortgagors make is failure to make mortgage payments, and that is the default a mortgagee is most likely to notice right away.

When you default on your mortgage, the full amount of your mortgage becomes payable immediately if the mortgagee wishes. The mortgagee has the right to collect that amount either by suing you on your promise to repay the loan or by taking steps to seize your home.

Legally, the mortgagee has the right to take action against you within a very short time after you miss a mortgage payment. Usually, though, the mortgagee will not actually do anything until you have missed more than one payment—but this is not to suggest that you should feel no concern at all about missing a mortgage payment.

If you know that you are going to miss a mortgage payment, you should contact your mortgagee as soon as you realize you have a financial problem—even if that's before the next payment is due. Maybe your inability to pay is only a short-term problem—you're off work for a while because of illness, or there's been an unexpected major expense. If you know that you will be missing only a payment or two and then everything will be back to normal, your mortgagee may be willing to let you make up the missed payments later. In fact, some mortgages have a special feature that permits you to miss occasional payments without penalty.

Even if your problems are long-term and you have no realistic hope of being able to afford your mortgage payments in the foreseeable future, it still makes sense to speak to your mortgagee. Your mortgagee will not turn a blind eye and allow you to stop paying your mortgage for an indefinite period of time. Your mortgagee may agree not to take action against you for a reasonable time to allow you to sell your house—and in this way get the money to pay back the mortgage. This might not seem like a big favour to you, but your house will probably sell for more if you sell it than if the mortgagee sells it. And the more you get for your house, the more money is available to pay off your mortgage. With luck, there may even be money left over that goes into your pocket.

If you default on your mortgage, it's never a good idea simply to wait and see what happens instead of getting in touch with your mortgagee.

When you default on your mortgage, the mortgagee has various options and can pursue one or more of them. The options are:

- foreclosure
- judicial sale
- power of sale
- getting possession
- suing on the covenant

Foreclosure

When a mortgagee chooses to **foreclose** under your mortgage, it is choosing to take your property in full satisfaction of the mortgage debt.

What is Foreclosure?

If the mortgagee forecloses and your home is worth more than the amount of the mortgage, the mortgagee doesn't owe you anything. If your home is worth less than the amount of the mortgage, in most provinces the mortgagee can't ask you to pay the difference.

A mortgagee has to start an action in order to get foreclosure. You will receive documents telling you that the mortgagee has started a foreclosure action. The documents will set out (although not necessarily in language you can understand) what you can do in response to the action. We tell you something about your possible options below, but to know exactly what to do in your situation, speak to your lawyer.

What Can You Do?

PAY OFF YOUR MORTGAGE: You can pay back the full amount of the mortgage. If you pay the mortgage, not only is the foreclosure action stopped, but your mortgage will be discharged. (Of course, if you couldn't even make your monthly payments, how on earth are you going to pay off the whole mortgage?) In almost every province, you may be able to stop the foreclosure action simply by making the mortgage payments you missed (plus a penalty). In that case, your mortgage is put back in good standing and it continues as before.

ASK TO REDEEM: You have the right to **redeem** the mortgage. (In most provinces you have to ask for it.) If you ask for the right to redeem, you will be given a period of time, from two to six months depending on the province, to come up with the money to pay the full amount of the mortgage (plus interest and your mortgagee's legal costs). You would ask to redeem if you thought you could find someone else to lend you the mortgage money (and you thought you would be in a position to pay that new mortgage back). During the redemption period, you can also try to sell your house for at least enough money to cover the amount owed to the mortgagee.

ASK FOR A SALE: You can ask for your home to be sold under court supervision, and the mortgagee must try to sell your home before it can foreclose. Your house must be offered for sale if you ask. In fact, in some provinces, you don't even have to ask, there will automatically be a sale. If your house is sold, the proceeds from the sale will be used to pay the mortgage, plus interest, and the mortgagee's legal costs. If any money is left, it will be used to pay off any other mortgages against your home; whatever is left after that is yours. If the proceeds are not enough to pay the mortgage, interest, and costs, in most provinces the mortgagee can go after you for the difference.

DEFEND: In rare cases, you may be able to defend the foreclosure action because you dispute the mortgagee's legal rights under the mortgage. For example, you may not have signed the mortgage in the first place—your signature was forged. Or you may already have paid the mortgage off.

Judicial Sale

In some provinces, instead of foreclosing, the mortgagee may from the outset choose to get your property sold under court supervision.

What is a Judicial Sale?

If your house is sold under judicial sale, the proceeds from the sale will be used to pay the mortgage, interest, and the mortgagee's legal costs. Any money left over will be used to pay off other mortgages against your home, and anything left after *that* is yours. If the proceeds of sale are not enough, in most provinces the mortgagee can recover the difference from you.

A mortgagee has to start a court action to get a judicial sale. You will receive court documents setting out what you can do in response to the action. Again, you should speak to your lawyer, but we'll tell you about your options. There aren't many.

What Can You Do?

PAY OFF YOUR MORTGAGE: You can pay back the full amount of the mortgage and stop the judicial sale that way. In most provinces, all you have to do is make the mortgage payments you missed (plus a penalty) to stop the sale.

ASK TO REDEEM: In some provinces you can ask for the right to redeem (see page 244) the mortgage, and the sale can't take place until the time for redemption has passed.

DEFEND: You can defend a judicial sale action on the same grounds as you can a foreclosure action.

Sale under Power of Sale

Almost all mortgages contain a provision that gives the mortgagee the power, if you default on your mortgage, to sell your property without having to go to court. As with a judicial sale, the proceeds from the sale will be used to pay the mortgage, plus interest, and the mortgagee's legal costs. If any money is left, it will be used to pay off any other mortgages against your home, and whatever is left after that is yours. If the proceeds of sale are not enough to pay the mortgage, interest, and costs, the mortgagee can go after you for the difference.

Before your property can be sold under power of sale, your mortgagee must give you written notice of its intention to sell. Once you receive the notice, you have a set period of time (it will be stated in the notice) to pay off the mortgage. In some provinces, you may be able to simply make the missed payments. If you don't pay, the mortgagee can sell your home after a specified period of time.

Sale under power of sale is used often in Manitoba, Newfoundland, Ontario, and Prince Edward Island.

Getting Possession of Your Home

Whether the mortgagee is selling your property or foreclosing, it will want you out of the house. The mortgagee has the right to ask the court for an order giving it **possession** of your home. You can't stop the mortgagee from getting an order for possession if it gets an order to foreclose or sell. Even if it gets an order for possession, most mortgagees won't actually take possession of your home if it looks as though you are going to redeem the property. If the mortgagee does decide to act on the order, force can be used to get you and your belongings out of your home, if you don't go peacefully.

If the mortgagee is suing for foreclosure or judicial sale, the claim for possession will be included in the same lawsuit. If your mortgagee is selling under its power of sale, the mortgagee will have to start a separate lawsuit for possession.

Suing on the Covenant

In most provinces the mortgagee may choose to simply sue you on your **covenant** (your promise) to pay the mortgage loan and not try to take or sell your house. A lawsuit on the covenant alone is unlikely because few mortgagees will ignore the other rights they have against your property.

Mortgagees usually combine suing on the covenant with selling the mortgaged property. They do this so they will have a judgment that will let them collect the shortfall from you if the proceeds from the sale of your house are not enough to pay off the mortgage. If the mortgagee is proceeding by way of judicial sale, the claim for payment on the covenant will be included in the same lawsuit. If the mortgagee is proceeding under its power of sale, it has to start a separate lawsuit.

Words of Wisdom

If you cannot make your mortgage payments, and in your heart of hearts you know you will not be able to make them soon, you have to face the fact that your future as a homeowner is in the hands of your mortgagee. You may hope that you can negotiate a deal with your mortgagee, but the mortgagee is only going to do something for you if that something will also get the mortgagee what it wants. What the mortgagee wants is to get back as much of its money as possible in the fastest, cheapest way.

Allowing the mortgagee to get its money in the fastest, cheapest way is usually in your best interest too. That's because the longer and harder you fight, the more interest accumulates on your unpaid debt and the higher the mortgagee's legal fees go. The interest and all of the mortgagee's legal fees get added to your mortgage debt and are ultimately paid by you. If your home is worth more than the mortgage, you want the amount you owe to stay as low as possible so that there will be some money left for you when the house is sold. You also want to sell your house for as much money as possible. You'll probably get more money for your home if *you* sell it rather than your mortgagee. So the best you may be able to do when you run into financial trouble is to persuade the mortgagee to let you sell your home yourself. The mortgagee is more likely to agree to this proposal if you make it early on.

FAMILY LAW CONSIDERATIONS

Being married or getting divorced may have an effect on your home.

If You Want to Sell or Mortgage Your Home

If you and your spouse are both registered owners of your home, you will not be able either to sell or mortgage it unless both spouses agree and sign all the necessary documents. Even if only one of you is the registered owner, if you are legally married, in most provinces you will almost certainly need the consent of your spouse before you can sell or mortgage your home. If your spouse won't consent to the mortgage or sale, speak to your lawyer. You may be able to get a court to approve the mortgage or sale without your spouse's consent. Of course, starting a lawsuit will not do wonders for your marriage. And the court may well order that your spouse is entitled to receive some of the mortgage money or sale proceeds.

Divorce and Separation

When husbands and wives separate or divorce, they must divide their property between them, including the home in which they live. Depending on the province you live in and your particular circumstances, the following may occur:

- Your home may have to be sold as part of an overall property settlement or order.

- Your spouse may have a right to a share in the home whether or not that spouse is an owner or made any financial contribution to it.

- Your spouse may be able to get an order to stay in the house and to keep you out of it, whether or not that spouse is an owner or made any financial contribution to the house.

Even if you are not legally married and your spouse is not a registered owner of your house, your spouse may be able to make a claim against it. For example, your spouse may seek a share of the house because he or she has made a financial contribution to the property or to your relationship.

If it looks like you and your spouse are going to separate you should speak to a lawyer.

HOW LITIGATION MAY AFFECT YOUR HOME

If you are involved in a lawsuit, it may have some effect on your home whether or not the lawsuit is about your home.

Construction, Builders', or Mechanics' Liens

We've already told you about construction, builders', or mechanics' liens and how a lien can be registered against the title to your home. As long as a lien is registered against your home, a prospective purchaser will not want to buy your home because it can be sold to pay off the lien. As well, a prospective mortgagee will not want to give you a mortgage for the same reason.

Notices of Pending Litigation

If you are sued by someone who is claiming an interest in your property, the person who is suing you may be able to register a notice on the title to your house that the lawsuit has been started. Such a notice advises any potential purchaser or mortgagee that the ownership of the property is in dispute. Most purchasers and mortgagees will not want anything to do with your property while this kind of lawsuit is outstanding.

Judgments against You

If you lose a lawsuit and a **judgment** is made against you ordering you to pay damages, the judgment may affect the title to your home. This is so even if the lawsuit had nothing to do with your property, for example, if you are sued for not making your credit card payments or for injuring someone in a car accident. The person who wins the lawsuit and gets the judgment against you has the right to take and sell as much of your property as necessary to pay off the judgment. In most provinces one of the things they can take and sell is your home, even if you own the property with another person. (They only get to keep your share of the money from the sale.)

After a judgment has been registered against you, the person with the judgment keeps the right to sell your home even if you sell it or mortgage it to someone else. Anyone who is buying your home or giving you a mortgage will check to see whether there are any judgments outstanding against you. If they find any, they will insist that the judgment be paid off either when you close the deal or before.

BANKRUPTCY AND INSOLVENCY

A lot of people are confused about the difference between **bankruptcy** and **insolvency**. If the amount of money you owe is greater than the value of what you own, or if you cannot pay your debts as they come due, you are insolvent. You are not bankrupt unless a court declares you bankrupt. A court can make a declaration that you are bankrupt at your request or at the request of one of your creditors. Before a court can declare you bankrupt you must be insolvent, and you must have debts of at least $1000.

If you are declared bankrupt, a **trustee in bankruptcy** is appointed by the court. The trustee gets all your property, with some very limited exceptions. The trustee's job is to sell that property and use the proceeds to pay your creditors. Because you owe more than you own, your creditors will not be fully paid. If this is your first bankruptcy, unless a creditor or the trustee objects, you will automatically be **discharged** from bankruptcy after nine months. Once you are discharged, all your debts, with a few exceptions, are wiped out.

What happens to your home if you go bankrupt? If you own a house, in most provinces the trustee will get it. If you own your house together with another person, the trustee in bankruptcy can sell it to get your share. If the house is mortgaged, your mortgagee will have the right to sell it or foreclose. If the mortgagee sells your house and there is any money left over, that money will go to the trustee in bankruptcy to pay the rest of your creditors. But if the house is sold for less than you owe the mortgagee, the mortgagee will not be able to sue you for the shortfall because you are bankrupt.

Not only will you lose your house, but you will lose most of your furniture and belongings as well. You are allowed to keep only furniture worth $2000 and personal effects (like clothing and jewellery) worth $1000. You can also keep "tools of your trade" worth $2000.

If you are insolvent, going bankrupt may be a blessing because it will get you out from under your debts and let you make a fresh start. On the other hand, bankruptcy may be very bad for you, depending on your financial position. If you are insolvent, you should seek the advice of a lawyer who specializes in bankruptcy or of a trustee in bankruptcy. They will be able to tell you whether or not it makes sense for you to choose to go bankrupt. If bankruptcy would be bad for you, they may be able to help you prevent it by assisting you in making a **consumer proposal** to your creditors that will allow you to repay your debts over time and, perhaps, at a reduced rate.

PROPERTY TAXES

We have told you that you will have to pay property taxes if you own a home. Your municipality uses property tax money to pay for municipal services and schools.

If You Don't Pay Your Property Taxes

If you don't pay your property taxes, the municipality will add interest charges and penalties to your property tax bill. If you still don't pay your property taxes, the municipality has the right to sell your home, similar to your mortgagee's right to sell if you don't pay your mortgage.

However, your municipality is not as fast-moving as your mortgagee. You will probably be able to leave your bill unpaid for several years before your municipality takes steps to sell your home. Before your house is sold, the municipality will send you a notice in writing and will give you an opportunity to pay your back taxes. The municipality doesn't get to keep all the money from the sale, only the amount that you owe in taxes.

If You're Having Trouble Paying Your Taxes

In some municipalities, you can ask for your property taxes to be reduced because of hardship—if you are ill, if you are extremely poor, or if your house has been destroyed. Contact your municipality for information.

If You Think Your Taxes Are Too High

We have told you that some municipalities have higher taxes than others. What we haven't yet told you is that, within each municipality, property taxes can vary from house to house. Property taxes are calculated for each property as a percentage of the value of that property. The percentage is the same for every house in the municipality, but the value of each house is different. Therefore, the higher the value placed on your house, the higher your taxes will be.

You can't dispute the percentage that is applied throughout the municipality, but you can dispute your house's **assessment**, which is the value your municipality has assigned to your home to calculate your taxes. The value that the municipality has given to your home may bear little or no resemblance to its actual market value. In theory, the assessed value is based on your home's market value, but it may be based on the market value ten or twenty years ago, depending on when the municipality last assessed your home.

If you think that your taxes are too high, check the records for your house at the assessment office. There may be a clerical error in the description of your house or property, or there may be an error in the calculation of your assessment. Errors like these should be corrected without your having to make a formal objection.

There are a number of grounds on which you can formally object to your assessment. You would have to show that the assessment was not "fair and equitable" because of at least one of the following things:

- Your house is not actually worth as much as the municipality says it is.
- Similar houses in the neighbourhood were assessed at a lower value because the municipality was using different standards.
- Your house was reassessed but other nearby similar houses were not reassessed at the same time.

Beware! Once you ask for your property to be reassessed, not only can it be reassessed downward as you hope, it can be reassessed upward. If you want to make an objection to your assessment, contact your municipality to find out what steps you must take.

EXPROPRIATION

The government (federal, provincial, or municipal) may up and decide that it needs all or part of your land for some public purpose or project, such as widening the street in front of your home, or building a highway or public building. They can get your property, whether you agree or not, by **expropriating** it. But they do have to pay you for it.

Expropriation is not an area of law for do-it-yourselfers. If you get notice of an intention to expropriate your property, you should speak to a lawyer who specializes in expropriations.

Can You Prevent the Expropriation?

The government has to give you notice of its intention to expropriate your property. Once you get that notice, you have some right to object to the expropriation. It's almost impossible to argue that the public project for the expropriation is not necessary. All you can really argue is that *your* property is not needed for the project. As you can imagine, this is a hard argument to make if your house is located smack in the middle of the proposed six-lane highway.

Unless you can convince the government to change its mind, the expropriation will go ahead whether you agree to it or not. The government will simply make itself the legal owner of the part of your property that it wants. Then, all you can do is to try to get a fair price for what was taken.

How Much Will You Be Paid?

If your land is expropriated, the government will pay you for it. Generally speaking, you will be paid an amount for your property that is calculated according to its market value before the expropriation. In some cases, though, giving you the market value of your property would not be the appropriate compensation. For example:

• There may be no market for your property, in which case you might be entitled to the cost of a replacement property.

• The land may be worth more than market value to you because you are using it for a special purpose, in which case you might be entitled to compensation for that extra value to you.

- You may suffer economic losses because you have to move, in which case you might be entitled to compensation for those losses.
- Only part of your property is expropriated and the value of the rest of your land is therefore decreased, in which case you might be entitled not only to compensation for the part of your land that is taken but also to compensation for the decrease in value of your remaining land.

In some cases, you may also be paid interest and some of what you spent on legal fees and on fees to determine the value of your property.

When Will You Be Paid?

In almost every province, the government must at least make you an offer of compensation or enter into negotiations with you before it has the right to take possession of your land. In fact, in some provinces, if an offer is made, you may be able to take the money and still fight for more.

If you don't accept the government's offer, or if you and the government do not agree on the amount you should be paid, you have the right to a hearing before a court or a special board to decide how much you should be paid. In that case, you won't be paid until the hearing is finished.

Don't think that you can delay the government's taking possession of your land by prolonging negotiations or by asking for a hearing. It's possible for the government to take possession of your land before the amount of compensation you are entitled to has been settled and paid to you.

All right, it's safe to come out from under the covers now. We have nothing more to say to you about money troubles—in fact, we have nothing more to say about being a homeowner. All that's left to talk about is what's involved when you decide to sell your home.

selling your home

17 GETTING READY TO SELL

People decide to sell their houses for many different reasons. Your family may be growing in number and size, and so your current house may be too small. You may want to sell your home and retire to a warmer climate now that your children have moved away. (Do it quickly before they decide to move back!) You may have to move because of a new job. You may have won the lottery and want to move into a mansion. Or you may have to sell because of less pleasant reasons, such as financial problems, divorce, or a death in the family.

No matter what your reason for selling your current home (unless, of course, you've won the lottery), you want the process to be as fast and painless as possible. And you want to get as much money as possible. Good news on that front! If your home has been your principal residence, you won't have to pay any capital gains tax on your profit from the sale.

WHEN IS THE BEST TIME TO SELL?

You've probably heard various kinds of advice about the best time to sell your home. Some people will say that you should time your sale based on the state of the economy. Others say you have to choose the right time of year. If your need to sell is not urgent, you can take some of the advice. In fact, we talk about some of the more common advice below. But if for some reason you must move right away, the best time for you to sell is now, no matter what the economy or season. Ultimately, your own circumstances determine the best time for *you* to sell.

Trends in the Real Estate Market

Over the past few decades, real estate prices have gone up and down in cycles, but the general movement has always been upward. Even with recent downturns in the market, real estate is worth far more now than it was in the 1950s. However, current wisdom holds that the days of steadily increasing real estate values are over. In fact, we may even be facing a long-term decrease in values when there are more ageing baby-boomers selling their homes than there are younger people buying them.

What we're saying is that real estate is not as attractive an investment as it was when people could make money speculating in houses. The best reason now to buy a house is to live in it, not to make a killing on the sale of it. However, since a house does represent such a large investment, it is only reasonable for you to want to get as much house as possible for your money when you buy, and as much money as possible for your house when you sell.

The long-term trends in real estate may not look great, but there are still some short-term changes or local conditions in the real estate market that you may be able to take advantage of, depending on your location and other circumstances.

On the national level, housing prices tend to be higher when the economy is strong and also when interest rates go down. On the local level, the popularity of a particular area of the country or within a city may also cause house prices to go up. Or the closing of a major employer in a community will cause house prices to drop as people who have lost their jobs try to sell their houses.

Here's something else to keep in mind. It's only natural to think that you should always try to sell your home when house prices are high. That's fine if you are getting out of the housing market altogether, or if you're planning to buy a less expensive house. But if you are trading up to a more expensive house, selling when prices are lower may be a better idea. While the house you are selling may not be worth as much as it might be in a better market, neither is the house you are buying. The more expensive house you're thinking about buying will probably go down in price more than the less expensive house you're thinking of selling.

Time of the Year

In Canada, the weather and the time of year have an effect on how many home buyers are out there looking. The more buyers there are, the higher the sale prices will be.

Almost no one wants to think about buying a house during Christmas or summer vacations. On the other hand, people with school-aged children like to move when school is over, and so are more likely to buy in the "spring." The spring real estate market in your area may or may not arrive at the same time as the tulips. In some regions, the spring market is over by the end of February. So, if you're hoping to take advantage of the spring market, ask a real estate agent when that would be.

Buy First or Sell First?

If you are selling your old house in order to buy a new one, you should start looking for your new home as soon as your old house is listed for sale, if not before. That way, you will know how hard or easy it's going to be to find a new home in your price range. Knowing what your new home is likely to cost will help you decide how much you need to get for your current home.

What if you find the new home you want before your old house is sold? If you sign an agreement to buy the new home, you are legally bound to buy it, even if you cannot find a buyer for your old house. You can end up owning and paying for two houses at the same time.

What if you sell your old house before you find a new house to buy? Even if you don't find a new house before the sale of your old house is scheduled to close, you are still legally bound to go through with the sale. You may have to rent until you find a house. That means rental payments *and* moving twice.

There are ways to avoid these two nightmare scenarios.

Buying First

If you find a house you want to buy before your old house is sold, you can make your offer to purchase **conditional** on your being able to sell your old house within a fixed period of time. If your offer to buy is accepted and you don't sell your house by the end of the fixed period, you can choose not to go through with the deal.

The vendor may not wish to agree to a condition like this. Or the vendor may insist that the fixed period be very short. Even if the vendor does agree, you may only be putting off having to make your decision if you have not sold your old house by the time the fixed period runs out.

Selling First

If someone offers to buy your old house before you have signed an agreement to purchase your new home, you can sign back the offer to make it conditional on your buying a new home within a fixed period of time. If you don't sign an agreement to purchase a new home by then, you can choose not to go ahead with the sale of your old house. A purchaser is more likely than a vendor to agree to make a sale conditional. Even if you haven't found a house by the end of the period, you may choose to go ahead with the sale if you believe that you won't have a problem finding a new house before the sale actually closes.

Think about this too. As a buyer, you will be in a stronger bargaining position if you can put in an unconditional offer to purchase. You may be better able to negotiate a good price if you have already sold your house.

The ultimate decision whether to buy first or sell first depends on which scenario you find more frightening—owning two homes or owning none. Our view is that it is less nerve-racking to sell first because you have more control over whether or not you buy than you have over whether or not you sell.

GETTING YOUR ACT TOGETHER

Once you decide that you are ready to sell your house, there are a number of documents and other material that you should collect. Your real estate agent will need some of them, and your lawyer will need others.

What Your Real Estate Agent Will Need

Title Documents

Your real estate agent will want to know the names of all the registered owners of your home, because all registered owners must consent to the sale. Your agent will also want information about the marital status of the owners, because their spouses may be required to consent to the sale. Gather together any of the following documents that you have:

- your deed or transfer of title document
- any separation agreement affecting your home
- any court order or judgment affecting your home
- any will or probate documents relating to your home

If you live in a condominium, you should also give your real estate agent copies of your condominium documents.

If your house is in a development with commonly owned land or recreational facilities, give your real estate agent a copy of the homeowner association rules and fee schedules.

Plan of Survey

If you have a plan of survey of your property, you should give it to your real estate agent too. Be sure to tell your agent whether there have been any changes made to your property since the date of the survey.

Mortgage Documents

If there is a mortgage outstanding against your home, your real estate agent will want to look at the documents to find out whether a purchaser would be allowed to assume it, or whether it can be discharged without a penalty if a purchaser insists on discharge of all mortgages.

Other Claims against Your Home

If you are aware of any claims or liens against your home, you should tell your real estate agent so that they can be dealt with in any agreement of purchase. These claims might include

- construction, builders', or mechanics' liens
- unpaid judgments against you
- unpaid taxes
- unpaid utility bills
- notice of pending litigation

Property Tax and Utility Bills

Give copies of your tax and utility bills to your real estate agent. People who are interested in buying your house will want to know the cost of taxes and utilities.

Things That Might Help Sell Your Home

You may have information that your real estate agent can use to market your house, such as:

- pictures or videos of your garden or pool (if you are selling during the winter)
- contracts or receipts that prove recent repairs or renovations
- the home inspection report that you had done when you bought your house
- any plans or drawings for renovations that you were considering

Private Sales

If you have decided to sell your house without using a real estate agent, you will need the same documents that you would give to a real estate agent. In addition, you will need information to help you decide what price you should sell your house for. Try to find out what other similar houses have sold for recently in your area. Or, for a fee, you can get an opinion from a real estate agent or real estate appraiser as to the value of your house.

What Your Lawyer Will Need

Your lawyer will want to see everything that you have collected for your real estate agent, other than the things that will help your agent to market your house.

If you are not using the same lawyer who acted for you when you bought your house, your lawyer will also want to see the reporting letter that your former lawyer gave you when you bought the house.

GETTING YOUR HOUSE'S ACT TOGETHER

Real estate agents have always given vendors advice about the little things they can do to make a house attractive when people come to view it. Lately, things have gotten a little out of hand. Real estate agents now have pamphlets and videos with detailed instructions that, if followed slavishly, would totally transform your ordinary home into a decorator's dream. You could wake up one morning and wonder where on earth you are! You might even decide that you'd be crazy to sell and let someone else enjoy this gorgeous house.

Let's face it. Your house is not perfect. If it were perfect, you wouldn't want to move. There are things that have needed doing for some time which you've kept putting off. In fact, you're probably moving to avoid doing these very things. Well, now you'll have to do some of them. Just don't go overboard with your time, effort, and money.

Look at Videos and Pamphlets

By all means, look at the pamphlets and videos and get some ideas. But don't actually *do* anything until you talk to your own agent. He or she will probably tell you not to get carried away and will give you advice on what steps it will make sense for you to take. If your real estate agent is a little too enthusiastic for your taste, follow your own instincts.

Clean and Unclutter

The first things you should do to get your house ready for sale are the ones that cost nothing. Start by cleaning your house and getting rid of unnecessary clutter. If you clean your house thoroughly, it will look better and smell better, and if you get rid of the clutter it will look bigger. When cleaning and uncluttering, keep in mind that, unlike polite house guests, prospective buyers will be looking in the closets, under the sink, and all around the basement.

Make Minor Repairs

After your house is clean and clutter-free, have a look around to see if there's anything that would put off a buyer. If you see something, think about what's involved in changing it. If it's a small problem that can be quickly and cheaply fixed, do it.

If fixing the problem would take a lot of effort or money, speak to your real estate agent first. Ask whether he or she thinks it is worthwhile for you to do the work. Will the problem affect the sale of your house? Will it make it take longer to sell, or even prevent your house from being sold at all? Will it reduce the price a buyer will pay? If your house won't sell until you fix the problem, then clearly you have to fix it. But if the problem will only delay the sale or reduce the price, you'll have to decide whether to invest the time and money involved in fixing it.

Don't Try to Hide Serious Problems

Whatever you do, if you have a major problem in your home, do *not* try to hide it. Either repair the problem properly or tell your real estate agent about it so that it can be disclosed to prospective buyers. For example, do not simply plaster and paint over a crack that you know is caused by a structural problem. If you have a pipe that leaks whenever you take a shower, don't just stop taking showers and then paint the stained wall.

☑Prepare Your Home Checklist

You can use this checklist to give you some ideas about what to do to get your house looking its best for prospective buyers. We start with things that are easy and cheap to do and move on to things that are more time-consuming or expensive.

How far should you go in beautifying your home? It's up to you, but we recommend that you stop when you feel yourself being overcome by a Martha Stewartish urge to create a spare bedroom out of a cantaloupe.

On the Outside

Gardens, Drives, and Walkways

❑ Depending on the season, mow your lawn, weed your flowerbeds, rake leaves, or shovel snow.
❑ Clean up any litter.
❑ Clean up after pets.
❑ Clean and arrange lawn furniture.
❑ Remove garden gnomes and pink flamingoes.
❑ Repair fences and gates.
❑ Repair or resurface driveways and walkways.

The House

❑ Clean windows, window ledges, and doors.
❑ Clean eavestroughs.
❑ Clean siding.
❑ Put out flower pots.

❑ Put down a new doormat.
❑ Paint trim.
❑ Repair broken windows or doors.
❑ Repair leaking roof.
❑ Repair crumbling chimney.

On the Inside

Walls, Ceilings, Windows, Doors, and Floors

❑ Wash walls.
❑ Touch up chipped paint.
❑ Plaster over minor cracks and holes and repaint.
❑ Repaint house in neutral colours.

❑ Remove ceiling cobwebs.
❑ Make sure all light fixtures are clean and change burnt-out light bulbs.
❑ Paint over any water damage (after you fix the leak).

❑ Clean windows, frames, sills, and blinds.
❑ Leave drapes and blinds open (or, if it's evening, turn on lights) during showings to make the house look bright.
❑ Make sure windows open and close properly; repair as necessary.
❑ Clean or replace window coverings.

❑ Clean doors and frames and polish doorknobs.
❑ Make sure that doors open and close properly; repair as necessary.
❑ Replace door hardware and knobs.

❑ Clean and polish floors.
❑ Vacuum carpets and steam clean, if necessary.
❑ Put down runners on carpets in high traffic areas.
❑ Replace flooring or carpets.

Closets, Storage Areas, and the Basement

❑ Remove clutter.
❑ Organize clothes, shoes, and other items neatly.
❑ Clean and deodorize pet areas.

Living Areas and Bedrooms

❏ Remove clutter.

❏ Dust and vacuum everything.

❏ Clean fireplace and stack logs neatly.

❏ Remove distracting pictures or posters.

❏ Set out flowers and plants.

❏ Rearrange furniture to make rooms appear larger.

❏ Store large items of furniture elsewhere.

❏ Purchase attractive bedspreads and curtains.

Kitchens and Bathrooms

❏ Clean to a sparkling shine.

❏ Clear off counter tops.

❏ Make sure everything smells good—remove garbage and don't cook smelly food just before a showing (bake cookies instead!).

❏ Remove embarrassing personal items from the bathroom before a showing.

❏ Replace mildewed shower curtain.

❏ Set out flowers, potpourri, or scented soap.

❏ Buy matching shower curtain and towels.

❏ Replace cracked toilet seat covers.

❏ Repair leaky faucets and toilets.

18 PUTTING YOUR HOUSE UP FOR SALE

You can sell your house with or without a real estate agent. In this chapter, we tell you about the sale process with an agent and without one. Since most people do use a real estate agent, most of the chapter deals with the process when you are selling with an agent.

THE SALE PROCESS WHEN YOU USE A REAL ESTATE AGENT

It's easier to sell your house if you have a real estate agent. A real estate agent will

- help you set a realistic asking price for your house
- find the greatest number of potential buyers for your house
- market your house
- arrange showings of your house to potential buyers
- help negotiate the terms of the sale of your house

Setting a Realistic Asking Price

When you put your house on the market, it is up to you to set the price you ask for the house. The asking price is a way of indicating what you would like to get for your house, if possible. An interested buyer doesn't have to offer the asking price.

The first step in setting your price is knowing what your house is worth. In order to know what your house is worth, you need information about recent sales of similar houses in your neighbourhood. A real estate agent has access to this information that you do not. A real estate agent also has the knowledge and objectivity to tell you how your house is different from those similar houses.

Knowing what your house is worth does not automatically tell you what price to list your house for. Real estate agents have the training to help you decide on the right asking price for your house and can also give you advice about how much higher or lower than the house's market value to set the asking price. It is a common practice to set a higher price than you actually expect to get because most people will offer less than your asking price. It's important not to ask for too much more because you can scare away potential buyers. If you are in a hurry to sell or if there are a lot of houses similar to yours on the market, you might want to ask exactly what you think your house is worth. You may even want to offer your house for sale for less than it's worth. Then you have to be careful because too low a price may cause buyers to think there is something wrong with the house.

Real estate agents say that a house that is properly priced will sell more quickly than a house that is improperly priced. If you price your house too high, it will take longer to sell. If your house stays on the market for too long, potential buyers may think that it has something wrong with it. They'll either not come to look at it at all, or they'll offer you far less money than they would have otherwise. Even if you reduce your asking price after a while, you may end up with less money than you would have received if you'd priced your house properly in the first place.

If your house has been listed for a while and no one has made an offer, your agent may suggest that you lower your asking price. This doesn't mean that your house wasn't properly priced in the first place. Pricing a house is an art, not a science, and market conditions can change.

Finding Potential Buyers

When you put your house on the market with a real estate agent, you have the option of using the **multiple listing service (MLS)** in your area. Only homes listed with real estate agents can be listed on the MLS. Details about your home will be made available to all real estate agents in the area. That means that every agent with a client looking for a house like yours can easily find out about it. In fact, your house will almost certainly be sold to someone whose real estate agent found out about it through the MLS.

Access to the MLS is the major advantage in using a real estate agent to sell your home. Without access to MLS, you are limited to a "For Sale" sign on your lawn and ads in the newspaper. Clearly, you cannot reach the same number of prospective buyers as you can through the MLS.

Marketing Your House

A real estate agent's major marketing tool is the MLS. But there are other things that your agent can do to help market your home.

Making Your House Attractive

The first thing your agent will do is advise you on how to make your house as attractive to buyers as possible. In the last chapter, we told you some of the things that people do to spruce up their homes for sale. Your agent should help you work out a plan for your house.

The Feature Sheet

Most agents will prepare a **feature sheet** that describes your house. A feature sheet is given to people who have viewed your house to help them remember it. It usually provides information about the size of the lot and the number and size of the rooms, and it highlights any especially attractive features of your home, like a newly renovated kitchen or bathroom. The feature sheet may also provide information about realty taxes, utility costs, and your mortgage. Some feature sheets are works of art, with colour photographs of your house and sparkling prose.

Open Houses

If your house is listed on the MLS, your agent will probably suggest an **open house** for real estate agents only. Experienced real estate agents constantly review the MLS for information about new listings that might be attractive to any of their clients. When an agent finds an interesting listing, he or she will make a point of going to the open house to see if any of the agent's clients would be interested in the house. Since your house is most likely to be bought by a client of another real estate agent, it is important to give other real estate agents this opportunity to see your house. If your house is attractive and well priced, many of the agents at the open house will make arrangements to bring their clients to see the house immediately.

In addition to open houses for other real estate agents, your agent may suggest that you have one or more open houses for the general public. Don't feel you have to agree. Just as you suspected, this kind of open house mostly attracts browsers and nosy neighbours. Agents like this kind of open house because it gives them a chance to find more clients. But you are not likely to find a buyer for your house through this kind of open house.

If you do have an open house, it's best for you not to be there. Your agent will ask for the name, address, and telephone number of everyone who comes to see your house and will try to walk through the house with each visitor. Even though your agent will be keeping an eye on things, you would be wise to put away valuable or fragile items.

Advertising Your House

Your agent will suggest that you place a "For Sale" sign on your lawn. Even though your house is most likely to be bought by a person who found out about it from a real estate agent, many buyers do drive around neighbourhoods looking for "For Sale" signs.

Don't worry too much that dozens of people may knock on your door because they have seen the sign. Your agent's name and telephone number will be on the sign, and most prospective buyers will either call your agent or their own agent. If someone does come to your door asking to look around your house, politely tell them to call your real estate agent.

Many vendors are very anxious to have their house advertised for sale in the newspaper. In fact, some real estate agents market themselves by promising to place lots of ads. However, experienced real estate agents will tell you that advertising in the newspaper will not usually sell your house. It's more of a way for the agents to market themselves. The thing that is going to sell your house is not newspaper ads but your listing on the MLS.

Showing Your House

Unless you are really fortunate, your house won't be sold until after a lot of people have looked at it. You can go through a period of weeks or months of people traipsing through your home on very little notice. You will be under constant pressure to keep your house looking its best. You'll have to keep the cat and the dog off the living-room sofa and pick up the socks and underwear that usually decorate the bedroom floors. You won't be able to cook fish *a la* garlic in case you get a call that someone wants to view your house after dinner. After the initial thrill of living in a neat, clean, sweet-smelling house wears off, having your house up for sale can seriously get on your nerves!

If someone wants to see your house your real estate agent will call you first to make an appointment. All appointments will be made through your agent's office, even though most of the people who come to see your house will not be clients of your agent. With luck, you will be given enough warning to tidy up your house and put away any valuables. If the prospective buyer is asking to come at a very inconvenient time, you can say no, but you shouldn't make it too difficult for people to view your house.

At the time of the appointment, the prospective buyer will come to your house with his or her own agent. Your agent will not be there. If your agent has prepared a feature sheet for your house, give it to the visiting agent. Then get out of the way—if the agent and the buyer have questions, they'll come and find you. Avoid any temptation to follow them around your house—it will make them uncomfortable. The agent will stay with the buyer, and this offers you some protection against theft or damage.

The prospective buyer's agent will give you a business card. Keep the cards of all the agents who come to your house so that your agent can collect them to make follow-up calls.

If you are away a lot of the time, you may want to give your agent permission to let other agents take buyers through when you're not there. In this case, give your agent a key to your house and make sure your house is always neat.

Negotiating the Terms of Your Sale

If someone wants to make an offer to buy your house, his or her real estate agent will contact your agent to make an appointment with you to review the offer. At that time, your agent and the buyer's agent will meet with you, usually at your house, to show you the offer and go over its terms with you. In the next chapter, we'll tell you what to look for when you review the offer.

If you want to discuss the offer privately with your own agent, you can ask the other agent to leave the room. You can ask your own agent to leave too, if you want to have a private discussion with family or friends.

You can accept the offer, reject the offer, or sign back a counter-offer (we'll have more to say about this in the next chapter). If you want to make a counter-offer, your agent will help you draft it.

HOW TO FIND A REAL ESTATE AGENT

If you are buying and selling at the same time, use the real estate agent you are house-hunting with to help you sell your old house.

If you don't have an agent, go back to Chapter 3—"Where Do You Want to Live?"—where we tell you how to find one. Your agent's job is to get you and your house set up for sale, but it's most likely going to be another agent who actually finds the buyer. You don't need an agent who has special talents at selling. You want someone whose judgment you trust about pricing your house, making it attractive to buyers, and accepting or rejecting an offer. You also want an agent who is pleasant to work with.

If you interview several agents, one of them may tell you that your house is worth a lot more than the others indicated. Don't choose an agent just because he or she suggests a high listing price. The agent may be doing this just to get your listing and may recommend that you lower the price very soon after.

Ask each agent you interview what commission he or she charges. Maybe you didn't know that commissions are negotiable. Well, they are. Talk to a few agents before you sign a listing agreement. You may find an agent who is willing to take a smaller commission in order to get your listing.

THE LEGAL RELATIONSHIP BETWEEN YOU AND YOUR REAL ESTATE AGENT

When you list your house for sale with a real estate agent, you and your agent enter into a legal relationship.

The Listing Agreement

The **listing agreement** is a form that you and your real estate agent fill out before your house is put up for sale. It will provide information to prospective buyers about such things as

- the legal description of the property
- the price you are asking
- the size of the lot
- the size, construction, and age of the house
- the size and number of rooms
- any fixtures excluded from the sale and any chattels included in the sale
- details of your mortgage
- the zoning that applies to your property

It's very important that the information you put in the listing agreement is absolutely correct because it will be relied on by prospective buyers.

Authority to Offer and Commission

The listing agreement is also the contract that sets out the legal relationship between you and your real estate agent. It gives the agent authority to offer your house for sale for a fixed period of time. If your house is sold during that period, no matter who actually sells it, you agree to pay a commission to your real estate agent. If the property is sold within a certain time after that period ends, you still agree to pay a commission to your agent if the buyer is someone who first saw your house through your agent or another MLS agent. The agreement also sets out what the rate of commission will be.

Exclusive Listing

The listing agreement states whether you want to use the multiple listing service or whether you want to give your agent an **exclusive listing**. An exclusive listing gives your agent alone the right to find buyers for your house. If you choose an exclusive listing, no other agent is going to bring potential buyers to your house because only your agent is entitled to receive a commission on the sale (other agents would have to negotiate with your agent to get some commission). The single advantage of an exclusive listing is that it's cheaper than an MLS listing. The big disadvantage is that fewer potential buyers will know about your house.

The only time you should consider an exclusive listing is if an agent approaches you when you aren't thinking about selling your house and tells

you he or she has a client who wants to buy it. If you are interested in seeing the offer, you might have to agree to list the property exclusively with
that agent. Such a listing should be for only a very short period of time.

Agency

All listing agreements create an agency relationship between the real estate
agent and the vendor. Once you have such a relationship, your agent has
certain duties to you, first and foremost to look after your best interest.
Some listing agreement forms set out these duties in detail and others
don't. These duties exist whether they're mentioned in the form or not.

Disclosure Statements

Some real estate agents in some provinces will ask you to complete a **disclosure statement** or **property information statement** which sets out
information about the condition of your house, in particular, information
about any problems you know about. This information will be made available to prospective buyers. If it contains any false statements, you can be
sued by the person who buys your house.

Your real estate agent wants this form as legal protection in case he or
she unknowingly passes on false information from you to the buyer. The
form makes it clear that you, and not the real estate agent, were the source
of the information.

Commissions

Real estate commissions are calculated as a percentage of the sale price of
your house. Commissions can be as high as 6 per cent. If you sell your house
for $100,000, the commission could be $6000. This is a lot of money, especially if your house sells quickly, and you may feel that your agent is being
very well paid for not doing very much.

If it makes you feel any better, your agent doesn't get to keep all that
money. First of all, if your house is sold on the MLS, the commission is split
between your agent and the agent working with the buyer. Then, those
agents only get to keep some of the money. A good chunk of it goes to the
real estate agency that they're working for. On a $6000 commission, your
agent might end up getting as little as $1500. Actually, now that you know
where the commission is going, you probably feel even crankier than before.

THE SALE PROCESS WHEN YOU SELL PRIVATELY

The reason for selling privately is to avoid paying a commission to a real estate agent. When you sell on your own, you will have to do for yourself all the things that an agent would have helped you with or done for you. You will have to

- set a realistic asking price
- make your house attractive
- find prospective buyers
- show your house to prospective buyers
- negotiate the terms of the sale of your house

Setting a Realistic Asking Price

If you set your asking price too high, you will scare away potential buyers. No matter what *you* think your house is worth, you would be wise to get a professional to tell you what the house's fair market value is. You can pay to get an opinion from a real estate agent or a real estate appraiser. You can also ask the professional to help you set your asking price. The price you set should be slightly above fair market value to leave a little room for negotiating.

Making Your House Attractive

In the last chapter, we made suggestions about how to make your house attractive to potential buyers. You can follow those suggestions. You just won't have a real estate agent to give you additional advice.

Finding Buyers

You should know that some buyers will be frightened off by a private sale. They fear that private sellers will be unreasonable about the price or that they will be generally difficult to deal with. On the other hand, there are buyers who will be attracted by a private sale. They will think that you may be willing to sell for a lower price because you don't have to pay a real estate commission. It's up to you to decide whether to pass on any part of what you save.

Place a "For Sale By Owner" or "Private Sale" sign on your lawn. You can buy or rent professional-looking signs. The sign should have your phone number on it.

Advertise in the local newspapers. Consider putting your address in the ad so that prospective buyers can drive by and look at your house. You may also want to include a picture of your house, although that will increase the cost of the ad. Don't forget to put your phone number in the ad.

Showing Your House

Prepare a feature sheet for your house and have copies available to give to prospective buyers.

Show your house by appointment only. For protection against break-ins, don't tell callers when you will be away from home. If real estate agents phone, tell them it's fine for them to bring a client if they agree that any commission will be paid by the buyer and not by you.

Before the appointment, put your house in order and put away any valuables or breakable items.

When someone comes to view your house, stay with that person at all times. You may want to have someone else with you in the house for your own safety and to guard against theft and damage. If a potential buyer makes a rude remark about the condition of your house, try not to act offended.

If a potential buyer asks you a question, answer it honestly. Don't make any false statements about the property.

If someone tries to negotiate the price with you during the showing, say that you will only consider written offers.

Negotiating

Speak to a lawyer before you put up your "For Sale" sign. Ask the lawyer to prepare an offer to purchase which contains blanks for things like the price and the closing date, but which contains all necessary clauses that an agreement to sell your particular house should have in it. These clauses might relate to things like a mortgage you can't discharge or a mutual driveway that gives your neighbour a legal right to drive over part of your property.

If you don't want to talk to a lawyer, you can get blank "Offer to Purchase" forms from a legal stationer.

If someone wants to make an offer, give him or her your offer to purchase form. The prospective buyer can either fill the offer in alone or with the help of a lawyer. To help the buyer draft the offer, provide a copy of your feature sheet. Also provide a legal description of the property, a survey if you have one, and details of your mortgage if the buyer asks about assuming it.

Don't accept any offer or sign back a counter-offer without legal advice. Once an offer is presented to you, take it to your lawyer.

19 FROM OFFER TO CLOSING

Someone has actually put in an offer to buy your house! You are (choose one): (a) amazed; (b) relieved; (c) horrified at the thought of moving; (d) all of the above. You can stop worrying about moving—because you've got lots of other things to think about and do first. In this chapter, we will tell you what you need to do from the time you receive an offer to purchase your house to the time that the deal closes. And *then* you can go back to worrying about moving.

REVIEWING AN OFFER TO PURCHASE

As we told you in the last chapter, if someone wants to make an offer to buy your house, it will be presented to you by your real estate agent and the buyer's agent. The agents will go through the offer with you to make sure that you understand it and that every detail in the offer is accurate. Even though the agents will explain the offer to you, we want to stress the importance of having your lawyer review it before you accept it or sign back a counter-offer.

Every offer contains an **irrevocable date**. You have until that date to decide whether you want to accept the offer, reject the offer, or sign back a counter-offer. If you do nothing, the offer will simply expire on that date.

The following information will help you understand the key terms of the offer and will help you to decide whether to accept the offer, reject it, or make a counter-offer.

The Names of the Purchaser and the Vendor

All owners of the property should be named as vendors. The owners' names are the only names that are important to you. It's up to the purchasers to figure out what their own names are.

Description of the Property

It is important that the size of your property is properly set out. The agreement must not set out a lot size that is bigger than the actual property.

You also want to make sure that any **easements** over your property are mentioned. An easement is a right that someone else has to use or cross over a portion of your property. If, for example, you share a mutual driveway with your next-door neighbour, your neighbour has an easement over your part of the driveway, and you have an easement over your neighbour's part of the driveway.

If the description of the property is not correct or does not mention an existing easement, the purchasers may be able to use that mistake later to get out of the deal or ask for a reduction in the purchase price.

The Purchase Price

The purchase price is probably the part of the agreement that you will look at first. It will probably be lower than your asking price. Just about every purchaser expects you to sign back a counter-offer asking for a higher price. If the offered price is reasonably close to what you want to get, it makes sense to sign back a counter-offer for the higher price, but if the offered price is much too low, it may make more sense to reject the offer.

Before you accept or reject an offered price, it's a good idea to sit down and figure out roughly how much of that money you will actually walk away with. Here's how you do it.

Start your calculation with the purchase price. At the time of closing you will probably have prepaid certain expenses that the purchaser will get the benefit of, such as realty taxes and fuel oil. The purchaser will have to pay you back for these prepaid expenses, so you can add these to the purchase price. You may also be able to get a refund for your homeowner's insurance.

After that you start subtracting. Out of the purchase price, you'll have to pay the real estate agent and your lawyer, you'll have to pay off your mortgage unless the purchaser is assuming it, you'll have to pay off any claims registered against your house, and you'll have to pay any taxes and utilities bills that are in arrears. It may turn out that you underpaid rather than overpaid your realty taxes, and you'll have to make an adjustment in the purchaser's favour for that. If the purchaser is assuming your mortgage, the amount of the outstanding balance of the mortgage has to be deducted from the purchase price.

The following table will help you do the calculation.

TABLE 1: ESTIMATING YOUR NET PROCEEDS FROM THE SALE

MONEY TO BE RECEIVED

Offered price $ _____
Plus adjustments for prepaid expenses
    realty taxes   _____
    fuel oil   _____
    unmetered utilities   _____
    condominium maintenance fees   _____
    home insurance (in some places)   _____

Total money you will receive   _____ (A)

MONEY TO BE SUBTRACTED

Real estate commission   _____
Legal fees   _____
Money required to discharge mortgages
    principal and interest   _____
    prepayment penalty   _____
    discharge fees   _____
Money required to discharge any claims
    (liens) against your property   _____
Money required to pay utilities arrears   _____
Money credited to the purchaser for
    assuming existing mortgages   _____
Adjustment for underpaid realty taxes   _____

Total money to be subtracted   _____ (B)

WHAT YOU'LL GET FROM THE SALE (A − B) $ _____

The Deposit

It is usual for the purchaser to pay a deposit if the offer is accepted. You want a substantial deposit. Handing over a large deposit makes a purchaser think twice before backing out of the deal without a good reason, because if the purchaser does, *you* may be able to keep the deposit. (Don't worry—most purchasers don't want to back out.)

The deposit will be held, usually by the real estate agent, until the deal is closed, at which time it will be applied against the commission you owe to your agent.

Assumed Mortgages and Vendor Take-Back Mortgages

Assumed Mortgages

The offer may state that the purchaser is to assume your existing mortgage. In such a case, the purchaser pays you less cash but takes over your mortgage payments.

If the offer states that the purchaser will assume your existing mortgage, make sure that the terms of the mortgage are accurately set out. If the offer promises something that does not match what your mortgage documents say, the purchaser may be able to force you to reduce the purchase price, or may even be able to get out of the deal.

The offer should set out the following information about your existing mortgage:

- outstanding principal
- interest rate
- monthly payments
- mortgage due date
- any prepayment privileges
- any limitations on a purchaser's right to assume the mortgage

OUTSTANDING PRINCIPAL: This is the amount of money that is still owing on your mortgage. The amount still owing will be less than the face amount of the mortgage (although maybe not very much less!) because you will have paid some of the mortgage principal back since you got the mortgage loan. The purchaser is relying on having this stated amount available to help finance the purchase. If the actual outstanding principal turns out to be less than stated in the offer, the purchaser will have to find money from other sources.

To find out how much is outstanding on your mortgage, ask your mortgagee. Make sure that this is the amount set out in the offer.

INTEREST RATE AND MONTHLY PAYMENTS: Make sure that the interest rate and monthly payments set out in the offer are the same as stated in your mortgage.

MATURITY DATE AND PREPAYMENT PRIVILEGES: The full remaining amount of the mortgage must be paid on the maturity date. At that time, the mortgage will have to be refinanced. It's important to the purchaser to know how long it is until refinancing will be necessary, so make sure that the date in the offer matches the one in your mortgage. The purchaser will also be relying on the prepayment privileges stated in the offer, so make sure that the description of these privileges is exactly the same as in the mortgage.

LIMITATIONS ON THE PURCHASER'S RIGHT TO ASSUME THE MORTGAGE: Not all mortgages can be assumed by a purchaser. Some mortgages become automatically payable on the sale of the mortgaged house. If the mortgage on your house cannot be assumed, you should not accept an offer that promises the purchaser the right to assume it. Other mortgages can be assumed by a purchaser only if the mortgagee approves, because the mortgagee wants to know that the purchaser is a good credit risk. In that case, the offer will usually be made conditional on approval of the purchaser by the mortgagee. If your mortgage gives your mortgagee the right to approve the purchaser, make sure the offer states that. If the offer is conditional on approval of the purchaser by the mortgagee, make sure that the offer states that the purchaser will take all reasonable steps necessary to get that approval. The purchaser will usually have to give the mortgagee financial information.

WARNING: You should know that in many provinces *you* remain liable on an assumed mortgage. If the purchaser does not make the mortgage payments and the house cannot be sold for enough money to cover the amount of the mortgage, you can be sued by the mortgagee for the shortfall. In fact, the mortgagee does not have to wait for a shortfall to start a lawsuit against you. Unless you get the mortgagee to agree otherwise, in most provinces there's nothing you can do to protect yourself against being sued by the mortgagee if you let the purchaser assume your mortgage. As long as the house is worth significantly more than the outstanding balance on the mortgage, there won't be a shortfall, and you won't have to pay the mortgagee anything.

Vendor Take-Back Mortgages

If the offer provides for a vendor take-back mortgage, the purchaser is asking you to lend some of the purchase price, usually as a second mortgage. The offer will set out the principal amount of the mortgage, the interest rate, the monthly payments, the due date, and any pre-payment privileges that the mortgage itself will contain.

You may like the idea of holding a mortgage as an investment. If you are thinking of taking back a mortgage, make sure it's a *good* investment. Calculate the value of your house. If the purchaser doesn't make mortgage payments and the house has to be sold, the value of the house should be high enough for the sale proceeds to cover any first mortgage, your mortgage, and the costs of selling the house. You should also ask your real estate agent to help you do a credit check on the purchaser.

If you don't want to hold the mortgage as an investment, you can still agree to take a mortgage back, and then find someone who is willing to buy the mortgage from you. If you sell your mortgage, you will have to do so at a discount—the person who buys it will pay you less than the face amount of the mortgage because that person has to wait to be repaid by the purchaser. Your real estate agent can probably find someone to buy the mortgage. Before you accept the purchaser's offer, make sure that you have a commitment from someone to buy the mortgage from you.

If you don't want to take back a mortgage, just delete the provision from the offer before you sign it back. (If you make this change to the purchaser's offer, you may lose the deal.)

Chattels and Fixtures

The purchaser may have put into the offer a list of certain chattels to be included in the purchase price, such as appliances or window coverings. Check this list carefully and decide whether or not you want to sell these things with the house.

If you want to take with you any items that are attached to the house (like ceiling lights and fans, built-in bookcases or shutters or heavy mirrors that are bolted to the wall), the offer must state your right to do so. These are called fixtures and are considered to be part of the house. If the offer does not state that you have a right to keep them, they are sold with the house.

If any equipment in the house is rented, for example, a water heater, the offer should say so. Otherwise, it's possible for the purchaser to claim he thought the equipment was being sold with the house and to ask for a reduction in the purchase price equal to the value of the equipment.

The Closing Date

The offer will set out a closing date of the purchaser's choice. Check the date to see that it satisfies your needs. You may want a longer time before you have to move, or you may want the sale to close as quickly as possible. If you are not happy with the closing date, change it before you sign the offer.

Use of the Property

The offer may contain a statement that the current use of the property may be lawfully continued and may state what that current use is, for example, single-family residential. Check to make sure that the stated use is correct. You may have to check with your municipal zoning department if you have any doubt about whether your current use is legal.

Conditions

The purchaser may have made the offer conditional on certain things, such as:

• being able to sell his or her own house

• being able to obtain financing

• being approved by your mortgagee

• getting a satisfactory professional home inspection report

It is very common for a purchaser to make the offer conditional on getting financing and getting mortgage approval within a certain time. Check with your real estate agent that the length of time asked for is reasonable.

More and more purchasers are also making their offers conditional on a satisfactory inspection report. The purchaser can only legally back out of the deal if the report shows significant problems with the house. (Dust bunnies under the beds are not a significant problem, although cracks in the foundations might be.) If you don't agree to an inspection, the purchaser will probably think that you have something to hide—something worse than dust bunnies, that is. Make sure that the offer requires the purchaser to have the inspection done right away.

The purchaser may have a house to sell too, and may make the offer conditional on selling it. Whether or not you agree to such a condition will depend on the length of time the purchaser wants to sell, and whether or not other people seem to be interested in your house. If there is a lot of interest in your house, it is silly to agree to this condition for *any* period of time. Even if the condition gives you the right to continue to list your house for sale and to consider other offers, many prospective purchasers will not even look at, let alone make an offer on, your house if it has been conditionally sold. On the other hand, if this is the only offer you have had in some time, and you have no reason to expect another offer any time soon, what do you have to lose?

Inspection Clauses

The offer may contain clauses giving the purchaser the right to visit the house to take measurements, to get estimates from contractors, or to inspect the condition of the property just before closing. As long as the clauses don't allow the purchaser to come too often and as long as you will be given enough notice of a visit beforehand, there is no reason not to agree to these clauses.

Other Special Clauses

The purchaser may (but realistically, probably won't) put in any number of clauses that could require you to provide things that you don't have, or to make changes to the property that you can't easily make.

For example, the offer might say that you will give the purchaser an up-to-date survey. That's fine if you have one, but if you don't, a clause like this would require you to have one done—at the cost of several hundred dollars! Or the offer may say that you will have the zoning changed. Agreeing to a zoning change could cost you a lot of time and money, and you still might not be able to get the change.

Be very careful of any special clauses. Don't promise to do things that you can't do easily—and especially don't promise to do things you can't do at all!

THE VENDOR'S LAWYER

As we told you before, you should get your lawyer involved as soon as you receive an offer to purchase your house. Whether or not you did so, you will need a lawyer once there is an accepted offer. Your lawyer will prepare all the necessary documents and answer any questions raised by the purchaser's lawyer.

Choosing a Lawyer

If you were happy with the lawyer you used when you bought your house, it is simplest to use that lawyer again for the sale. That lawyer will already have most of the information and documents necessary for the sale. Besides that, this is the lawyer who certified that you had a good and marketable title to your house. If the purchaser's lawyer finds any title problems, this is the lawyer who is responsible for correcting them.

If for any reason you decide to use a different lawyer, go back to Chapter 6 for information about how to choose a lawyer.

Once you have chosen a lawyer, you should immediately give him or her a signed copy of your agreement of purchase and sale. A new lawyer will want to see the reporting letter, your deed, and any other documents that you received from the lawyer who helped you buy the house. Your lawyer, new or old, may also need the following documents when he or she starts to work on your sale:

- any mortgage documents
- your most up-to-date plan of survey of the property
- your most recent property tax and utility bills
- any separation agreement affecting your home
- any court order or judgment affecting your home
- any will or probate documents affecting your home

What Your Lawyer Will Do

Legal fees for selling houses are lower than legal fees for buying houses. They will still be at least several hundred dollars, so you should know what you are paying for. Your lawyer will

- review the agreement of purchase and sale
- answer any questions the purchaser's lawyer has about your title to the property
- calculate exactly how much money you should receive from the purchaser
- prepare the documents needed to transfer title to the purchaser and arrange for you to sign them
- close the transaction
- review and register any vendor take-back mortgage
- pay off any claims against your house or any mortgages that are not being assumed by the purchaser
- pay the real estate commission
- pay you the balance of the purchase money
- provide you with a reporting letter

Reviewing the Agreement of Purchase and Sale

Whether or not your lawyer reviewed the offer before you signed it, it must be reviewed now. This time your lawyer will be looking mainly at the kind of title you promised to transfer to the purchaser on closing. Your lawyer needs to know what the purchaser is entitled to ask for.

Answering Questions about Title

The purchaser's lawyer will search the title to your house. If the purchaser's lawyer discovers any problem with the title, he or she will ask your lawyer to correct it by the closing date. It's up to your lawyer to determine whether or not the problem is one that you as the vendor are responsible for fixing. If so, the lawyer must try to fix the problem. Occasionally, there are problems that cannot be fixed easily. If there is a serious problem that you cannot or will not fix, it is up to the purchaser whether or not to complete the deal. Your lawyer will tell you whether a problem is serious enough to give the purchaser a legally valid reason not to complete the deal.

Calculating the Money to be Paid by the Purchaser

Your lawyer will calculate exactly how much money the purchaser must pay to you when the deal closes and will prepare a document that sets out these **adjustments** to the purchase price and give it to the purchaser's lawyer.

The purchaser agreed to pay the purchase price but will be credited with certain amounts against the price. First of all, there is a credit for the deposit. In addition, the purchaser will receive a credit for the amount of any mortgage being assumed. There are other items that must be taken into account which may increase or decrease the amount the purchaser pays, such as realty taxes and some utility charges. Whether these last items increase or decrease the amount the purchaser pays on closing depends on whether you have overpaid or underpaid for them.

Preparing Documents

In order to transfer ownership of your house to the purchaser, you will have to sign a deed. Your lawyer will prepare the deed and will prepare and explain to you any other documents necessary for the sale of your house. Because you will have to sign documents, it is important for you not to disappear—let your lawyer know where you can be reached up to and including the day of closing.

Closing the Transaction

On the day of closing, you lawyer will meet the purchaser's lawyer to hand over the deed and the keys to your house. In most provinces, you will receive the final purchase money then (in some you may have to wait).

Dealing with a Vendor Take-Back Mortgage

If you agreed to take back a mortgage from the purchaser, the mortgage itself will usually be prepared by the purchaser's lawyer. Your lawyer will review the mortgage to make sure that it matches the terms you were promised in the agreement of purchase and sale. At the closing of the transaction, your lawyer will register the mortgage on the house's title.

Paying off Mortgages and Other Claims

If you have a mortgage that is to be paid off when your house is sold, your lawyer will contact the mortgagee to find out exactly how much money must be paid. Usually, your lawyer will be able to arrange to pay off the mortgage after you have received the purchase money. Your lawyer will tell the purchaser's lawyer to make part of the purchase money payable directly to the mortgagee. Your lawyer will then arrange to deliver the money to the mortgagee and get and register a discharge of the mortgage.

Occasionally, the purchaser will insist that the mortgage be paid off and discharged *before* the deal closes. In that case, you may have to borrow money to pay off the mortgage and repay that loan when the deal closes. Whether a purchaser may take this position depends on the wording of the agreement of purchase and sale. Your lawyer will tell you early on in the transaction if the purchaser is taking this position.

If there are any other outstanding claims against the property (such as a judgment against you, a construction or mechanics' lien, back taxes, or unpaid utility accounts), your lawyer will arrange for these claims to be paid out of the purchase money.

Paying the Real Estate Commission

The purchaser pays a deposit at the time the agreement of purchase and sale is signed, and that deposit is generally held in trust by your real estate agent. When the deal is completed, the real estate commission is paid out of that deposit. If any deposit money is left, it will be sent to you. If the deposit is not enough to cover the commission, your lawyer will pay your real estate agent the balance of the commission out of the purchase money.

Paying You the Balance of the Purchase Money

After paying off any mortgages and claims, after paying the real estate commission, and after scooping something from what's left to cover the legal fees, your lawyer will pay you the balance of the purchase money.

If you are buying another house, the money will be used for that purchase. If you aren't buying another house, think about what you want to do with the money. Make arrangements with your lawyer to deposit it directly into your bank account or into an investment certificate. You want to start earning interest on your sale proceeds as soon as possible.

Providing You with a Reporting Letter

When the sale of your house has been completed, your lawyer will send you a reporting letter. This letter will show how the amount paid by the purchaser was calculated by explaining the adjustments that were made. The letter will also set out in detail the money received by your lawyer and what money was paid out and to whom it was paid.

YOUR RESPONSIBILITIES UNTIL CLOSING

Signing an agreement of purchase and sale means that on the closing date, you not only have to transfer title to the property but also have to hand over possession of your house. The closing date can be weeks or months away, and you remain responsible for the house even though you are not going to own or live in it for very much longer.

You Can't Take It with You (Unless You Must Take It with You)

You've signed an agreement to sell your house (and perhaps some of the contents too). When you move out of the house, you can't take any of the contents you agreed to sell. You also can't take any fixtures out of the house, other than those you specifically mentioned in the agreement of purchase and sale.

When you hand over possession to the purchaser, you have to hand over **vacant possession**. That means you can't leave behind any family members (no matter how much you would like to), and you also can't leave behind any possessions the purchaser did not agree to buy. Resist the temptation to leave your broken-down freezer in the basement or your National Geographic magazine collection (started in 1953) that has been residing in your attic. The purchaser doesn't want to find these things in the house for the same reason you did not want to take them with you—it costs money to get rid of them.

If you remove things that you should have left behind, you may be sued for the value of the items you took. If you leave things behind that you should have taken, you can be sued for the cost of having them removed. As a practical matter, though, it's rarely worth the cost for the purchaser to sue for these items alone. But if the purchaser finds enough problems with the house, a lawsuit against you becomes more worthwhile and therefore more likely.

In the Event of Damage or Destruction

You're not just required to hand things over to the purchaser—you must hand them over to the purchaser at closing in the same condition they were in when the agreement of purchase and sale was signed, except for normal wear and tear. This rule applies not only to the chattels and fixtures in the house but to the house itself.

If something in the house breaks or is damaged, you must fix it. If your roof develops a leak, you must repair it, although you don't have to replace the roof if it is possible to simply patch the leak. You are not required to repair damage the way you would do it if you were going to keep the house. If you have agreed to sell your fifteen-year-old refrigerator, and it stops working before closing, you must either repair the refrigerator or replace it. But, you don't have to get a new refrigerator—just a fifteen-year-old refrigerator that works.

If the house is destroyed or suffers major damage before closing, you must tell the purchaser. The purchaser has the right to walk away from the deal and get his deposit back. Or instead, the purchaser can choose to complete the deal and receive any insurance proceeds paid to you as a result of the damage or destruction. As you can see, it's in your interest to keep your house and contents properly insured right up until closing. You should not make any repairs until you find out what the purchaser wants to do.

THE RESPONSIBILITY TO CLOSE

If the Vendor Refuses to Close

On the day of closing, you have a legal obligation to transfer your house to the purchaser and hand over possession. If you've changed your mind about selling since you signed the agreement of purchase and sale—maybe because house prices have risen since then and you think you might get more from a new purchaser—you may not be able to get out of the deal.

If you refuse to close, the purchaser can sue you for **specific performance** and if successful will get a court order forcing you to hand over the house and title on exactly the terms set out in the agreement. The purchaser may also be able to get money from you by way of court-ordered **damages**, to compensate for the trouble you've caused. And on top of that, you'll have to pay not only your own legal fees but a good part of the purchaser's too.

While a court action is going on, the purchaser will probably be able to prevent you from selling your house to anyone else by registering notice of the lawsuit against the title to your house.

If the Purchaser Refuses to Close

On the day of closing, the purchaser has a legal obligation also—to pay you for the house. If the purchaser refuses to close the deal without a valid reason, you can claim the purchaser's deposit. You may have to sue to get it.

Instead of claiming the deposit, in most provinces you can sue for damages. If you are successful, the money you get in damages will amount to the difference between what the purchaser was supposed to pay and what you actually receive by selling the house to someone else. You'll also get some of your legal fees paid back by the purchaser.

But if it turns out that you sell the house for the same amount the purchaser was to pay, or for more, you don't have any damages and a court won't order the purchaser to pay you anything. It could turn out that you would get more money by going after the deposit than you would by suing for damages.

Don't Panic

Most deals close without a hitch. Even if a problem does arise, it can usually be solved.

GOODBYE AND GOOD LUCK

Well, much to your relief and ours, we don't have a lot left to say.

We hope that this book has given you enough information to let you go into home ownership with your eyes open. We hope that we have not opened your eyes so wide that you don't go at all.

APPENDIX

SAMPLE INVENTORY LISTS

	Description	Quantity	Original Cost	Date of Purchase
Living room:				
sofas				
chairs				
tables				
desks				
lamps				
musical instruments				
mirrors, paintings, and wall decorations				
ornaments and clocks				
plants				
books				
stereo equipment				
CDs, tapes, and records				
television and VCR				
videotapes				
computer equipment				
draperies				
carpets				
fan				
air-conditioner				
other				

	Description	Quantity	Original Cost	Date of Purchase
Family room:				
sofas				
chairs				
tables				
desks				
lamps				
musical instruments				
mirrors, paintings, and wall decorations				
ornaments and clocks				
plants				
books				
stereo equipment				
CDs, tapes, and records				
television and VCR				
videotapes				
computer equipment				
sewing machine				
draperies				
carpets				
fan				
air-conditioner				
other				
Dining room:				
table				
chairs				
buffet, server, or sideboard				
cabinet				
sidetables				
lamps and chandeliers				
china				
silverware–flatware				
silverware–dishes				

	Description	Quantity	Original Cost	Date of Purchase
glass and crystal				
mirrors, paintings, and wall decorations				
ornaments				
plants				
draperies				
carpets				
wallpaper				
Bedrooms:				
bed, including mattress				
dresser				
chairs				
tables				
lamps				
computer equipment				
stereo equipment				
television and VCR				
radio				
alarm clock				
books				
bed linens				
draperies				
carpet				
mirrors, paintings, and wall decorations				
ornaments				
plants				
wallpaper				
fan				
air-conditioner				
humidifier				
other				
Kitchen:				
table				
chairs				

	Description	Quantity	Original Cost	Date of Purchase
cabinets and countertops				
sideboard or server				
dishes				
glassware				
cutlery				
pots and pans				
utensils				
clock				
radio				
television				
mirrors, paintings, and wall decorations				
wallpaper				
linens				
draperies				
flooring and carpet				
plants				
food				
appliances:				
stove and oven				
microwave oven				
refrigerator				
freezer				
electric kettle				
electric coffee pot				
electric coffee grinder				
toaster				
food processor or blender				
electric juice maker				
electric can opener				
electric knife				
deep fryer				
washing machine				

	Description	Quantity	Original Cost	Date of Purchase
dryer				
vacuum cleaner				
iron				
sewing machine				
other				
Bathroom:				
towels				
mirrors, paint-ings, and wall decorations				
lamps				
table				
chair				
scale				
ornaments				
curtains and shower cur-tains				
plants				
cosmetics				
appliances:				
electric razors				
hairdryer				
electric tooth-brush				
curling iron				
Women's clothing and jewellery:				
dresses				
suits				
skirts				
pants				
shorts				
blouses and shirts				
sweaters				
shoes				
belts				
scarves				
gloves				

	Description	Quantity	Original Cost	Date of Purchase
coats				
hats				
boots				
purses				
undergarments				
stockings				
night clothes				
swimsuits				
other				
jewellery:				
rings				
earrings				
necklaces				
brooches				
bracelets				
watches				
glasses and sun-glasses				
other				
suitcases				
Men's clothing and jewellery:				
suits				
pants				
shorts				
jackets				
shirts				
sweaters				
belts				
ties				
handkerchiefs				
shoes				
gloves				
underwear				
night clothes				
coats				
hats				
boots				
other				

	Description	Quantity	Original Cost	Date of Purchase
jewellery:				
rings				
watches				
cufflinks				
tie pins				
glasses and sun-glasses				
other				
suitcases				
Children's clothing, equipment, and toys:				
pants				
tops				
sweaters				
dresses				
skirts				
shoes				
coats and snowsuits				
hats				
gloves				
boots				
underwear				
night clothes				
swimsuits				
glasses				
toys and games				
equipment:				
carriage				
stroller				
car seat				
playpen				
crib				
swing				
other				

	Description	Quantity	Original Cost	Date of Purchase
Sports equipment:				
bicycles				
camping equipment				
fishing equipment				
golf clubs and bags				
hunting equipment				
outboard motor				
shoes (running, aerobics etc.)				
skis, boots, and poles; ski clothes				
tennis and squash racquets				
other				
Basement:				
pool or ping-pong table				
exercise equipment				
bar and liquor				
furniture				
carpets				
tools				
stored valuables				
appliances:				
furnace				
air-conditioning system				
dehumidifier				
Garage and outbuildings:				
lawnmower				
snowblower				
garden tools				
other				

INDEX